Accounting for Inventory

Second Edition

Steven M. Bragg

For more information about AccountingTools® products, visit our Web site at www.accountingtools.com.

ISBN-13: 978-1-938910-64-7

Printed in the United States of America

Table of Contents

Chapter 1 - Overview of Inventory 1

The Definition of Inventory 1

Accounting for Inventory 3

Inventory Transactions 6

Inventory Flow in a Push Environment 7

Inventory Flow in a Pull Environment 8

Chapter 2 - Periodic and Perpetual Inventory Systems 10

The Periodic Inventory System 10

The Perpetual Inventory System 12

Summary 13

Chapter 3 - Inventory Record Accuracy 14

Inventory Record Errors 14

Environmental Factors Impacting Record Accuracy 16

Employee Factors Impacting Record Accuracy 17

Labeling Issues Impacting Record Accuracy 17

Inventory Naming Conventions Impacting Record Accuracy 18

Excessive Data Recordation 19

Inventory Data Collection Methods 19

The Data Entry Backlog Problem 22

Back Flushing 23

Controls over Record Accuracy 24

Inventory Review Reports 25

The Negative Inventory Balance 26

Inventory Auditing 26

The Corrective Action System 27

Chapter 4 - Inventory Counting and Reconciliation 29

How to Set Up Inventory Record Keeping 29

The Physical Inventory Count 30

Concerns about the Physical Inventory Count 33

Physical Count Improvements 33

Cycle Counting..34

Control Group Analysis 38

100% Count Analysis 39

Inventory Reconciliation 40

Chapter 5 - Estimating Ending Inventory........................44

The Gross Profit Method..44

The Retail Inventory Method..45

The Effect of Overstated Ending Inventory.............................46

Chapter 6 - Inventory Cost Layering.................................49

Inventory Costing...49

The First in, First Out Method..50

The Last in, First Out Method...51

The Dollar-Value LIFO Method..53

The Link-Chain Method...55

The Weighted Average Method...58

The Specific Identification Method 59

Chapter 7 - Standard Costing of Inventory 61

Overview of Standard Costing..61

How to Create a Standard Cost 61

Historical, Attainable, and Theoretical Standards...................62

How to Account for Standard Costs.......................................63

Overview of Variances..65

The Purchase Price Variance 65

Material Yield Variance..66

Labor Rate Variance..67

Labor Efficiency Variance 68

Variable Overhead Spending Variance..................................69

Variable Overhead Efficiency Variance.................................70

Fixed Overhead Spending Variance 70

Problems with Variance Analysis 71

The Controllable Variance...72

The Favorable or Unfavorable Variance.................................72

Where to Record a Variance *73*

Which Variances to Report *74*

How to Report Variances *75*

Chapter 8 - Job Costing **77**

Overview of Job Costing *77*

When Not to Use Job Costing *78*

Accounting for Direct Materials in Job Costing *79*

Accounting for Labor in Job Costing *80*

Accounting for Actual Overhead Costs in Job Costing *81*

Accounting for Standard Overhead Costs in Job Costing *82*

The Importance of Closing a Job *84*

The Role of the Subsidiary Ledger in Job Costing *84*

Chapter 9 - Process Costing **86**

Overview of Process Costing *86*

The Weighted Average Method *87*

The Standard Costing Method *89*

The First In, First Out Method *90*

The Hybrid Costing System *92*

Process Costing Journal Entries *93*

Problems With Process Costing *95*

Chapter 10 - Overhead Allocation **97**

Overhead Allocation *97*

Averaging of Overhead Rates *101*

Chapter 11 - Obsolete Inventory **103**

Expected Dispositions Method *103*

Reserve Method *105*

Expensing Method *107*

Issues with Obsolete Inventory Recognition *108*

Chapter 12 - Lower of Cost or Market Rule **110**

Lower of Cost or Market Rule *110*

Inventory Translation Adjustment *113*

Practical Application..*114*

Chapter 13 - Inventory Spoilage, Rework, and Scrap...**115**

Definition of Spoilage...*115*

Accounting for Normal Spoilage...*116*

Accounting for Abnormal Spoilage..*117*

Accounting for the Sale of Spoilage..*117*

Cost Allocation to Spoilage..*118*

Definition of Rework...*118*

Reporting Rework..*119*

Accounting for Rework..*120*

Definition of Scrap...*120*

Accounting for Scrap..*120*

Chapter 14 - Joint and By-Product Costing..**123**

Split-Off Points and By-Products..*123*

Why We Allocate Joint Costs..*124*

Joint Cost Allocation..*124*

Joint Product and By-Product Pricing..*125*

Special Concerns With By-Product Costing..*126*

Chapter 15 - Inventory Disclosures..**128**

Inventory Disclosures...*128*

Chapter 16 - Inventory Transactions..**130**

Initial Cost Recognition..*130*

Acquired Inventory Transactions..*131*

Backflushing Transactions..*131*

Bill and Hold Transactions...*132*

Consignment Transactions..*132*

Cross Docking Transactions..*133*

Drop Shipping Transactions..*133*

Engineering Change Order Transactions...*134*

Goods in Transit Transactions..*134*

Kitting Transactions..*134*

Lower of Cost or Market Adjustments..*135*

Obsolete Inventory Adjustments...*135*

Overhead Allocation Transactions...*136*

Physical Count Adjustments..*136*

Receiving Transactions...*137*

Sale Transactions...*137*

Scrap and Spoilage Adjustments..*138*

Chapter 17 - Internal Revenue Code for Inventory **139**

IRC Section 471 – General Rule for Inventories...*139*

IRC Section 472 – Last In, First Out Inventories..*139*

IRC Section 473 – Qualified Liquidations of LIFO Inventories.........................*142*

IRC Section 474 – Simplified Dollar-Value LIFO Method *144*

IRC Section 1504(a) – Affiliated Group...*147*

Chapter 18 - Inventory Transfer Pricing **149**

Overview of Transfer Pricing..*149*

Market Price Basis for Transfer Pricing...*151*

Adjusted Market Price Basis for Transfer Pricing...*152*

Negotiated Basis for Transfer Pricing *152*

Contribution Margin Basis for Transfer Pricing *153*

Cost Plus Basis for Transfer Pricing *153*

Cost Anomalies in a Cost-Based Transfer Price..*154*

Pricing Problems Caused by Transfer Pricing..*155*

The Tax Impact of Transfer Prices..*156*

Chapter 19 - Inventory Controls..**159**

Purchasing Process Overview *159*

In-Process Purchasing Controls *161*

Additional Purchasing Controls – Fraud Related *163*

Additional Purchasing Controls – Periodic Actions..*165*

Receiving Process Overview..*166*

In-Process Receiving Controls..*168*

Additional Receiving Controls – Fraud Related *170*

Additional Receiving Controls – Periodic Actions...*170*

Shipping Process Overview...*171*

In-Process Shipping Controls *174*

Additional Shipping Controls – Fraud Related.......................................*175*

Additional Shipping Controls – Periodic Actions *176*

Intercompany Controls...*177*

Inventory Valuation Controls..*178*

Warehouse Controls...*180*

Production Controls...*181*

Chapter 20 - Fraudulent Inventory Transactions **183**

Those Who Commit Fraud *183*

Financial Statement Fraud – Labor Component *183*

Financial Statement Fraud – Materials Component.................................*184*

Financial Statement Fraud – Overhead Component.................................*188*

Revenue Fraud...*189*

Inventory Theft..*190*

Common Fraud Risk Factors...*192*

Fraud Prevention Tactics..*193*

Chapter 21 - Inventory Policies...**196**

Inventory Policies *196*

    Receiving Policy...196

    Point of Ownership Policy...197

    Responsibility for Inventory Policy..197

    Inventory Access Policy 197

    Inventory Owned by Third Parties Policy...198

    Consigned Inventory Identification Policy 198

    Physical Count Policy...198

    Cycle Counting Policy...198

    Inventory Record Access Policy 199

    Bill of Material Updates Policy 199

    Standard Costing Updates Policy...199

    Lower of Cost or Market Updates 200

    Obsolete Inventory Updates..200

    Bill and Hold Policy 200

    Collections Take-Back Policy 200

Chapter 22 - Inventory Budgeting **202**

The Production Budget *202*

Other Production Budget Issues *203*

Budgeting for Multiple Products..*205*

Ending Inventory Concepts...*206*

Impact of Changes in Ending Inventory..*207*

The Ending Finished Goods Inventory Budget...*208*

Direct Materials Budgeting Overview...*210*

The Direct Materials Budget (Roll up Method)..*210*

The Direct Materials Budget (Historical Method)......................................*212*

The Direct Materials Budget (80/20 Method)..*214*

Anomalies in the Direct Materials Budget...*215*

The Role of the Direct Materials Budget...*216*

Chapter 23 - Inventory Measurements...**218**

Overview of Inventory Measurements..*218*

Average Inventory Calculation...*219*

Inventory Turnover Measurements..*220*
   Inventory Turnover Ratio 220
   Raw Materials Turnover 221
   Work-in-Process Turnover 222
   Finished Goods Turnover 223

Inventory Accuracy Percentage..*224*

Excess Inventory Measurements...*225*
   Obsolete Inventory Percentage 225
   Percent of Inventory Greater than XX Days..226
   Returnable Inventory Valuation...228
   Opportunity Cost of Excess Inventory..228

Glossary..**231**

Index **236**

Preface

Inventory can be the largest asset that a company owns, and is one of the most complex to track and value. This presents a risk to the accountant, since an inventory misstatement could be large enough to seriously alter the financial statements. In *Accounting for Inventory*, we present every issue that the accountant might need to create and maintain an accurate and comprehensive system of inventory accounting. The topics covered include inventory record accuracy, how to count inventory, the costs to assign to inventory, when to adjust recorded balances, and a great deal more. As examples of the topics covered, *Accounting for Inventory* provides answers to the following questions:

- What causes inventory records to become inaccurate?
- How do I manage a physical inventory count?
- What methods are available for estimating the amount of ending inventory?
- What types of cost layering systems are available?
- How can I use standard costs to value inventory?
- Which costs can be included in factory overhead?
- What methods are available to account for obsolete inventory?
- How do I calculate the lower of cost or market rule?
- What are the accounting treatments for normal and excessive spoilage?
- What is the journal entry for each type of inventory transaction?
- Which controls should be installed to improve inventory recordation?
- How can someone commit fraud using inventory?
- How do I budget for inventory?

Accounting for Inventory is intended for accountants, auditors, and students, who can benefit from its broad range of topics related to inventory. The book also provides references to the author's popular Accounting Best Practices podcast, which provides additional coverage of several inventory topics. As such, it may earn a place on your book shelf as a reference tool for years to come.

Centennial, Colorado
November 2015

About the Author

Steven Bragg, CPA, has been the chief financial officer or controller of four companies, as well as a consulting manager at Ernst & Young. He received a master's degree in finance from Bentley College, an MBA from Babson College, and a Bachelor's degree in Economics from the University of Maine. He has been a two-time president of the Colorado Mountain Club, and is an avid alpine skier, mountain biker, and certified master diver. Mr. Bragg resides in Centennial, Colorado. He has written the following books and courses:

Accountants' Guidebook	Financial Analysis
Accounting Changes and Error Corrections	Financial Forecasting and Modeling
Accounting Controls Guidebook	Fixed Asset Accounting
Accounting for Derivatives and Hedges	Foreign Currency Accounting
Accounting for Earnings per Share	GAAP Guidebook
Accounting for Inventory	Hospitality Accounting
Accounting for Investments	Human Resources Guidebook
Accounting for Managers	IFRS Guidebook
Accounting for Stock-Based Compensation	Interpretation of Financial Statements
Accounting Procedures Guidebook	Inventory Management
Bookkeeping Guidebook	Investor Relations Guidebook
Budgeting	Lean Accounting Guidebook
Business Combinations and Consolidations	Mergers & Acquisitions
Business Insurance Fundamentals	New Controller Guidebook
Business Ratios	Nonprofit Accounting
Capital Budgeting	Payables Management
CFO Guidebook	Payroll Management
Closing the Books	Project Accounting
Constraint Management	Public Company Accounting
Corporate Cash Management	Purchasing Guidebook
Corporate Finance	Real Estate Accounting
Cost Accounting Fundamentals	Revenue Recognition
Cost Management Guidebook	The Soft Close
Credit & Collection Guidebook	The Year-End Close
Developing and Managing Teams	Treasurer's Guidebook
Enterprise Risk Management	Working Capital Management
Fair Value Accounting	

On-Line Resources by Steven Bragg

Steven maintains the accountingtools.com web site, which contains continuing professional education courses, the Accounting Best Practices podcast, and hundreds of articles on accounting subjects.

Accounting for Inventory is also available as a continuing professional education (CPE) course. You can purchase the course (and many other courses) and take an on-line exam at:

www.accountingtools.com/cpe

Chapter 1
Overview of Inventory

Introduction

Inventory can be one of the largest assets that a company owns. It also requires a considerable amount of skill and effort by the accountant to be properly valued. In many cases, a flaw in inventory accounting represents the difference between the reporting of profits and losses for a business.

In this chapter, we introduce the concept of inventory, the types of accounting activities that relate to it, and how the accounting for inventory can vary, depending upon the complexity of the underlying systems and the presence of a push or pull production flow. This basic level of knowledge is required in order to decide which of the accounting activities described in the following chapters are actually needed.

The Definition of Inventory

Inventory is the raw materials, work-in-process, finished goods, and merchandise that a business has on its premises or out on consignment at any given time. These components of inventory are defined as follows:

- *Raw materials.* This is the source material for a company's manufacturing process. It can literally be "raw" materials that require a major transformation to become a product (such as sheet metal) or it can be components purchased from a supplier, and which can simply be bolted onto a product that is being assembled.
- *Work-in-process.* This is raw materials that are in the process of being transformed into finished products through a manufacturing process. This can be quite a small amount if the manufacturing process is short, or a massive amount if the item being created requires months of work (such as an airliner or a satellite).
- *Finished goods.* This is products that have successfully completed the manufacturing process, and which are ready for sale.
- *Merchandise.* This is finished goods that have been purchased from a supplier, and which are ready for immediate resale. Examples of merchandise are clothes sold at a retailer, or tires sold at a local automobile repair shop.

The preceding list does not reveal the functional reasons *why* inventory is being held. The following classifications do a better job of revealing why an organization needs inventory:

- *Batch replenishment inventory.* Some inventory is created simply because the production system is designed to create inventory in batches, rather than one at a time. For example, if the setup interval for a machine is quite lengthy, the production manager may elect to process 1,000 units of inventory through it in order to justify the long setup, rather than the 100 units that are actually needed at the moment. The remaining 900 units are batch replenishment inventory, and will sit in the warehouse until needed at some later date. The same logic applies to volume discounts that can be obtained from a supplier. The purchasing manager buys 500 units at a discounted price, instead of the 50 units that are actually needed. The 450 unused units are all batch replenishment inventory.

- *Safety stock.* Some inventory is kept on hand as a buffer to guard against shortages. For example, the high variability of customer demand dictates that 80 units of a green widget be maintained to avoid imposing backorders on customers. Similarly, if there is a risk of having a shortfall of raw materials before a supplier can replenish them, a certain amount of safety stock is maintained. The need for safety stock is eliminated if a company has perfect information about future customer orders, and knows exactly how long it will take for a supplier to fulfill an order. Since the reduction of lead times reduces forecasting uncertainty, such a reduction also reduces the need for safety stock.
- *Seasonal inventory.* When sales are seasonal, production continues through low-sale months, so that inventory levels will be high enough to sustain customer orders during high-demand months. A company may elect to avoid some of this inventory by instead incurring overtime costs to produce for longer periods of time during high-demand months.
- *Work-in-process inventory.* This is the only case where the accounting designation for inventory matches its actual function. This inventory type refers to the inventory passing through the production system. Large amounts of work-in-process inventory tend to build up between work stations in a production process. This buildup can be caused by the distance between work stations, and can be mitigated by compressing the distance.
- *Investment inventory.* Some types of inventory can increase in value over time, such as wines, precious metals, and precious stones. Oil and gas and other commodities may also be held over the short term in order to take advantage of spikes in spot rates. If management wants to engage in this type of speculation, it may hold substantial amounts of inventory for prolonged periods.

Inventory does not include supplies, which are charged to expense in the period purchased. Also, customer-owned inventory is not recorded as inventory owned by the company. Further, supplier-owned inventory located on the premises is also not recorded as inventory.

Inventory can be located in three places, which are:
- *In company storage.* By far the most common of the three inventory location types, this is inventory kept in any location that is under the direct control of the business. This may be anywhere at a company facili-

ty, in trailers in the company parking lot, in leased warehouse space, and so forth.

- *In transit.* A business technically takes ownership of inventory if the delivery terms from the supplier are FOB shipping point, which means that ownership passes to the buyer as soon as the goods leave the shipping dock of the supplier. At the other end of the delivery pipeline, a business also owns inventory until it reaches the customer's receiving dock if it is shipped under FOB destination terms. However, from a practicality perspective, a company does not attempt to account for inventory that is either in transit to it or from it.

- *On consignment.* A company may retain ownership of inventory at a retailer or distributor location, with its ownership interest continuing until such time as the inventory is sold. This inventory is much more difficult to track, since it is off-site.

We now turn to an overview of the accounting required for the inventory asset.

Accounting for Inventory

There is a notable amount of accounting associated with the inventory asset. It is necessary to first determine the correct unit counts comprising ending inventory, and then assign an appropriate value to those units. Overhead costs are also added to the inventory valuation. These actions are needed to record an ending inventory value, as well as to calculate the cost of goods sold for the reporting period. We expand upon these basic issues in the following bullet points:

- *Determine ending unit counts.* A company may use either a periodic or perpetual inventory system to maintain its inventory records. A periodic system relies upon a physical count to determine the ending inventory balance, while a perpetual system uses constant updates of the inventory records to arrive at the same goal. We address this topic in Chapter 2, Periodic and Perpetual Inventory Systems.

- *Improve record accuracy.* If a company uses the perpetual inventory system to arrive at ending inventory balances, the accuracy of the transactions is paramount. In Chapter 3, Inventory Record Accuracy, we make note of the many types of inventory record errors, how they are caused, and how to correct them.

- *Conduct physical counts.* If a company uses the periodic inventory system to create ending inventory balances, the physical count must be conducted correctly. This involves the completion of a specific series of activities to improve the odds of counting all inventory items. In Chapter 4, Inventory Counting and Reconciliation, we delve into not only the physical count, but also how to set up a system of inventory record keeping and roll out a cycle counting program (which involves ongoing daily counts).

- *Estimate ending inventory.* There may be situations where it is not possible to conduct a physical count to arrive at the ending inventory balance. If so, the gross profit method or the retail inventory method can be used to derive an approximate ending balance. The mechanics of these methods are covered in Chapter 5, Estimating Ending Inventory.

- *Assign costs to inventory*. The main role of the accountant on a monthly basis is assigning costs to ending inventory unit counts. There are a number of methods for doing so, which we cover in Chapters 6 through 9. The basic concept of cost layering, which involves tracking tranches of inventory costs, is addressed in Chapter 6, Inventory Cost Layering. This chapter makes note of the first in, first out (FIFO) layering system, the last in, first out (LIFO) system, and several related approaches to how historical costs can be assigned to units as they move into and out of inventory. A different approach is covered in Chapter 7, Standard Costing of Inventory, which describes the assignment of a standard cost to each inventory item, rather than a historical cost. In addition, we make note of two alternative ways to aggregate costs; job costing is used to compile costs for small production runs or unique products, and is described in Chapter 8. Process costing is used to compile costs for large production runs of identical products, and is described in Chapter 9.
- *Allocate inventory to overhead*. The typical production facility has a large amount of overhead costs, which must be allocated to the units produced in a reporting period. In Chapter 10, Overhead Allocation, we describe the contents of factory overhead and various ways to allocate it.

The preceding bullet points cover the essential accounting for the valuation of inventory. In addition, it may be necessary to write down the inventory values for obsolete inventory, or for spoilage or scrap, or because the market value of some goods have declined below their cost. There may also be issues with assigning costs to joint and by-product inventory items. We expand upon these additional accounting activities in the following bullet points:

- *Write down obsolete inventory*. There must be a system in place for identifying obsolete inventory and writing down its associated cost. In Chapter 11, we cover several alternative methods for writing down the cost of obsolete inventory.
- *Review lower of cost or market*. The accounting standards mandate that the carrying amount of inventory items be written down to their market values (subject to various limitations) if those market values decline below cost. In Chapter 12, The Lower of Cost or Market Rule, we describe how this calculation is performed, and how to limit its use.
- *Account for spoilage, rework, and scrap*. In any manufacturing operation, there will inevitably be certain amounts of inventory spoilage, as well as items that must be scrapped or reworked. In Chapter 13, we cover the accounting for normal and abnormal spoilage, the sale of spoiled goods, rework, scrap, and related topics.
- *Account for joint products and by-products*. Some production processes have split-off points at which multiple products are created. The accountant

must decide upon a standard method for assigning product costs in these situations. We give guidance on the topic in Chapter 14, Joint and By-Product Costing.

- *Disclosures.* There are a small number of disclosures about inventory that the accountant must include in the financial statements. We make note of these disclosure rules and provide examples in Chapter 15, Inventory Disclosures.

In addition, the related journal entries for many of the preceding transactions are described in Chapter 16, Inventory Transactions.

The preceding points cover the essentials of accounting for inventory. In addition, several other topics relate to the inventory asset. For example:

- *Internal revenue code.* The regulations of the Internal Revenue Service contain specific authorizations for the use of the last in, first out cost layering method in the reporting of taxable income. We discuss these regulations in Chapter 17, Internal Revenue Code for Inventory.
- *Transfer pricing.* When a company has several subsidiaries that buy goods from each other, a methodology must be adopted for setting the prices at which these goods are sold. There can be a significant impact on the amount of taxable income that each subsidiary reports. We discuss the types of transfer pricing methodologies in Chapter 18, Inventory Transfer Pricing.
- *Inventory controls.* Inventory is one of the most difficult assets to control, given the large number of items involved, their dispersal over a large area, and the multiple types of costs that can be applied to them. In Chapter 19, Inventory Controls, we cover a multitude of controls related to the purchasing, receiving, shipping, and valuation of inventory.
- *Inventory fraud.* The accountant should be aware of the numerous ways in which someone can either steal inventory or alter the inventory records in order to boost reported financial results. In the latter case, fraud is likely being perpetrated within the accounting department. The topic is addressed in Chapter 20, Fraudulent Inventory Transactions.
- *Supporting policies.* The work of the accountant can be supported by a set of policies that mandate how inventory is to be received, accessed, counted, valued, billed, and so forth. Sample policies are noted in Chapter 21, Inventory Policies.
- *Budgeting.* The accountant is likely to be deeply involved in creating the annual budget, and may even be in charge of the process. A large part of the budget model is driven by the estimation of inventory levels and how inventory is to be used in the production process. In Chapter 22, Inventory Budgeting, we describe the related budgeting models and a number of conceptual issues that impact the estimated amounts of inventory that should be included in a budget.
- *Measurements.* The accountant should be aware of several inventory measurements, particularly turnover and record accuracy, since these measures relate to usage levels and the overall investment in inventory.

Chapter 23, Inventory Measurements, describes these and other measurements for the inventory asset.

Clearly, there are a large number of functions related to inventory that the accountant must be either directly involved in or at least have some knowledge of. In the next section, we make note of those operational activities in a business that may call for the recordation of an inventory asset.

Inventory Transactions

There are numerous places in the flow of inventory through a company that may call for the recordation of formal inventory transactions. The most basic areas in which the accountant will be involved are:

- *Receiving*. When raw materials or merchandise arrive from a supplier, the receiving department forwards receiving documentation to the accounts payable department. The payables staff records these receipts once it also receives an invoice from the supplier, as well as a confirming purchase order from the purchasing department (known as three-way matching).
- *Shipping*. When goods are shipped to a customer, the shipping department forwards a copy of the daily shipping log to the billing department. The billing staff records a sale transaction from the log and the related sales order. Depending on the accounting system, the cost of the goods may also be charged to the cost of goods sold expense at this point.
- *Period-end adjustments*. At the end of each reporting period, the accountant adjusts the recorded ending inventory valuation to match the actual inventory valuation (typically using standard costs), and applies factory overhead to the goods produced during the period. Some of this allocated overhead will end up being charged to the cost of goods sold and some will appear in ending inventory, depending upon the extent to which the produced goods were sold during the period. The derivation of costs for work-in-process inventory includes capitalized labor costs, depending on their stage of completion. Similarly, capitalized labor costs are included in the valuation of finished goods.

These three transactions represent the absolute minimum level of accounting needed for inventory. However, they do nothing to record changes to the inventory while it is on the premises, nor do they slot the inventory into any reporting categories, such as the raw materials, work-in-process, and finished goods classifications noted earlier in this chapter. To engage in this more fine-grained level of accounting, the following additional areas can be considered:

- *Write downs*. It may be necessary to write down the value of inventory for spoilage, scrap, rework, obsolescence, or lower of cost or market adjustments. All of these activities are encompassed by the period-end adjustments just noted, but there is no segregation of each type of cost. At a more advanced level, the accountant can identify each type of write down and record it in a separate account, which can be used by management to investigate the underlying causes of these expenses.

- *Reserves.* A more refined form of accounting for write downs is to create reserves for these items based on estimates of probable losses, and then write down the reserves as actual losses are encountered.
- *Classifications.* If there is a need to report inventory by classification, the ending inventory count must be segregated into raw materials, work-in-process, and finished goods inventory, with cost assignments to each classification for capitalized labor and overhead costs.
- *Cost layering.* The accuracy of inventory costs can be increased by using a cost layering methodology (see the Inventory Cost Layering chapter), such as the FIFO or LIFO methods. Doing so requires the tracking of costs incurred to obtain each inventory item, and the order in which these costs are charged to the cost of goods sold.
- *Perpetual inventory adjustments.* If a company is using a perpetual inventory system (see the next chapter), separate entries are made to document the flow of goods through the various inventory classifications, as well as any write downs of inventory.

The volume of accounting transactions is quite low when just the most basic inventory events are being recorded. However, as the system becomes more sophisticated, the number of accounting events skyrockets. The volume level of transactions is especially high when there is a perpetual inventory system and adjustments to this system are rolled forward into the accounting system.

Inventory Flow in a Push Environment

The most common production system is one in which a forecast of expected customer demand is generated, and is used to schedule production. This is known as a push system, since a production planner is pushing production orders into the manufacturing process.

The production module used to plan production around a forecast is called material requirements planning (MRP). MRP links computer-driven planning with the bills of material for all items to be produced, records of on-hand inventory balances, and a production schedule. The output of this system is a listing of dates on which orders are released to production, as well as a set of purchase orders issued to suppliers for raw materials to be delivered to the company in order to support the planned production. An MRP system is a marvel of interlinked schedules, and can yield significant output improvements over a less organized system. However, it is also highly dependent upon having accurate inventory records and bills of material; if there is a data error anywhere in the system, MRP planning breaks down.

The use of a push system has a profound impact on the amount of inventory in a company. The following areas are affected:

- *Finished goods.* The accuracy of the forecast used to schedule production directly impacts the amount of finished goods on hand. If the forecast is lower than actual demand, finished goods inventory levels will be near zero. If the forecast is too high, these inventory levels will be quite high as well, and there is an increased risk of having obsolete inventory on hand.

- *Work-in-process.* There can be a substantial amount of goods in the production process, depending upon the extent to which the system assumes that goods are batched at a work station prior to being moved to the next work station for additional processing. There can also be significant queue times in front of each work station, allowing work-in-process to pile up.
- *Raw materials.* If large safety stocks are built into the MRP system, there may be substantial raw material inventory balances on hand to guard against shortages. This can result in obsolete raw materials, if the products for which the raw materials are intended are cancelled.

An MRP system is a boon to the accountant. The system emphasizes a high degree of accuracy in inventory records and bills of materials, and requires the use of a perpetual inventory system. This means that the accountant does not need to conduct physical counts, and can instead run an inventory report at the end of each reporting period that is likely to contain highly accurate unit counts. Since the bill of material records have a high level of accuracy, the accountant can combine these records with standard costs to compile accurate standards-based inventory valuations. Also, it is quite difficult for anyone to fraudulently alter inventory unit counts in an MRP system, since such an action would likely be detected by the system's control points in short order. Finally, when properly used, the system can reduce inventory levels by paying close attention to ordering requirements and parts usage. With a lower inventory investment, the inventory asset as a whole comprises a smaller proportion of the balance sheet, so it takes a larger inventory accounting error to create a material error in the financial statements.

Inventory Flow in a Pull Environment

We have just discussed the flow of materials in a push environment, where raw materials are essentially pushed into the front end of the production process. An alternative production system employs the "pull" approach, where production is pulled from the back end of the process by actual customer orders. The pull concept is incorporated into the just-in-time production system, which focuses on reducing waste in the production process. Under a just-in-time system, waste is defined as excess inventory in the system. Inventory is reduced by the following means:

- *Reduced production runs.* Fast equipment setup times make it economical to create very short production runs, which reduce the investment in finished goods inventory.
- *Production cells.* Employees walk individual parts through the processing steps in a work cell, thereby reducing scrap levels. Doing so also eliminates the work-in-process queues that typically build up in front of a more specialized work station.

- *Compressed operations*. Production cells are arranged close together, so there is less work-in-process inventory residing between cells.
- *Delivery quantities*. Deliveries from suppliers are made in the smallest possible quantities, possibly more than once a day, which nearly eliminates raw material inventories.
- *Certification*. Supplier quality is certified in advance, so their deliveries can be sent straight to the production area, rather than piling up in the receiving area to await inspection.
- *First pass production quality*. A pull system can only work if the quality of first-pass production is extremely high. Otherwise, so many goods will be rejected that additional production orders must be run through the system, thereby delaying the fulfillment of customer orders.
- *Local sourcing*. When suppliers are located quite close to a company's production facility, the shortened distances make it much more likely that deliveries will be made on time, which reduces the need for safety stocks.

The impact of a just-in-time system on the accounting function is profound. Since this approach emphasizes the elimination of waste, and the time spent to record accounting transactions can be considered waste, there are very few accounting actions being output from the system – essentially just receiving and shipping transactions. The system is designed to produce so little scrap, spoilage, and rework that there is no point in separately recording these items – they are simply rolled into the general cost of goods sold account. Similarly, the amount of inventory kept on hand is so low that the amount of obsolete inventory should also be low. In addition, the cycle time required to manufacture a product is minimized – to the point where there is no reason to separately record any work-in-process. Instead, there are only classifications for raw materials and finished goods. Finally, a just-in-time system requires so little on-site inventory that there are no cost layers to track; instead, there is only the cost of the most recent purchase of raw materials in the accounting records. In short, the general reduction of inventory levels and increase in production speed yields a leaner environment in which accounting activities can be reduced.

Summary

The overwhelming volume of topics related to inventory should make it clear that the accountant must be deeply concerned with the accuracy of the inventory asset. There are an inordinate number of ways in which inventory can be incorrectly recorded or subsequently modified, as well as ways in which the asset value can be fraudulently altered. In the following chapters, we show how these concerns can be mitigated by installing a robust system of counting, valuation, controls, and measurements.

Chapter 2
Periodic and Perpetual Inventory Systems

Introduction

The accounting for inventory is highly dependent upon the type of inventory system that a company has in place. In this chapter, we discuss the periodic and perpetual inventory systems, which form the basis for reliable inventory accounting processes. We make note of the process flows in these systems, as well as the circumstances in which each one is most applicable.

The Periodic Inventory System

The minimum inventory accounting system is the periodic system. It is impossible to devise an ending inventory valuation without having a functioning periodic inventory system in place. The system is dependent upon just two activities, which are:

- Compiling the cost of all inventory-related purchases during the reporting period; and
- Conducting a physical count of the ending inventory.

The compilation of inventory-related purchases is quite easy in any accounting system, and is only dependent upon recording targeted purchases in an inventory purchases account as the offsetting debit to each accounts payable transaction.

Since physical inventory counts are time-consuming, few companies do them more than once a quarter or year. In the meantime, the inventory asset account continues to show the cost of the inventory that was recorded as of the last physical inventory count; the balance is not adjusted until there is another physical count or an ending valuation is estimated. The longer it takes to conduct a replacement physical inventory count, the longer the time period in which errors and inventory losses of various kinds can pile up undetected. As a result, there is an increasing risk of overstating ending inventory and understating the cost of goods sold over time. Given this problem, we recommend frequent physical counts.

To operate a periodic inventory system, follow these steps:

1. Compile all inventory-related purchases during the reporting period in a separate account.
2. At the end of the period, conduct a physical count to derive the ending inventory valuation.
3. Calculate the cost of goods sold for the period, using the following formula:

Beginning inventory + Purchases = Cost of goods available for sale

Cost of goods available for sale – Ending inventory = Cost of goods sold

4. Complete the following entry to zero out the balance in the purchases account, adjust the inventory account to match the ending physical count, and record the cost of goods sold:

	Debit	Credit
Cost of goods sold	xxx	
Inventory purchases		xxx
Inventory		xxx

EXAMPLE

Milagro Corporation has beginning inventory of $100,000, has paid $170,000 for purchases, and its physical inventory count reveals an ending inventory cost of $80,000. The calculation of its cost of goods sold is:

$100,000 Beginning inventory + $170,000 Purchases - $80,000 Ending inventory

= $190,000 Cost of goods sold

Milagro's controller records the following journal entry to document this calculation:

	Debit	Credit
Cost of goods sold	190,000	
Purchases		170,000
Inventory		20,000

The periodic inventory system is most useful for smaller businesses that maintain minimal amounts of inventory. For them, a physical inventory count is easy to complete, and they can estimate cost of goods sold figures for interim periods. However, there are several problems with the system:

- *Inaccuracy in the absence of a count.* The system does not yield any information about the cost of goods sold or ending inventory balances during interim periods when there has been no physical inventory count.
- *Subsequent catch-up adjustments.* The accounting staff must estimate the cost of goods sold during interim periods, which will likely result in a significant adjustment to the actual cost of goods whenever the company eventually completes a physical inventory count.
- *Obsolete inventory and scrap adjustments.* There is no way to adjust for obsolete inventory or scrap losses during interim periods, so there tends to be a significant (and expensive) adjustment for these issues when a physical inventory count is eventually completed.

A more up-to-date and accurate alternative to the periodic inventory system is the perpetual inventory system, which is described in the next section.

The Perpetual Inventory System

Under the perpetual inventory system, an entity continually updates its inventory records to account for additions to and subtractions from inventory for such activities as received inventory items, goods sold from stock, and items picked from inventory for use in the production process. Thus, a perpetual inventory system has the advantages of both providing up-to-date inventory balance information and requiring a reduced level of physical inventory counts. However, the calculated inventory levels derived by a perpetual inventory system may gradually diverge from actual inventory levels, due to unrecorded transactions or theft, so the warehouse staff should periodically compare book balances to actual on-hand quantities with cycle counting (as explained in the Inventory Counting and Reconciliation chapter). The following example shows how a perpetual system functions.

EXAMPLE

This example contains several journal entries used to account for transactions in a perpetual inventory system. Milagro Corporation records a purchase of $1,500 of widgets that are stored in inventory:

	Debit	Credit
Inventory	1,500	
Accounts payable		1,500

Milagro records $250 of inbound freight cost associated with the delivery of widgets:

	Debit	Credit
Inventory	250	
Accounts payable		250

Milagro records the sale of widgets from inventory for $2,000, for which the associated inventory cost is $800:

	Debit	Credit
Accounts receivable	2,000	
Revenue		2,000
Cost of goods sold	800	
Inventory		800

Milagro records a downward inventory adjustment of $300, caused by inventory theft, and detected during a cycle count:

	Debit	Credit
Inventory shrinkage expense	300	
Inventory		300

The net effect of these entries, assuming a zero beginning balance, is an ending inventory balance of $650.

The downside of using a perpetual inventory system is a massive increase in the number of inventory-related transactions that must be recorded. This burden may require the addition of warehouse clerks to record transactions, or the use of bar code scanning, portable data entry terminals, or other labor-saving devices. These concepts are addressed in the Inventory Record Accuracy chapter.

The initial comparison of a perpetual system's recorded inventory valuation to the physical count will likely reveal a significant disparity. This variance will be caused by a number of transactions not being recorded or recorded incorrectly. If the causes of these variances are tracked down and corrected (usually with procedural changes and training updates), the perpetual system will eventually become quite reliable. However, if a company has a small and low-cost inventory that rarely experiences much turnover, it is possible that the increased reliability of a perpetual system will not be worth its added cost. If so, the periodic inventory system may be the more applicable system.

Summary

If a company has any real investment in inventory, the long-term goal of the accounting department should be to install a perpetual inventory system, coupled with a long-term cycle counting program. This system is the only one that offers a reliable level of inventory record accuracy on a day-to-day basis. Unfortunately, these systems are under the control of the warehouse manager, not the controller. Ensuring that these systems will be installed calls for a campaign to point out to all parts of the company the exceptional benefits of a perpetual system, including having a reliable flow of materials into the production process, being able to close the books faster, and possibly even reducing the investment in inventory. Presenting a strong case in favor of the system will make it much easier to obtain multi-departmental support for installing the system and ensuring that record accuracy remains high. For more information about record accuracy, see the Inventory Record Accuracy chapter.

Chapter 3
Inventory Record Accuracy

Introduction

It is impossible to properly account for inventory without first having highly accurate inventory records. The accounting staff cannot create a proper inventory valuation unless it has reliable inventory information. In this chapter, we describe the nature of inventory errors, factors that cause the errors, data entry methods that mitigate errors, and similar issues.

> **Related Podcast Episode:** Episode 56 of the Accounting Best Practices Podcast discusses inventory record accuracy. It is available at: **accounting-tools.com/podcasts** or **iTunes**

Inventory Record Errors

Many of the techniques available for valuing inventory are predicated on the existence of highly accurate inventory records. Unfortunately, there are an extraordinary number of ways in which inventory transactions can be incorrectly recorded. Here are a number of examples:

Receiving and putaways

- Received goods are not recorded at all
- A receipt is recorded against the wrong item, or in the wrong quantity
- Goods are putaway and the location is not recorded
- Goods are putaway and the location is incorrectly recorded

Picking activities

- The wrong quantity or the wrong product is picked
- A picker correctly picks an item, but scans the wrong bar code
- A picking transaction is not recorded, or recorded twice
- Picked goods are assigned to the wrong customer order
- A counting scale is incorrectly used, resulting in the wrong pick quantity

Data entry

- The quantity picked is transposed when entering the information
- Data entry does not occur until the following day

<u>Cycle and physical counting</u>

- A counting error is discovered that is actually caused by late data entry of a prior transaction, resulting in a correcting entry that compounds the problem
- An inexperienced person incorrectly counts inventory during a physical count, resulting in the "correction" of an on-hand balance
- A data entry person assumes the wrong unit of measure, such as rolls instead of inches

Another major factor that impacts record accuracy is, curiously, the capacity level at which a facility is operating. If there is little storage space left in the warehouse, the number of transactions increases in proportion to the amount of inventory, as goods are constantly shuffled in and out of temporary storage. Similarly, if the receiving and shipping areas do not have sufficient space for staging operations, more transactions are needed to move inventory in and out of temporary storage locations. Error rates are closely tied to the volume of transactions, so the error rate will increase as capacity levels approach their maximum theoretical limits. Consequently, a sudden spike in error rates can signal an immediate need for more storage space.

Another factor that impacts record accuracy is the speed of operations. If goods are picked from stock and immediately sent to customers, transactions are only needed to record the pick and the shipment. Similarly, if items are picked for inclusion in the production process, a rapid manufacturing flow may require only transactions for the picking of raw materials and the putaway of finished goods. However, if these processes are slowed down, inventory must also be recorded in the temporary storage locations where it may reside. Each of these additional transactions increases the risk of recording a transaction error. For example:

- Goods are picked from stock early, and are not expected to be delivered to the customer until the next day. This requires that the goods be recorded in a staging area prior to shipment the following day.
- Goods are taken from one customer order to satisfy another order. This means that the first order is shunted aside to temporary storage until the goods can be replaced. The remaining goods must be recorded in temporary storage until shipped. Alternatively, the goods may be returned to stock until the order can be fulfilled, which requires an extra putaway transaction.
- The production process requires that many subassemblies be delivered from suppliers before final assembly can be completed. The process allows for partially-completed assemblies to be held in temporary storage until subassemblies arrive. Each instance of temporary storage requires a transaction to track the location of the goods.

In short, there are a multitude of areas in which inventory record errors can arise. In the next few sections, we note how a variety of factors can have a negative impact on record accuracy.

Environmental Factors Impacting Record Accuracy

A number of issues involving the warehouse environment can impact inventory record accuracy. Environmental factors to be aware of include the following:

- *Floor and aisle lighting.* Information can be misread or incorrectly entered if there is poor lighting in the warehouse. Poor lighting can refer to both dim lighting and excessively bright lighting. For example, a fork lift driver may have to squint up into the overhead lights in an aisle to putaway a pallet, and puts it in the wrong location. Or, the lighting is so dim in an aisle that workers cannot see location tags or identification numbers. There are many ways to improve or compensate for lighting, including localized spot lights on forklifts, backlit displays on portable computers, and using much larger fonts on inventory tags.

- *Direct sunlight.* If scanners are being used to read bar code labels, direct sunlight on the labels can make it impossible for the scanners to see any information. In addition, direct sunlight can rapidly fade labels, making them impossible to read. The fading problem can be mitigated by using more robust labels. Items stored in direct sunlight may have to be moved elsewhere if scanners are to be used.

- *Temperature.* Computer equipment is only designed to work within certain temperature ranges, outside of which they may not be usable. Colder temperatures make it difficult for employees to write legibly or key information into a computer. If pick and pack to voice systems are available for cold weather applications, they can overcome the low-temperature problem. If temperature ranges are extreme, it may be necessary to only use computer equipment within temperature-controlled parts of the warehouse.

- *Housekeeping.* When there is little attention to how goods are stored, they may routinely be placed in the wrong locations or span several locations, or be tucked away into corners and not recognized in the computer system at all. Poor housekeeping in staging areas can lead to the mixing of inventory among different customer orders or production kits. Poor housekeeping also applies to computer workstations, where paper-based transactions can easily be mixed up or lost. The only solution is an ongoing emphasis on housekeeping within the warehouse area.

While each of these items can cause record accuracy to decline, an ongoing remediation program that targets each issue can yield excellent results.

Employee Factors Impacting Record Accuracy

There are major differences in the ability of certain individuals to correctly record transactions. These differences are not immediately apparent when someone is hired, but will become apparent over a relatively short period of time. The following factors all contribute to an employee causing inventory record inaccuracies:

- *Attachment to work*. Those employees that truly care about what they do have a much higher level of record accuracy than those who are disinterested.
- *Feedback acceptance*. When employees receive feedback about an incorrect inventory transaction, some immediately accept the feedback and others become defensive.
- *Experience*. A person with minimal experience will inevitably make more mistakes than someone with years of experience in the same environment.

Only the last of the preceding factors (experience) will improve record accuracy over time. The other factors are ones that an employee must make the decision to correct.

Ultimately, everyone who is involved with inventory is responsible for the accuracy of the associated records. This means that there is no place in a company where minimally-accurate employees can be parked. Unfortunately, some employee turnover will likely be required before a company arrives at the point where inventory record inaccuracies are no longer associated with the incompetence of employees.

Labeling Issues Impacting Record Accuracy

The types and durability of the labels used to identify inventory and storage locations can have a profound impact on inventory record accuracy. Labels can easily be ripped or destroyed in the high-impact environment of a warehouse, making it much more difficult for the warehouse staff to record transactions. To mitigate problems with labels, follow these practices:

- *Label adhesion*. Buying inventory labels is a serious business, since the wrong ones may not adhere to cardboard or shrink wrap, or fall off after minimal impact or due to high humidity levels. Consequently, obtain a sample of the labels to be used, and subject them to the full range of adhesion scenarios that are likely to be encountered. The testing may last for several months, to see if adhesion wears off over time.
- *Label durability*. Subject a set of test labels to rigorous inventory handling practices, and determine the extent to which they are damaged. This can be impacted by the thickness and fiber content of the labels.
- *Scanability*. Packing tape is frequently run over labels, especially location labels in the storage racks. If so, and bar codes are used, determine how many layers of packing tape (if any) can be used without interfering with the ability of a bar code scanner to access bar code information.

- *Label placement.* Develop standards for where labels are to be placed on inventory items, so that they are easily accessible by the staff. For example, placing a label on the backside of a pallet does little good if it cannot be seen from the front of a storage rack.
- *Font size.* There is no such thing as an excessively large font, especially in a low-light or dirty environment. If there is excess space on a label, use it to more prominently display information with a larger font.

Proper attention to these issues can largely eliminate labeling issues as a source of inventory record accuracy problems.

Inventory Naming Conventions Impacting Record Accuracy

A key element in the record accuracy problem is the complexity of the information being entered. If inventory identification numbers, units of measure, and location codes are excessively complex, there is an increased chance that they will be entered incorrectly. For example:

- *Inventory names.* Instead of using random digits to identify an item, consider the inclusion of at least some meaning in the name, so that a data entry person will understand what they are entering. For example, a large blue widget could be identified as Widget-Blue-L instead of 123ABC04#. However, the result can be extremely long part numbers. Also, a numbering scheme that made sense several years ago may no longer be practical, as a business transitions to new product lines and configurations.
- *Location codes.* A typical location code describes the aisle, rack, and bin in which inventory is located. For example, location 04-M-03 signifies aisle four, rack M, bin three. Or, if goods are to be located in a bulk storage area, use just an aisle address to denote a lane in which all pallets containing a specific item are to be stored. These approaches are simple and widely-used naming conventions. Trouble can arise when the coding system varies by section of the warehouse, or for different warehouses using the same computer system. Instead, do everything possible to require the same coding convention for all storage areas.
- *Units of measure.* It may seem simple enough to record a unit of measure, such as EA for each. However, some companies obfuscate the obvious by including too much information. For example, a label stating "8/20 LB" might be intended to convey that there are eight units in a box, each of which weighs 20 pounds. This label can be misinterpreted, such as 8/20ths of a pound, or 20 units weighing eight pounds. Consequently, do not include too much information in the unit of measure.

> **Tip:** Exclude all special characters, such as hyphens, from inventory records. These characters are especially difficult to access on a portable keyboard. Instead, have the data entry software automatically insert these characters in a specific position in a data entry sequence. For example, the entry of location code B-04-T only requires a person to enter B04T, with the computer entering the applicable hyphens automatically.

There are other benefits of having simplified naming conventions. Stock pickers will have a much easier time finding and picking the correct goods from stock. It is also less likely that incorrect pack sizes will be sent to the production area or to customers.

One might believe that the issues raised in this section do not apply when the entire data collection system is automated. For example, if scanners are used to extract information from bar code labels, who cares about the complexity of the labels? This is an incorrect assumption, for information must at some point be encoded into the labels, and this can be done incorrectly. If a bar code label is incorrect, all subsequent scans of that label will also be incorrect. Thus, the use of automated data collection simply makes errors more widespread.

> **Tip:** There is no such thing as an excessively large label that identifies an inventory item. Use the largest possible font sizes and the cleanest information layout, so the warehouse staff has a better chance of reading the label information from a distance.

Excessive Data Recordation

The typical inventory management system requires that a standard set of information be entered for each new inventory item. This can involve dozens of data fields, especially in more complex systems that seek to provide every conceivable feature to users. The result is that users must tab their way through a massive number of fields to enter the information that is actually needed. It is quite easy for a user to inadvertently tab through to the wrong field to enter information, or to skip entering needed information.

To avoid this data entry problem, configure all data entry screens to contain only those fields for which information must be entered. Also, set the system to require information to be entered in each of these required fields, thereby sidestepping the problem of missing information. Depending on the capabilities of the software, it may also be possible to reconfigure the layout of the fields on the screen, to cluster together groups of similar information and to generally speed up the data entry process.

Inventory Data Collection Methods

The method chosen to collect information about inventory transactions can have a profound impact on the accuracy of inventory records. In the following table, we note the issues and benefits associated with the most common inventory data collection methods:

Inventory Data Collection Methods

Data Collection Method	Description, Issues and Benefits
Paper-based	Description: All transactions are recorded on paper and forwarded to a warehouse clerk for entry in a manual ledger. Advantage: Can be maintained under primitive conditions and high-stress environments where computer systems are not available or usable. Disadvantages: Subject to data entry error at the point of origin as well as by the warehouse clerk. Notification documents may also be lost or seriously delayed before they reach the clerk. These delays can interfere with cycle counting.
Bar code scanning	Description: Bar codes are assigned to all bin locations and inventory items. The bar codes for other commonly-used information, such as employee identification numbers, quantities, and activity descriptions can be included on bar code scan boards that employees carry with them. The warehouse staff scans bar codes to initiate a transaction, and then uploads the information to the computer system. No manual entries are required. Advantages: Eliminates data entry errors, reduces the time of the warehouse staff in recording transactions, and eliminates the data entry work of the warehouse clerk. Disadvantages: Scanners are moderately expensive and can be broken. There is a risk of data loss if the memory component of a scanner is broken before scanned transactions can be uploaded. Does not work if there is no direct line of sight access to a label. Labels are subject to tearing, which can make them unreadable. If a label is encoded incorrectly, this will result in the recordation of incorrect information for as long as the label is used.
Radio frequency terminals	Description: This is a portable scanning unit that also accepts instructions by wireless communication from the warehouse management system. Scanned transactions are uploaded in real time. Advantages: An excellent technique for maintaining a mobile workforce in the warehouse that sends back and receives transactional information from anywhere in the facility. Disadvantages: Terminals are expensive and can be broken. Transmissions do not always work in hostile environments where there are stray radio signals.

Data Collection Method	Description, Issues and Benefits
Radio frequency identification	Description: Transponder tags are attached to inventory items, which emit an encoded set of information to a receiver when inventory items pass a receiving station. These tags are usually passive, which means they only transmit information when impacted by a transmission signal. Active tags contain their own power source, and so can transmit at any time. Advantages: Can automatically receive information from passing inventory, so that inventory movements are tracked in real time without operator intervention. Can operate even if there is no direct line of sight communication with the receiver. Receivers can accept high volumes of information within a short period of time, and can collect information from tags located relatively far away. Disadvantages: Relies upon the ability of transponder tags to properly transmit information and of receiving units to receive the information, which does not always happen. The result is incomplete transactions from data dropout. Tags are not individually expensive, but so many are needed to track all items that the total tag cost can be prohibitive; the cost currently limits their use to unit-loads.
Voice	Description: The warehouse management system (WMS) sends wireless instructions to an employee, who is wearing a headset and microphone attached to a small portable computer. The computer converts the instructions to voice commands. The employee can respond with a specific set of words that the WMS can understand. Advantages: Useful in environments where hands-free communication is necessary, such as cold storage. Increases record keeping accuracy and employee productivity, while eliminating rekeying errors. Has a lower error rate than bar code scanning. A minimal training period is required. Disadvantages: Can be difficult to communicate with the WMS if there are stray signals in the warehouse environment. Not usable if the WMS must capture long strings of random numbers.
Pick to light	Description: A picking person receives a tray that contains a bar coded order number. After the order number is scanned, a display panel mounted above each storage bin flashes a light, indicating that a pick should be made; a display shows the number of units to pick, and a button is pressed when the pick is complete. The tray containing all picked items then moves to the next picking zone, where the order bar code is scanned again and all items to be picked from that area are lit up. The system can also be used to make on-the-spot cycle counting adjustments. Advantages: Can be retrofitted onto existing rack space. Works well for high-speed picking operations, and eliminates any need for the manual entry of transactions. There is also no need for a pick list. Requires minimal training. Disadvantages: Requires a linkage to the WMS, which controls the

Data Collection Method	Description, Issues and Benefits
	operation in real time. Can be expensive when large numbers of bins must be outfitted with display panels. The cost tends to limit its use to higher-volume picking operations.

The bar code scanning approach noted above can be expanded upon by requiring suppliers to label all goods shipped to the company with designated bar codes that identify the part number and quantity shipped. Then, when the goods are received, their attached bar codes are immediately scanned, and the stored information is loaded into the company's WMS. This approach is more accurate than having the receiving staff attempt to decipher the contents of each incoming load and create bar code labels on site.

The Data Entry Backlog Problem

Much of the last section contained descriptions of high-speed, automated data entry systems. What if a company cannot afford these systems, and continues to use a manual record keeping system? This is quite likely in smaller organizations with lower inventory turnover levels. In this situation, the single most important issue impacting inventory record accuracy is the data entry backlog problem.

In a manual system, paper-based transaction documents are continually arriving from all over the warehouse, documenting receipts, putaways, picks, restocking transactions, scrapped items, kitting activity, shipments, and so forth. If the warehouse data entry staff cannot keep up with this incoming flood, here are some of the resulting anomalies:

- Cycle counters routinely find that the recorded amount for an inventory location diverges from the on-hand count, since any transactions impacting that bin from the previous day(s) have not yet been recorded. Cycle counters then make adjustments to the inventory records based on what they have counted, which further reduces the accuracy of the records.
- Customers place orders based on the availability of inventory. However, the customer service staff is basing their promises on inventory records that are out of date, so that inventory may not actually be on the shelf. The result is either cancelled orders or expedited production activities to create replacement goods.
- Production is planned based on recorded parts availability. When the parts are not actually in stock, production must be rescheduled on a rush basis or overnight air freight used to obtain replacement parts from suppliers.

Given the significance of these issues, a great deal of effort should be put into erasing any data entry backlog. This can be done by overstaffing the data entry function, so that any backlog is eliminated in short order, and there is sufficient staff on hand to deal with a sudden surge in transaction volume. In addition, consider having data entry staff in any shift during which there is warehouse activity, so that the records are always up-to-date by the start of the next shift's work.

The best solution to the data entry backlog problem is to not use paper-based transactions at all. If the warehouse is a small one and transaction volumes are low, the automated systems required to avoid data entry issues will appear to be too expensive. However, if the cost of data entry staff and the time required to correct errors are included in the analysis, the cost-benefit of implementing a non-paper system may become more apparent. If not, continue to examine the situation if warehouse transaction volume grows over time, to see if paper-based transactions can be eliminated at a later date.

Back Flushing

Backflushing is the concept of waiting until the manufacture of a product has been completed, and then recording all of the related issuances of inventory from stock that were required to create the product. This approach has the advantage of avoiding all manual assignments of costs to products during the various production stages, thereby eliminating a large number of transactions and the associated labor. It also eliminates the need to manually record production picks, which is an area in which errors are particularly difficult to eradicate.

Backflushing is entirely automated, with a computer handling all transactions. The backflushing formula is:

$$\text{Number of units produced} \times \text{Unit count listed in the bill of materials for each component} = \text{Pick total}$$

Backflushing is a theoretically elegant solution to the complexities of assigning costs to products and relieving inventory, but it is difficult to implement. Backflushing is subject to the following problems:

- *Accurate production count.* The number of finished goods produced is the multiplier in the back flush equation, so an incorrect count will relieve an incorrect amount of components and raw materials from stock.
- *Accurate bill of materials.* The bill of materials contains a complete itemization of the components and raw materials used to construct a product. If the items in the bill are inaccurate, the back flush equation will relieve an incorrect amount of components and raw materials from stock.
- *Accurate scrap reporting.* There will inevitably be unusual amounts of scrap or rework in a production process that are not anticipated in a bill of materials. If these items are not separately deleted from inventory, they will remain in the inventory records, since the back flush equation does not account for them.
- *Rapid production.* Backflushing does not remove items from inventory until after a product has been completed, so the inventory records will remain incomplete until such time as the backflushing occurs. Thus, a very rapid production cycle time is the best way to keep this interval as short as possi-

ble. Under a backflushing system, there is no recorded amount of work-in-process inventory.

Backflushing is not suitable for long production processes, since it takes too long for the inventory records to be reduced after the eventual completion of products. It is also not suitable for the production of customized products, since this would require the creation of a unique bill of materials for each item produced.

We make note of the backflushing topic in this chapter in order to emphasize how easily it can be incorrectly implemented to spawn a large number of inventory record errors. However, the cautions raised here do not mean that it is impossible to use backflushing. Usually, a manufacturing planning system allows for the use of backflushing for just certain products, so that it can be run on a compartmentalized basis. This is useful not just to pilot test the concept, but also to use it only under those circumstances where it is most likely to succeed. Thus, backflushing can be incorporated into a hybrid system in which multiple methods of transaction recordation may be used.

Controls over Record Accuracy

Ideally, it should only be necessary to record an inventory-related transaction once, and then assume that the entry was made correctly. Doing so achieves a massive decline in data entry labor. However, the amount of errors actually experienced is likely to drive an additional need for controls that examine whether transactions were initially handled correctly. The following table shows the nature of a potential record accuracy problem, and the related controls that can mitigate the error rate.

Controls over Record Accuracy

Potential Error	Offsetting Control
Suppliers send incorrect quantities	• Count all pallets, cases, or units as received, or a selection of these items • Weigh pallets, cases or units as received • Visual inspection of received goods for obvious errors
Shipping department sends incorrect quantities	• Clearly delineate staging areas for each truckload, so that orders are not mixed • Second person independently counts pallets, cases, or units prior to delivery • Weight pallets, cases, or units prior to delivery • Visual inspection of goods to be shipped for obvious errors • Count the number of pallets or cases shipped and match to customer order • Do not load a truck until the entire shipment has been staged; otherwise, it is difficult to ascertain what has already been loaded

Potential Error	Offsetting Control
Putaway errors	• Match recorded putaways to actual locations from the prior day • Run report showing locations with zero inventory, and match to actual locations to see if they contain inventory
New employee errors	• Sort transaction logs by employee number and verify all transactions associated with new employees
General transaction errors	• Conduct cycle counts to look for general errors • Match what is on the shelf back to inventory report

Other controls than the ones noted here may be of more use, depending on the structure of the process flow and the types of inventory being handled.

When deciding upon a set of controls to install, always consider their impact on the process flow. A number of labor-intensive controls may indeed improve record accuracy, but at the price of slowing down the record-keeping process. Ideally, there should be a balance between adding additional controls and losing process efficiency.

Inventory Review Reports

There are a small number of reports that can be used to track down possible inventory record errors. The reports themselves will not pinpoint exactly why an error is occurring, but can at least point the user in the right direction. The reports are:

- *Empty location report.* Run a report that shows all locations in the warehouse in which there should be no inventory. Then check each of these locations. If inventory is located in one of these bins, there is a guaranteed record accuracy problem.
- *Multi-location report.* Run a report that shows all pallet-storage locations for which more than one item is supposedly being stored. The chances are good that one of the items is not really in storage, since there is no room for it. This report does not work in locations where cases and broken cases are stored, since many items could actually be kept in these areas.
- *Negative balance report.* Run a report that shows negative inventory unit quantities. An investigation can reveal that a key transaction has not yet been entered that will correct the balance, but this report will likely also reveal several situations where transactions have not been recorded at all. This report is described in more detail in the next section.
- *Sorted valuation report.* Calculate the total valuation of each inventory item, and sort the report in descending order of total valuation. The first page of the report can reveal situations where unit counts are grossly too high. A likely cause is that the incorrect unit of measure is being used.

Inventory review reports are detective controls, and so are only useful for locating errors after they have already occurred. These reports do not prevent errors from occurring in the first place.

The Negative Inventory Balance

An unfortunately common occurrence is that the inventory records indicate a negative on-hand balance. This situation always arises from either a delay or an error in data entry. Here are several situations that can cause a negative inventory balance:

- Goods are cross-docked from the receiving area, straight through to a truck for delivery to a customer. The shipment transaction is entered but not the receipt, resulting in a negative balance.
- Goods are replenished from reserve storage and then picked. The pick transaction is recorded but not the replenishment move, resulting in a negative balance.
- A receipt is incorrectly recorded with too small a quantity or with the wrong unit of measure, and then picked from stock. The receipt amount is too low, resulting in a negative balance.
- Goods are removed from stock, and the forklift operator accidentally records the transaction twice. With a double pick recorded, the on-hand balance appears to be negative.

As the examples indicate, a negative balance is sometimes a case of transaction documentation being delayed. If so, waiting a short period of time for the transaction to be recorded will yield a corrected inventory balance. However, other negative balances are indicative of more serious problems where transactions are lost or entered incorrectly. Since it is impossible to tell which scenario applies to a negative balance, it is best to immediately investigate every negative balance as soon as it is detected.

> **Tip:** Create an inventory report that only lists negative inventory balances, have the warehouse manager run it every day, and follow up on any negative items found.

Inventory Auditing

Given the massive number of transactions involved in the receipt, handling, and shipment of inventory, it may be useful to schedule a periodic audit by the internal audit department. These audits are usually highly targeted, so that specific activities are reviewed in detail. For example, the warehouse manager might be concerned about record accuracy related to picking activities, and so requests an audit to investigate these transactions. Even more specifically, the manager may ask for an audit of picking within a certain aisle, where error rates are unusually high.

Inventory audits are particularly useful when there is a suspicion that some employees in the warehouse area are stealing inventory. In this situation, cycle counting may not work, since the people counting goods may also be engaged in theft. By using the audit staff instead, there is a higher probability of locating specific fraudulent activity.

A variation on the auditing concept is self-auditing. Essentially, self-auditing means that employees review the transactions recorded by each other, either through the review of a small inventory count or a full-blown transaction reconstruction. This approach is only feasible if there is a sufficient amount of excess staff time available for self-auditing. Possible self-auditing methods include:

- *Cycle counting*. Have the warehouse staff review any exceptions found by their fellow cycle counters. This can also include a mutual review of any changes made to the inventory database for location or unit count altera-tions.
- *Picking*. Have inventory pickers compare what they picked to what is stated on their pick tickets.
- *Transaction entry*. The data entry staff can compare the paper transactions from which information was entered to a log of entered information from the computer system.

While useful, it is difficult to enforce the use of self-auditing, for several reasons. First, it is difficult to monitor auditing activities. Also, employees may pressure each other to not report any errors found. These issues can be reduced by paying a bonus to the warehouse staff that is based on the accuracy of inventory records.

The Corrective Action System

Any error found in the production and materials handling functions will likely have a negative impact on inventory. Either inventory must be scrapped, or more must be ordered, or a customer must be informed that an order cannot be shipped. In all three cases, the company loses – either because it must invest in more inventory or forego a sale. The best way to deal with these situations is to install a corrective action system.

A corrective action system is essentially a database of logged errors that are examined for corrective solutions. Every error is entered into this system, and is then assigned to an investigative team, with the goal of deriving a solution that will either eliminate or mitigate the incidence of the error. At a minimum, the database should contain the following information:

- Unique case identification number
- Complete description of the problem
- Identification information for the impacted inventory
- The area of the business in which the error occurred
- Person responsible for investigating the error
- Results of the investigation
- Actions taken to correct the error
- Scheduled date of follow-up review

In addition, someone should be responsible for reviewing the status of all open corrective action events. If an examination appears to be languishing, this fact can then be boosted to a higher level of management for more aggressive follow-up.

If an error is causing unusually significant problems, the presence of a follow-up review may be particularly important. In this case, management wants to ascertain whether the corrective action is sufficient, or if additional steps must be taken. In addition, the type of corrective action taken may itself be causing additional problems, which the follow-up review can spotlight. The trouble with corrective actions is that they represent a patch to the existing system, and so may not have been designed to fit seamlessly into the existing systems. If so, the follow-up review is intended to note any issues requiring additional examination. In short, the follow-up review is not intended to be a cursory review – instead, it can be a major re-examination of the changes made.

The end result of a corrective action system should be an ongoing reduction in the number of issues impacting inventory. However, this does not mean that all errors will eventually vanish. The introduction of new products, product lines, and processes will always trigger new error types. Also, there will be occasional outlier events that cause less-common errors. Consequently, there will always be a need for a corrective action system, even in the finest production and materials handling environment.

Summary

The inventory record accuracy issue is not an insignificant one. It is entirely possible that a mix of many environmental, technology, and employee issues all contribute to different types of errors. It may take a detailed investigation to discern the base-level reason for a particular issue, and even more time to determine a reasonable correction that will eliminate the problem. In one case, the author worked with a food processing company that estimated there were 65 ways to cause inventory record errors! When there are so many possible ways to cause errors and so much time is required to correct them, it is essential to focus on the largest classifications of errors first, and gradually work through to those problems causing the fewest errors. Doing so generates the most immediate return on investment, and also provides an immediate improvement to the many activities that depend on record accuracy in order to function properly, such as purchasing, production, and shipping.

Chapter 4
Inventory Counting and Reconciliation

Introduction

The inventory information generated by an accountant is useless if the underlying inventory records are incorrect. Consequently, the accountant may be deeply involved in periodic inventory counts or more frequent cycle counts, to ensure higher levels of record accuracy. In this chapter, we discuss how to set up a system of inventory record keeping, the various methods for counting inventory, and ways to improve these counts. We also describe the investigation of incorrect inventory counts, to ascertain the underlying problems that cause inaccurate inventory records. Only by implementing these systems can the accountant have a reasonable level of assurance that the inventory records being used are accurate.

How to Set Up Inventory Record Keeping

There must be an organizational and record keeping structure in place to support inventory records. Otherwise, the records will be hopelessly inaccurate in all respects; it will be difficult to locate inventory items, and unit quantities will be suspect. The following steps describe how to set up a warehouse structure that can support an inventory tracking and counting system:

1. *Identify inventory.* Create a part numbering system, and ensure that every item in inventory has been properly labeled with a part number. There should also be a procedure for identifying and labeling all new inventory as it is received or manufactured.
2. *Clean out miscellaneous accumulations.* Stray inventory items may accumulate in out-of-the-way locations, such as around work stations, in corners, and under conveyors. Return these items to their designated locations, and institute procedures to ensure that these stray areas are regularly swept clear of goods.
3. *Consolidate inventory.* If the same inventory items are stored in multiple locations, consolidate them into one place. This makes the counting process easier.
4. *Package inventory.* Where possible, put loose inventory items in boxes or bags, seal the containers, and mark the quantity on the sealing tape. Also put partial cases in front of or on top of full cases. This greatly reduces any subsequent counting effort.
5. *Create locations.* Create a system of inventory locations throughout the warehouse, which state the aisle, rack, and bin number in a logical manner. Verify that all locations in the warehouse have a prominently displayed location tag.

6. *Segregate the warehouse.* Install a fence around the warehouse, so that inventory can only pass through a central gate. The warehouse staff then counts and records inventory as it passes through the central gate.

7. *Count inventory.* After all of the preceding steps have been completed, conduct a physical inventory count (see the following Physical Inventory Count section).

8. *Record information.* Record the inventory quantities and locations in the inventory database.

Once an inventory record keeping system is in place, work on upgrading the accuracy of the inventory records. This can be done by installing a daily cycle counting program, which is discussed in the Cycle Counting section.

The accountant typically works on the initial setup of inventory records in an advisory role, though it is possible that some accounting staff may be transferred to the warehouse for the duration of the project.

The Physical Inventory Count

A physical inventory count provides the unit totals that form the basis for the ending inventory valuation, and can also be used to update inventory unit count records. A physical count is most necessary when inventory record accuracy levels are quite low, but can be avoided when there is an effective system of cycle counts in place.

Follow these steps when administering a physical inventory count:

Prior to the count:

1. *Tags.* Order a sufficient number of sequentially numbered count tags for the count. These should be two-part tags, and include line items for the product name, product identification number, quantity, and location. Also consider adding space for the counter's initials. There may be a punch hole in the top center, which can be used to tie the count tag to an inventory item. A sample count tag follows.

Sample Inventory Count Tag

2. *Part numbers.* Identify all inventory items that do not have a legible part number, and have the warehouse staff properly identify them prior to the count.

3. *Pre-counts.* Where possible, count items in advance, seal them in containers, and mark the quantities on the outside of the containers.

4. *Management area.* Set up management areas within the warehouse where counters are to assemble for instructions, as well as to collect and return all reports and forms needed for the count.

5. *Segregation.* Move all items not to be counted out of the counting area, or identify them with "Do not count" tags.

6. *Cutoff.* Segregate all received goods if they arrive after the cutoff date for the physical inventory count. Doing so ensures that only items properly logged into the inventory system will be counted.

7. *Outside locations.* Notify all outside locations to count their inventory and send in their count totals.

8. *Finalize data entry.* Have the warehouse staff complete all manual data entry of inventory transactions by the close of business before the count is scheduled to begin.

Counting activities:

1. *Train teams.* Instruct the counting teams regarding counting procedures, and issue them count tags that are numerically sequential. Keep track of which team has been issued a set of tags.

> **Tip:** Consider conducting a short practice count with anyone who has not been involved in a physical count before, so that problems can be corrected before actual counts are taken.

2. *Count inventory.* Each counting team must count the inventory in the area assigned to it, fill out the count information on an inventory tag, and tape a tag to each inventory item, retaining the copy of each tag. One person should count inventory, while a second person writes down the information on tags. When a count team is done, it turns in its copies of the tags, as well as any unused tags.
3. *Track tags.* A person responsible for tags verifies that all used and unused tags have been received, and accounts for any missing tags.
4. *Data entry.* Enter all tags into a database or spreadsheet, and summarize the quantities by part number and location.
5. *Comparison.* If the company uses a perpetual inventory system, compare the count totals to the inventory records. Investigate any variances by recounting the inventory.
6. *Reporting.* Print a final report that summarizes the unit quantities of all counted inventory items.
7. *Review the process.* Examine the entire physical count process, identify areas in which it could be improved, and write down these issues for consideration as part of the next physical count.
8. *Subsequent counts.* Create a list of the largest variances noted during the physical inventory count, and return to these items for cycle counts. It is entirely possible that a counting error caused the variances, and will require correction.

The amount of staff time required to complete a physical count tends to limit their use. Few organizations will conduct a count more frequently than on a quarterly basis. Far more organizations will only do so when the auditors require one as part of the year-end audit.

Concerns about the Physical Inventory Count

One might think that the effort required to organize and complete a physical inventory count would at least result in accurate inventory records. This is not necessarily the case. There are several reasons why the information generated by a physical count may be incorrect. Consider the following:

- *Staff quality.* If the count process is a large one, or if management wants to complete the count as quickly as possible, staff from outside the warehouse may be brought in to count inventory. These people may not know how to properly identify inventory items or count them, resulting in worse information than if the records had been left alone.
- *Data entry.* A massive amount of information from the count tags is keypunched into a database. Given the volume of information involved, it is very likely that there will be keypunching errors.
- *Duplicate and no counts.* There are many storage locations in a warehouse. Even in the best-organized physical count, some locations may be counted twice, while other locations are not counted at all.

Warehouse employees frequently look upon physical counts with dread, because the resulting information worsens inventory record accuracy to such an extent that they may spend weeks correcting records. Consequently, we strongly recommend moving away from physical inventory counts, and instead using an ongoing program of cycle counts to achieve higher levels of inventory record accuracy.

Physical Count Improvements

If a company finds that it cannot get away from the physical count process, there are some techniques available for streamlining the process flow in order to compress the counting process to the minimum possible time period, and to reduce error rates. Consider the following possibilities:

- *Counter qualifications.* Only warehouse employees are allowed to count inventory. No one else is allowed to do so, since they are unfamiliar with the inventory, and will make an unusually large number of errors. Given the time required to fix errors, using a smaller number of experienced counters is faster than using a large number of inexperienced counters.
- *Cycle count in advance.* A company may have already instituted cycle counting procedures, but accuracy levels are not yet sufficiently high to warrant the elimination of a physical count. If so, accuracy levels are likely much higher already than would have been the case without the cycle counting. Consequently, continue to run cycle counts right up to the start of the physical count. This should reduce the number of adjustments found during the physical count.
- *Hold receipts.* If an unusually large amount of inventory has just been delivered to the company, consider leaving it in the receiving area and not logging it into the record keeping system until the physical count is com-

pleted. This leaves less inventory to count, and reduces the chance of having a receiving error impact the counting process.

- *Inventory software interface.* Design a data entry program for the company's inventory records database, so that count tags can be entered directly into the system. Once aggregated, the program compares the balances to the on-hand amounts recorded in the system, and issues a variance report. This is a substantial improvement on entering tag information into an electronic spreadsheet, which is then compared by hand to the balances in the computer system.
- *Bar code tags.* Print a bar code on each tag issued, which contains the unique tag number. The data entry staff can then scan the bar code rather than manually entering the information, which eliminates a possible transposition error.
- *Record tag locations.* Have the count team note the exact aisle-rack-bin location of each inventory item on the related count tag. Then, if there is an issue with a tag, it is quite easy to locate where the tag was used in the warehouse, saving search time.
- *Pre-print tags with quantities.* Print a count tag in advance for each location that contains inventory, along with a bar coded tag number and the number of units stated in the inventory database. Counters then circle the stated inventory amount if it is correct, or enter a different number. A removable portion of the tag is then peeled off and stuck on the inventory to show that a count was completed. Once the entire count is done, aggregate all tags for which the stated quantity was correct. Design a data entry program for these items that only requires a scan of the bar coded tag number to enter the indicated quantity. Then use a different data entry program to enter all remaining tags for which different amounts were counted.

The last of the suggested improvements requires a large amount of up-front design work, but can yield the best overall improvement, since it streamlines counts and yields a massive reduction in data entry work.

Cycle Counting

Cycle counting is the process of counting a small proportion of the total inventory on a daily basis, and not only correcting any errors found, but also investigating the underlying reasons why the errors occurred. An active cycle counting program should result in a gradual increase in the level of inventory record accuracy.

Tip: Only the more experienced warehouse staff should engage in cycle counting, since they have the most experience with the inventory. Anyone else would probably make so many mistakes that they would *decrease* the level of inventory record accuracy.

There are multiple methods used for selecting the inventory items to be counted each day for a cycle counting program. They are:

- *By location*. Simply work through the warehouse, section by section. This approach ensures that all inventory items will be counted, and is a simple way to coordinate the daily counts. Once the entire warehouse has been counted, start back at the beginning and do it again.

- *By usage*. The materials management department places a higher emphasis on the inventory record accuracy of those items used most frequently in the production process, since an unexpected shortage of one of these items could stop production. Consequently, high-usage items would be counted more frequently.

- *By criticality*. Some items must be on hand, or production cannot proceed. Also, these items may be extremely difficult to obtain, perhaps because suppliers require long lead times, or because the only supplier is selling goods on an allocation basis. In this situation, the very small number of critical items should be continually monitored, with all other goods receiving less cycle counting attention. A variation on this concept is to give counting priority to those items scheduled to go into production in the near future; under this approach, cycle counts should be scheduled earlier than the lead time required to replace a part, in case the counts reveal missing parts, and replacements must be ordered in time to meet the production schedule.

- *By valuation*. The accounting department is most concerned with the record accuracy of those inventory items having the largest aggregate cost, since an error here would impact reported profits. Consequently, high-valuation items would be counted more frequently.

A further refinement of these concepts is to conduct cycle counts at the low point of on-hand quantity levels. Doing so reduces the amount of counting effort by the warehouse staff, thereby reducing the time required to complete a series of counts. A variation on this concept is to conduct cycle counts after a production run has been completed. Doing so catches any reporting errors associated with the last production run. Also, since production has just been completed, raw material unit counts should be at a low point, which facilitates counting.

Some inventory items may move so slowly that there is little need to subject them to cycle counts. In these situations, one could create a single annual cycle count for them, and exclude them from all other counts during the year.

Once a cycle counting methodology is in place, use the following steps to conduct daily cycle counts:

1. *Complete transactions*. Verify that all prior inventory transactions have been recorded in the inventory database. If cycle counts are allowed when there are still some unrecorded transactions, counters will find differences between their counts and the cycle counting report and make adjustments, after which the original transactions are also recorded, resulting in reduced inventory record accuracy.

2. *Print reports.* Print cycle counting reports for the cycle counters, which itemize the counts to be made based on the cycle counting methodology (e.g., by location, usage, criticality, or valuation). The typical report is sorted by location code, so that counters can most efficiently locate items to be counted. A sample format follows:

Sample Cycle Counting Report

Location	Item Number	Description	Unit of Measure	Quantity
B-08-A	B1234	Widget, Titanium, Green – Medium Size	EA	_____
B-08-B	Q1420	Widget, Steel, Blue – Small Size	EA	_____
B-08-C	Z0998	Widget, Aluminum, Yellow – Large	EA	_____
B-08-D	H6320	Widget, Stainless Steel, Red – Large	EA	_____

3. *Count.* Each cycle counter traces the items listed on his or her cycle counting report to their locations, counts the units in the storage bin, and marks any corrections on the report. Further, the counters trace items from the bin back to the report, to see if there are any items in stock that are not in the inventory database.

> **Tip:** Only count a few items when the cycle counting program is just getting under way, since there will likely be a large number of problems to investigate and correct. The sample size can be increased once there are fewer errors to investigate.

> **Tip:** A good way to reduce count inaccuracies is to have counters move counted items into a separate container for the duration of a count, thereby avoiding double counts or missed counts. A variation is to dump all items out of a bin and then count them as they are replaced into the bin.

4. *Recount.* Have a second person conduct a recount of any indicated errors. Someone else's viewpoint may be needed to discover that an initial count was incorrect, perhaps due to an improper inclusion or exclusion, or the use of an incorrect unit of measure.

> **Tip:** Anyone assigned to recount possible record errors should have an excellent knowledge of the inventory and the counting process, thereby increasing the probability that an incorrect initial count is detected. This person is frequently a senior warehouse staff person.

5. *Reconcile errors.* Investigate any differences between the inventory record and the amounts counted. This process is discussed in the following Inventory Reconciliation section.

6. *Correct errors.* The warehouse staff adjusts the inventory database for any errors found. These adjustments should be clearly designated as cycle counting corrections.
7. *Take preventive action.* If certain errors are appearing on a repetitive basis, the warehouse manager should adjust the warehouse procedures to keep them from arising in the future.

Tip: Reinforce the importance of cycle counting by having an accounting or internal audit person conduct a weekly audit of the inventory, and calculate an overall inventory accuracy percentage that is posted for the warehouse staff to see. In addition, consider paying bonuses to the warehouse staff for continuing improvements in inventory record accuracy.

When is the best time of day in which to conduct cycle counts? The main consideration is that they only be conducted after all inventory transactions for the day have been inputted into the inventory records. Otherwise, the amounts counted during cycle counts cannot be compared to any valid record quantity. Other than this consideration, the best time of day is at the beginning of a shift, before the warehouse staff becomes overwhelmed by the daily round of activities. Otherwise, there is a strong chance that a sudden crisis will divert the warehouse staff from their counting responsibilities until another day.

If there is an ongoing pattern of cutting cycle counts short to deal with other issues, a different approach is indicated. In this situation, assign cycle counting to a small group that does nothing but cycle counts and the associated investigation of errors found. This approach ensures that cycle counting will continue at all times. This approach also yields an extremely experienced group that develops great expertise in tracking down inventory record accuracy problems.

Tip: If a permanent cycle counting group is formed, consider rotating them out to other duties from time to time. Doing so keeps the staff from becoming bored, and also spreads the importance of inventory record accuracy among the entire warehouse staff.

There may be situations in which the warehouse operates at all hours, every day of the week. If so, it can be quite difficult to ensure that all records have been entered and activity frozen long enough to engage in cycle counting at all. Under these circumstances, consider using the following techniques to squeeze in cycle counts:

- *Rely on exception reports.* Focus a large amount of attention on counting those inventory items that have been flagged by exception reports as being possibly in error. See the Inventory Review Reports section in the Inventory Record Accuracy chapter for more information.
- *Schedule counts around activity.* If there is a schedule of picks and putaways, use programming logic to assign counts to those areas that are not scheduled to be impacted during specific time periods. This approach also

works for the production area; schedule count activity for those periods when machinery is scheduled to be down for preventive or other scheduled maintenance.

- *Schedule counts around shift changes.* There is usually a work stoppage that coincides with the end of one shift and the beginning of the next. Schedule the shifts of the cycle counters to overlap with the normal shift change, so they can count inventory when the warehouse is effectively shut down.
- *Use intermediate storage.* If goods are about to be picked for any reason, pick in advance to an intermediate storage location to get them out of the way, and then count the residual balance in a location.

After cycle counting corrections have been implemented over a period of time, the incidence of inventory record errors should decline considerably, yielding higher inventory accuracy levels. To see if this is happening, create an inventory accuracy report that is sorted by responsibility area, noting audited accuracy levels over a period of time. This report should be widely distributed, so the warehouse staff is fully aware of how much importance is assigned to a high level of accuracy. A sample report format follows, with key accuracy declines noted in bold:

		Audited Inventory Accuracy Percentage			
Aisle	Responsibility	Today	Last Week	Last Month	Last Quarter
A	Jeff B.	69%	63%	58%	42%
B	Allen R.	**51%**	68%	45%	20%
C	Anya K.	75%	**70%**	80%	33%
D	Sara C.	23%	19%	12%	12%
E	Devon Q.	45%	40%	**12%**	27%
F	Michael J.	28%	24%	20%	19%
G	Nora G.	**40%**	50%	35%	25%

Over time, the error correction process associated with cycle counts may eliminate so many procedural and other issues that the count teams are no longer finding any errors. If so, it is permissible to gradually scale back the amount of effort allocated to cycle counting. However, the counting effort must continue at *some* level, since new errors may arise that must be spotted and counteracted.

Control Group Analysis

Cycle counting is a never-ending process, which can be a problem. Someone assigned to always count inventory every day may eventually adopt slipshod habits while trying to rush through this task. Likely results are inattention to minor differences in account balances, and not bothering to follow up on errors found. A way to break through this malaise is to use control groups, either as a supplement to or in place of cycle counting.

Under the control group concept, a small number of inventory items are blocked out for study. These items typically have high transaction volumes, and are subject to a particular error that requires detailed investigation. A team of those employees most knowledgeable in inventory record accuracy issues monitors this control group, waiting for an error to appear. The group then reviews the situation, locates the problem, derives a solution, implements it, and follows up to ensure that the error has been eliminated. In short, this process is targeted at locating specific problems, rather than the cycle counting approach of scanning the entire inventory for any types of errors at all.

The control group concept works well when record accuracy is being notably impacted by a particular problem. However, it has no effect on incidental problems, unless the review team decides to specifically target them.

The control group concept can also be pursued prior to laying out a large cycle counting program. By doing so, management can see if the cycle counters have sufficient knowledge to identify and correct record accuracy problems. If not, the issues can be addressed within the control group. Otherwise, cycle counters might make a number of improper correction entries across the entire inventory that end up reducing total record accuracy.

EXAMPLE

Entwhistle Electric is having trouble with the record keeping associated with its inventory putaway operations. It appears that some of the putaways are not being recorded. Currently, putaways are conducted using any available storage location in the facility outside of the main picking area. To concentrate attention on the problem, putaways for the next week are only allowed in Aisle A, with putaways in the following week restricted to Aisle B, and so on. By using this approach, location audits can be concentrated in a small area, and errors traced back to putaway operations that span a relatively brief period of time.

100% Count Analysis

In some inventories, there are a very small number of extremely high-value items. These items typically have quite small cubic volumes, and yet comprise a significant part of the value of the entire inventory. If this is the case, it is not sufficient to review count balances with cycle counting, since reviews may only take place at long intervals. Instead, consider engaging in a 100% count of these items on a very frequent basis, perhaps daily.

By engaging in such an oppressively frequent review, any transaction errors or fraudulent withdrawals will be spotted immediately, thereby allowing for prompt corrective action. This approach is not cost-effective for less-valuable items, and so should be confined to considerably less than one percent of the items listed in inventory.

Inventory Reconciliation

Inventory is reconciled when the inventory counts in an organization's records are compared to the actual amounts on the warehouse shelves, the differences between the two amounts are resolved, and the inventory records are adjusted to reflect this analysis.

Inventory reconciliation is an extremely important part of cycle counting, since the warehouse staff uses it to continually update the accuracy of its inventory records. Inventory reconciliation is not as simple as adjusting the book balance to match the physical count. There may be other reasons why there is a difference between the two numbers that cannot be corrected with such an adjustment. In particular, consider following any or all of these steps:

- *Recount the inventory.* It is entirely possible that someone incorrectly counted the inventory. If so, have a different person count it again (since the first counter could make the same counting mistake a second time). Further, if the physical count appears to be significantly lower than the book balance, it is quite possible that there is more inventory in a second location - so look around for a second cache of inventory. Recounting is the most likely reason for a variance, so consider this step first. Also, it can make sense to wait a day or two to see if a missing transaction turns up that can explain the difference.

- *Match the units of measure.* Are the units of measure used for the count and the book balance the same? One might be in individual units (known as "eaches"), while the other might be in dozens, or boxes, or pounds, or kilograms. If a recount has already been conducted and there is still a difference that is orders of magnitude apart, it is quite likely that the units of measure are the problem. This is especially likely if goods are recorded using an unusual unit of measure.

- *Verify the part number.* It is possible that the part number of the item on the shelf is being misread, or its identification is a guess because there is no part number at all. If so, get a second opinion from an experienced warehouse staff person, or compare the item to the descriptions in the item master records. Another option is to look for some other item for which there is a unit count variance in the opposite direction - this could be the missing part number.

- *Look for missing paperwork.* This is an unfortunately large source of inventory reconciliation issues. The unit count in the inventory records may be incorrect because a transaction has occurred, but no one has yet logged it. This is a massive issue for cycle counters, who may have to root around for unentered paperwork of this sort before they feel comfortable in making an adjusting entry to the inventory records. Other examples of this problem are receipts that have not yet been entered (so the inventory record is too low) or issuances from the warehouse to the production area that have not been entered (so the inventory record is too high).

- *Investigate backflushing records.* If the organization uses backflushing to alter inventory records (where inventory is relieved based on the number of finished goods produced), the bill of materials and the finished goods production numbers had better both be in excellent condition, or the reconciliation process will be painful. Backflushing is not recommended unless the level of manufacturing record keeping is superb.

The preceding points cover the most obvious issues that can impact inventory record accuracy. In addition, there are many transaction-specific issues that can cause an error. Consider the following additional investigation steps:

- *Examine transaction history.* Review the flow of transactions that were recorded since the last cycle count. There may be an obvious change in the number of units used somewhere in the flow. For example, 100 units are received, but only 50 are put away. Also, there may be a transfer between locations, with the unit count changing as part of the transfer.
- *Examine scrap.* Scrap can arise anywhere in a company (especially production), and the staff may easily overlook its proper recordation in the accounting records. If there is a modest variance where the inventory records are always just a small amount higher than the physical count, this is a likely cause.
- *Investigate possible customer ownership.* If there is no record of an inventory item at all in the accounting records, there may be a very good reason for it, which is that the company does not own it – a customer does. This is especially common when the company remodels or enhances products for its customers.
- *Investigate possible supplier ownership.* To follow up on the last item, it is also possible that there are items in stock that are on consignment from a supplier, and which are therefore owned by the supplier. This is most common in a retail environment and highly unlikely anywhere else.
- *Investigate data entry person.* There may be a high incidence of errors associated with the person logging in to record transactions. This could be an actual error, or could be indicative of a fraudulent transaction where goods are being removed from the warehouse.
- *Investigate variance trends.* If a series of variances are always negative, this is a strong indicator of either incorrect bill of material records or fraud. If there is no trend, with an equal number of positive and negative variances, look for variances that offset each other. This can indicate that inventory items are being misidentified, such as through picking errors.
- *Investigate canceled actions.* There may be a record of a cancelled purchase order, shipment, or production job. If the amount of the variance matches this cancelled activity, it is possible that the action actually occurred, and the cancellation was never reversed.
- *Investigate production errors.* If a shortage of raw materials coincides with the production of an excess amount of finished goods, it is possible that a

withdrawal of raw materials from stock for the production process was not recorded. This investigation requires detailed matching of bills of material to the missing amount of raw materials.

- *Investigate quality withdrawals*. If a product has a history of significant quality rejections and finished goods are missing from stock, it is entirely possible that the quality assurance staff rejected some finished goods and never recorded the withdrawal. This is an especially likely scenario, since the quality staff is unaccustomed to the detailed level of transaction recording that other employees consider to be routine.
- *Investigate payables*. A supplier may have invoiced the company for substantially more than the receiving department says was received. If so, the supplier may be correct, and the amount that should have been recorded as received is substantially higher. This is a rare case where an issue raised in the accounting department can point toward a record accuracy issue.
- *Investigate temporary storage*. There may be a record of goods that have been received, but which never appeared in a normal storage location. These items were likely recorded correctly, but no putaway transaction was ever recorded. A search of supposedly empty bins may find the missing goods.
- *Investigate prior cycle counting adjustments*. If the amount of a detected error approximately offsets a previous cycle counting adjustment, the error may be due to incorrect cycle counting procedures. This is a particularly pernicious error, since just one inexperienced cycle counting person can cause a large number of record errors.

If all forms of investigation fail, then there is no choice but to alter the inventory record to match the physical count. It is possible that some other error will eventually be found that explains the discrepancy, but for now the variance should be addressed; when in doubt, the physical count is correct. A variation under which the variance should also be accepted is when count scales are used to count goods, and the amount of the variance is within the accuracy tolerance of the counting scales.

Tip: Do not ignore a small variance. Even a variance that is immaterial on a percentage basis may be the first indicator of what may grow into a large accuracy problem.

The preceding points give a solid grounding in the reasons why there are errors in inventory records, but they are not the only reasons; other errors may be caused by unique record keeping systems or in particular industries, so compile a list of errors that have been discovered in the past, and use it when conducting an inventory reconciliation.

Summary

We cannot emphasize enough that some form of inventory counting will always be necessary – it is not sufficient to rely upon a perpetual inventory system, no matter how perfect the underlying inventory procedures may be. It takes very little to reduce inventory record accuracy, perhaps just a lack of training of a new employee in one type of transaction. Inventory counting is the last line of defense in ensuring that accuracy problems are detected in a timely manner. For more information about the causes of inventory record inaccuracy, see the Inventory Record Accuracy chapter.

Chapter 5
Estimating Ending Inventory

Introduction

The ending inventory figure is needed to derive the cost of goods sold, as well as the ending inventory balance to include in the balance sheet. It may not be possible to count the amount of inventory on hand, or assign a value to it. This situation can arise when there is too much shipping activity at month-end to conduct a physical count, or when the staff is too busy to take the time to conduct a physical count. If so, there are two methods available for estimating the ending inventory. These methods are not foolproof, since they rely upon historical trends, but they should give a reasonably accurate number, as long as no unusual transactions occurred during the period that might alter the ending inventory.

The Gross Profit Method

The *gross profit method* is the most generic method used to estimate the amount of ending inventory. Follow these steps to estimate ending inventory using the gross profit method:

1. Add together the cost of beginning inventory and the cost of purchases during the period to arrive at the cost of goods available for sale.
2. Multiply (1 - expected gross profit percentage) by sales during the period to arrive at the estimated cost of goods sold.
3. Subtract the estimated cost of goods sold (step 2) from the cost of goods available for sale (step 1) to arrive at the ending inventory.

EXAMPLE

Mulligan Imports is calculating its month-end golf club inventory for March. Its beginning inventory was $175,000 and its purchases during the month were $225,000. Thus, its cost of goods available for sale is:

$175,000 beginning inventory + $225,000 purchases
= $400,000 cost of goods available for sale

Mulligan's gross margin percentage for all of the past 12 months was 35%, which is considered a reliable long-term margin. Its sales during March were $500,000. Thus, its estimated cost of goods sold is:

(1 - 35%) × $500,000 = $325,000 cost of goods sold

By subtracting the estimated cost of goods sold from the cost of goods available for sale, Mulligan arrives at an estimated ending inventory balance of $75,000.

There are several issues with the gross profit method that make it unreliable as a long-term method for determining the value of inventory, which are:

- **Applicability**. The calculation is most useful in retail situations where a company is simply buying and reselling merchandise. If a company is instead manufacturing goods, the components of inventory must also include labor and overhead, which make the gross profit method too simplistic to yield reliable results.
- **Historical basis**. The gross profit percentage is a key component of the calculation, but the percentage is based on a company's historical experience. If the current situation yields a different percentage (as may be caused by a special sale at reduced prices), the gross profit percentage used in the calculation will be incorrect.
- **Inventory losses**. The calculation assumes that the long-term rate of losses due to theft, obsolescence, and other causes is included in the historical gross profit percentage. If not, or if these losses have not previously been recognized, the calculation will likely result in an inaccurate estimated ending inventory (and probably one that is too high).

In short, this method is most useful for a small number of consecutive accounting periods, after which the estimated ending balance should be updated with a physical inventory count.

The Retail Inventory Method

The retail inventory method is sometimes used by retailers that resell merchandise to estimate their ending inventory balances. This method is based on the relationship between the cost of merchandise and its retail price. To calculate the cost of ending inventory using the retail inventory method, follow these steps:

1. Calculate the cost-to-retail percentage, for which the formula is (Cost ÷ Retail price).
2. Calculate the cost of goods available for sale, for which the formula is (Cost of beginning inventory + Cost of purchases).
3. Calculate the cost of sales during the period, for which the formula is (Sales × cost-to-retail percentage).
4. Calculate ending inventory, for which the formula is (Cost of goods available for sale - Cost of sales during the period).

EXAMPLE

Mulligan Imports sells golf clubs for an average of $200, and which cost it $140. This is a cost-to-retail percentage of 70%. Mulligan's beginning inventory has a cost of $1,000,000, it paid $1,800,000 for purchases during the month, and it had sales of $2,400,000. The calculation of its ending inventory is:

Beginning inventory	$1,000,000	(at cost)
Purchases	+ 1,800,000	(at cost)
Goods available for sale	= 2,800,000	
Cost of sales	-1,680,000	(sales of $2,400,000 × 70%)
Ending inventory	= $1,120,000	

The retail inventory method is a quick and easy way to determine an approximate ending inventory balance. However, there are also several issues with it:

- *Estimate*. The retail inventory method is only an estimate. Do not rely upon it too heavily to create results that will compare with those of a physical inventory count.
- *Consistency*. The retail inventory method only works if there is a consistent mark-up across all products sold. If not, the actual ending inventory cost may vary wildly from what was derived using this method.
- *Subsequent changes*. The method assumes that the historical basis for the mark-up percentage continues into the current period. If the actual mark-up was different (as may be caused by an after-holidays sale), the results of the calculation will be incorrect.

Tip: If the mark-up percentage varies by groups of products or departments, set up separate retail method calculations for each of these groups. Doing so also creates a more reliable ending inventory calculation for the company as a whole.

As was the case with the gross profit method, this approach is most useful for a small number of consecutive accounting periods, after which the estimated ending balance should be updated with a physical inventory count.

The Effect of Overstated Ending Inventory

The primary caution with using either of the preceding methods is the risk of overstating ending inventory. There are many factors that can drive down actual inventory valuations – so many that they cannot be fully incorporated into a simplistic gross profit or retail method calculation. Thus, the result of either method is usually an ending inventory balance that is too high.

When ending inventory is overstated, this reduces the amount of inventory that would otherwise have been charged to the cost of goods sold during a period, so the cost of goods sold expense declines.

EXAMPLE

Dude Skis has beginning inventory of $1,000,000, purchases of $5,000,000, and a correctly counted ending inventory of $2,000,000, which results in the following cost of goods sold calculation:

$1,000,000 Beginning inventory + $5,000,000 Purchases - $2,000,000 Ending inventory
= $4,000,000 Cost of goods sold

But what if the controller did not insist on a physical count, and instead relied on the retail inventory method to arrive at an ending inventory figure of $2,500,000? The cost of goods sold calculation now changes to the following:

$1,000,000 Beginning inventory + $5,000,000 Purchases - $2,500,000 Ending inventory
= $3,500,000 Cost of goods sold

Thus, the $500,000 overstatement of ending inventory translates into a reduction of the cost of goods sold of the same amount. This effect carries forward into profits, net of a subtraction for income taxes.

If an ending inventory overstatement is corrected in a future period, this problem will reverse itself when the inventory figure is dropped, thereby shifting the overstatement back into the cost of goods sold and overstating the cost of goods sold in whichever future period the change occurs.

When an ending inventory overstatement occurs, the cost of goods sold is stated too low, which means that net income before taxes is overstated by the amount of the inventory overstatement. A business then pays income taxes on the amount of the overstatement. Thus, the impact of the overstatement on net income after taxes is the amount of the overstatement, less the applicable amount of income taxes.

EXAMPLE

To return to the preceding example, Dude Skis overstates its ending inventory by $500,000. Since Dude has an incremental income tax rate of 35%, Dude must now pay an additional $175,000 in income taxes, so the overstatement generates a notable cash outflow for the company.

Summary

Under no circumstances will auditors allow the gross profit or retail inventory methods to be used as the basis for determining year-end inventory balances, since the results will not be entirely correct. Also, for a number of reasons, it is entirely possible that either of these methods will yield an inaccurate result, especially if used over a number of consecutive periods (which allows assumption errors to pile up). Consequently, we strongly recommend the use of cycle counting or physical inventory counts to obtain better ending inventory information, reserving the gross profit and retail inventory methods for occasional use.

Chapter 6
Inventory Cost Layering

Introduction

The single most critical concept in inventory accounting is cost layering, which is a system for determining which tranche of costs are charged to expense when an inventory item is sold. The accountant must decide upon a methodology for determining which cost layering system to follow, and then employ that system consistently when compiling financial statements. In this chapter, we describe the concept of cost layering, the types of cost layering systems, and how they function.

Inventory Cost Layering Overview

The typical inventory asset is comprised of many identical parts that may have been acquired or constructed during different time periods. In each of these time periods, it is likely that the costs incurred varied somewhat from those incurred in other time periods. The result is a mish-mash of inventory items that all look the same, but which have different costs associated with them. How is the accountant to decide which costs to assign to goods when they are sold? A possible solution is the cost layering concept. Under cost layering, we assume that different tranches of costs have been incurred to construct or acquire certain clusters of inventory. The following example illustrates the concept.

EXAMPLE

Milford Sound acquires speakers from a contract manufacturer, for sale through Milford's on-line store. An especially popular speaker is the home theater subwoofer model. Over the past three months, Milford made the following purchases of this model from its contract manufacturer:

Date	Quantity	Price/each
1/05/X3	3,200	$89.00
1/29/X3	850	90.25
2/15/X3	1,700	91.00
3/09/X3	1,350	91.00

Since the first two purchases were made at different prices, the units in each of these purchases can be considered a separate cost layer. Since the last two purchases were made at the same price, they can be aggregated into the same cost layer, or they may be treated as separate cost layers.

Depending on the cost layering system that Milford chooses to use, the company can assume that the cost of a subwoofer that is charged to the cost of goods sold may come from the first of these cost layers (the first in, first out system), from the last of the cost layers (the last in, first out system) or from an average of these costs (the weighted-average system).

Several methods for calculating the cost of inventory that employ the cost layering concept are shown in this chapter. Of the methods presented, only the first in, first out method and the weighted average method have gained worldwide recognition. The last in, first out method cannot realistically be justified based on the actual flow of inventory, and is only used in the United States under the sanction of the Internal Revenue Service; it is specifically banned under international financial reporting standards. We also make passing note of the specific identification method, which is an acceptable alternative to the cost layering methods, but which is usually only applicable to a small number of organizations.

The First in, First Out Method

The first in, first out (FIFO) method of inventory valuation operates under the assumption that the first goods purchased are also the first goods sold. In most companies, this accounting assumption closely matches the actual flow of goods, and so is considered the most theoretically correct inventory valuation method.

Under the FIFO method, the earliest goods purchased are the first ones removed from the inventory account. This results in the remaining items in inventory being accounted for at the most recently incurred costs, so that the inventory asset recorded on the balance sheet contains costs quite close to the most recent costs that could be obtained in the marketplace. Conversely, this method also results in older historical costs being matched against current revenues and recorded in the cost of goods sold, so the gross margin does not necessarily reflect a proper matching of revenues and costs.

EXAMPLE

Milagro Corporation decides to use the FIFO method for the month of January. During that month, it records the following transactions:

	Quantity Change	Actual Unit Cost	Actual Total Cost
Beginning inventory (layer 1)	+100	$210	$21,000
Sale	-75		
Purchase (layer 2)	+150	280	42,000
Sale	-100		
Purchase (layer 3)	+50	300	15,000
Ending inventory	= 125		$78,000

The cost of goods sold in units is calculated as:

100 Beginning inventory + 200 Purchased − 125 Ending inventory = 175 Units

Milagro's controller uses the information in the preceding table to calculate the cost of goods sold for January, as well as the cost of the inventory balance as of the end of January. The calculations appear in the following table:

	Units	Unit Cost	Total Cost
Cost of goods sold			
FIFO layer 1	100	$210	$21,000
FIFO layer 2	75	280	21,000
Total cost of goods sold	175		$42,000
Ending inventory			
FIFO layer 2	75	280	$21,000
FIFO layer 3	50	300	15,000
Total ending inventory	125		$36,000

Thus, the first FIFO layer, which was the beginning inventory layer, is completely used up during the month, as well as half of Layer 2, leaving half of Layer 2 and all of Layer 3 to be the sole components of the ending inventory.

Note that the $42,000 cost of goods sold and $36,000 ending inventory equals the $78,000 combined total of beginning inventory and purchases during the month.

From a database management perspective, the FIFO method results in the smallest number of cost layers to track, since the oldest layers are constantly being eliminated.

The Last in, First Out Method

The last in, first out (LIFO) method operates under the assumption that the last item of inventory purchased is the first one sold. Picture a store shelf where a clerk adds items from the front, and customers also take their selections from the front; the remaining items of inventory that are located further from the front of the shelf are rarely picked, and so remain on the shelf – that is a LIFO scenario.

The trouble with the LIFO scenario is that it is rarely encountered in practice. If a company were to use the process flow embodied by LIFO, a significant part of its inventory would be very old, and likely obsolete. Nonetheless, a company does not actually have to experience the LIFO process flow in order to use the method to calculate its inventory valuation.

The reason why companies use LIFO is the assumption that the cost of inventory increases over time, which is reasonable in inflationary periods. If one were to use LIFO in such a situation, the cost of the most recently acquired inventory will always be higher than the cost of earlier purchases, so the ending inventory balance will be valued at earlier costs, while the most recent costs appear in the cost of goods sold. By shifting high-cost inventory into the cost of goods sold, a company can reduce its reported level of profitability, and thereby defer its recognition of income taxes. Since income tax deferral is the only justification for LIFO in most situations, it is banned under international financial reporting standards (though it is still allowed in the United States under the approval of the Internal Revenue Service).

EXAMPLE

Milagro Corporation decides to use the LIFO method for the month of March. The following table shows the various purchasing transactions for the company's Elite Roasters product. The quantity purchased on March 1 actually reflects the inventory beginning balance.

Date Purchased	Quantity Purchased	Cost per Unit	Units Sold	Cost of Layer #1	Cost of Layer #2	Total Cost
March 1	150	$210	95	(55 × $210)		$11,550
March 7	100	235	110	(45 × $210)		9,450
March 11	200	250	180	(45 × $210)	(20 × $250)	14,450
March 17	125	240	125	(45 × $210)	(20 × $250)	14,450
March 25	80	260	120	(25 × $210)		5,250

The following bullet points describe the transactions noted in the preceding table:
- *March 1*. Milagro has a beginning inventory balance of 150 units, and sells 95 of these units between March 1 and March 7. This leaves one inventory layer of 55 units at a cost of $210 each.
- *March 7*. Milagro buys 100 additional units on March 7, and sells 110 units between March 7 and March 11. Under LIFO, we assume that the latest purchase was sold first, so there is still just one inventory layer, which has now been reduced to 45 units.
- *March 11*. Milagro buys 200 additional units on March 11, and sells 180 units between March 11 and March 17, which creates a new inventory layer that is comprised of 20 units at a cost of $250. This new layer appears in the table in the "Cost of Layer #2" column.
- *March 17*. Milagro buys 125 additional units on March 17, and sells 125 units between March 17 and March 25, so there is no change in the inventory layers.
- *March 25*. Milagro buys 80 additional units on March 25, and sells 120 units between March 25 and the end of the month. Sales exceed purchases during this period, so the second inventory layer is eliminated, as well as part of the first layer. The result is an ending inventory balance of $5,250, which is derived from 25 units of ending inventory, multiplied by the $210 cost in the first layer that existed at the beginning of the month.

Before implementing the LIFO system, consider the following points:

- *Consistent usage.* The Internal Revenue Service states that a company using LIFO for its tax reporting must also use LIFO for its financial reporting. Thus, a company wanting to defer tax recognition through early expense recognition must show those same low profit numbers to the outside users of its financial statements. This may not be a problem in a privately-held company that does not release its financial results to outsiders.
- *Covenant compliance.* When LIFO has been used for a long period of time and materials prices have increased during that period, the reported inventory asset may be so low that a company has trouble meeting the terms of its loan covenants that require a certain amount of current assets.
- *Just-in-time conversion.* If a company using LIFO subsequently converts to a just-in-time production system that emphasizes minimal on-hand inventories, it is likely that the oldest inventory layers will be accessed, resulting in the recognition of many out-of-date costs.
- *Layering.* Since the LIFO system is intended to use the most recent layers of inventory, earlier layers may never be accessed, which can result in an administrative problem if there are many layers to document.
- *Profit fluctuations.* If early layers contain inventory costs that depart substantially from current market prices, a company could experience sharp changes in its profitability if those layers are ever accessed.

In summary, LIFO is only useful for deferring income tax payments in periods of cost inflation. It does not reflect the actual flow of inventory in most situations, and may even yield unusual financial results that differ markedly from reality.

The Dollar-Value LIFO Method

A variation on the LIFO concept is to calculate a conversion price index that is based on a comparison of the year-end inventory to the base year cost. In essence, the dollar-value LIFO method is designed to aggregate cost information for large amounts of inventory, so that individual cost layers do not need to be compiled for each item of inventory. Instead, layers are compiled for pools of inventory items.

The key concept in the dollar-value LIFO system is the conversion price index. To calculate the index, follow these steps:

1. Calculate the extended cost of the ending inventory at base year prices.
2. Calculate the extended cost of the ending inventory at the most recent prices.
3. Divide the total extended cost at the most recent prices by the total extended cost at base year prices.

These calculations yield an index that represents the change in prices since the base year. The calculation should be derived and retained for each year in which a business uses the LIFO method. Once the index is available, follow these additional steps to determine the cost of the LIFO cost layer in each successive period:

1. Determine any incremental increases in units of inventory in the next reporting period.
2. Calculate the extended cost of these incremental units at base year prices.
3. Multiply the extended amount by the conversion price index. This yields the cost of the LIFO layer for the next reporting period.

The concept is illustrated in the following example:

EXAMPLE

Entwhistle Electric has had the same cell phone battery version in stock for the past four years. The company uses the dollar-value LIFO method. Entwhistle's inventory database contains the following quantity and pricing information for the battery:

Year	Year-end Quantity	Year-end Price	Extended Price
1	1,000	$15.00	$15,000
2	2,500	16.50	41,250
3	2,200	17.25	39,750
4	3,500	18.10	63,350

The first year is designated as the base year for purposes of creating the index in later years. The current price index for Year 2 is calculated as follows:

Year	Year-end Quantity	Base Year Cost	Year 2 Cost	Extended Base Year Cost	Extended Year 2 Cost	Index
2	2,500	$15.00	$16.50	$37,500	$41,250	110%

In Year 2, the incremental amount of cell phone batteries added to stock is 1,500 units. To arrive at the cost of the Year 2 LIFO layer, Entwhistle's controller multiplies the 1,500 units by the base year cost of $15.00 and again by the 110% index to arrive at a layer cost of $24,750. In total, at the end of Year 2, Entwhistle has a base layer cost of $15,000 and a Year 2 layer cost of $24,750, for a total inventory valuation of $39,750.

In Year 3, there is a decline in the ending inventory unit count, so there is no new layer to calculate. Instead, the controller assumes that the units sold off are from the most recent inventory layer, which is the Year 2 layer. To calculate the year-end inventory valuation, we multiply the presumed residual balance of 1,200 units from the Year 2 layer by the $15.00 base year cost, and again by the 110% index, to arrive at a revised layer cost of $19,800. When combined with the $15,000 cost of the base layer, Entwhistle now has an ending inventory valuation of $34,800.

In Year 4, the inventory level has increased, which calls for the calculation of a new index. The calculation for the Year 4 current price index is:

Year	Year-end Quantity	Base Year Cost	Year 4 Cost	Extended Base Year Cost	Extended Year 4 Cost	Index
4	3,500	$15.00	$18.10	$52,500	$63,350	121%

There is an incremental increase in Year 4 from Year 3 of 1,300 units. The controller multiplies this amount by the $15.00 base year cost and again by the 121% current cost index to arrive at a cost for this new inventory layer of $23,595.

After four years of inventory accumulation under the dollar-value LIFO method, the ending inventory is comprised of the following LIFO inventory layers:

Layer Identification	Layer Price Index	Layer Valuation
Base layer	--	$15,000
Year 2 layer	110%	19,800
Year 4 layer	121%	23,595
Total		$58,395

Tip: The method can be used to create separate indexes for a number of different pools of inventory. However, since doing so increases the labor associated with calculating and applying conversion price indices, it is better to minimize the number of inventory pools employed.

The dollar-value method is not commonly used to derive inventory valuations, for the following reasons:

- *Calculation volume.* A large number of calculations are required to determine the differences in pricing through the indicated periods.
- *Base year issue.* Under IRS regulations, a base year cost must be located for each new inventory item added to stock, which can require detailed research. Only if such information is impossible to locate can the current cost also be considered the base year cost.

The Link-Chain Method

The main problem with the dollar-value LIFO method is that a base year cost must be compiled for each inventory item, which can be difficult or impossible to do. In situations where there is a high level of turnover in the types of inventory kept in stock, tax regulations allow for the alternative use of the link-chain method. This method eliminates the use of a base year cost, instead using a price index whose baseline is the immediately preceding year. Since each successive pricing index is compiled from the index in the immediately preceding year, there is said to be a link between the years being used, hence the name of this method.

The calculation steps for this method closely follow those just noted for the dollar-value LIFO method. The calculation flow is illustrated in the following example.

EXAMPLE

The controller of Entwhistle Electric is frustrated with the amount of work associated with tying current period costs back to base year costs under the dollar-value LIFO method, and so is experimenting with what would be required if the company were to instead use the link-chain method. He begins with the same information noted in the last example, which is replicated here, along with beginning-of-year information:

Year	Year-end Quantity	Year-end Price	Extended Ending Price	Beginning Price	Extended Beginning Price
1	1,000	$15.00	$15,000	$--	$--
2	2,500	16.50	41,250	15.00	37,500
3	2,200	17.25	39,750	16.50	36,300
4	3,500	18.10	63,350	17.25	60,375

Year 1 is considered the base year, so there is no index associated with it. The price index for Year 2 is 110%, which is the extended ending price of $41,250 divided by the extended beginning price of $37,500. Thus far, there is no difference between the outcome of this method and the dollar-value LIFO method.

The valuation of the Year 2 inventory layer is then derived by dividing the $41,250 ending extended price by the 110% price index, which yields an extended base year cost of $37,500. The base year layer of $15,000 is subtracted from this amount to yield a Year 2 LIFO layer at the base year cost of $22,500. This amount is then multiplied by the price index to bring its cost back to the Year 2 pricing level, which is $24,750. At the end of Year 2, the LIFO layering situation is as follows:

Layer Identification	Cumulative Price Index	Layer Valuation	Base Year Valuation
Base layer	--	$15,000	$15,000
Year 2 layer	110%	24,750	22,500
Total		$39,750	$37,500

In Year 3, the price index is calculated as the extended price based on the year-end price, divided by the extended price based on the beginning-of-year price, which is 109.5%. To arrive at the cumulative price index, the original price index of 110% is multiplied by the next-year price index of 109.5% to arrive at 120.5% (calculated as 110% × 1.095).

To determine the base year cost of the Year 3 ending inventory, the Year 3 ending inventory price of $39,750 is divided by the cumulative price index of 120.5% to arrive at $32,988. Since this amount is less than the ending valuation for Year 2, there is no new LIFO layer to record. Instead, the base year layer of $15,000 is subtracted from the $32,988 Year 3 year-end figure to arrive at the $17,988 base year cost of the remaining Year 2 layer. This base year cost is then multiplied by the Year 2 price index of 110% to determine the revised Year 2 inventory valuation of $19,787. At the end of Year 3, the LIFO layering situation is as follows:

Layer Identification	Cumulative Price Index	Layer Valuation	Base Year Valuation
Base layer	--	$15,000	$15,000
Year 2 layer	110.0%	19,787	17,988
Year 3 layer	120.5%	--	--
Total		$34,787	$32,988

In Year 4, the price index is calculated as the extended price based on the year-end price, divided by the extended price based on the beginning-of-year price, which is 104.9%. The cumulative index is derived by multiplying the preceding cumulative price index of 120.5% by the next-year price index of 104.9% to arrive at 126.4% (calculated as 120.5% × 1.049).

To determine the base year cost of the Year 4 ending inventory, the Year 4 ending inventory price of $63,350 is divided by the cumulative price index of 126.4% to arrive at $50,119. This amount is then netted against the existing base year valuation of $32,988 to determine the base year valuation of the LIFO layer associated with Year 4, which is $17,131. The last step is to multiply the base year valuation of this newest layer by the cumulative price index of 126.4% to determine the current year valuation of the Year 4 layer, which is $21,654. At the end of Year 4, the LIFO layering situation is as follows:

Layer Identification	Cumulative Price Index	Layer Valuation	Base Year Valuation
Base layer	--	$15,000	$15,000
Year 2 layer	110.0%	19,787	17,988
Year 3 layer	120.5%	--	--
Year 4 layer	126.4%	21,654	17,131
Total		$56,441	$50,119

Tip: The tax regulations allow a company to derive a link-chain index based on a subset of the total inventory. This subset must include those inventory items whose values collectively comprise at least half of the total inventory valuation.

A comparison of the calculation steps involved in the determination of the dollar-value LIFO and link-chain methods will reveal that many of the steps are the same or similar. The primary difference between the two methods is that knowledge of the base year cost is not needed under the link-chain method to determine the price index in later reporting periods.

The Weighted Average Method

When using the weighted average method, divide the cost of goods available for sale by the number of units available for sale, which yields the weighted-average cost per unit. In this calculation, the cost of goods available for sale is the sum of beginning inventory and net purchases. This weighted-average figure is then used to assign a cost to both ending inventory and the cost of goods sold.

The singular advantage of the weighted average method is the complete absence of any inventory layers, which avoids the record keeping problems encountered with either the FIFO or LIFO methods described earlier.

EXAMPLE

Milagro Corporation elects to use the weighted-average method for the month of May. During that month, it records the following transactions:

	Quantity Change	Actual Unit Cost	Actual Total Cost
Beginning inventory	+150	$220	$33,000
Sale	-125		
Purchase	+200	270	54,000
Sale	-150		
Purchase	+100	290	29,000
Ending inventory	= 175		$116,000

The actual total cost of all purchased or beginning inventory units in the preceding table is $116,000 ($33,000 + $54,000 + $29,000). The total of all purchased or beginning inventory units is 450 (150 beginning inventory + 300 purchased). The weighted average cost per unit is therefore $257.78 ($116,000 ÷ 450 units).

The ending inventory valuation is $45,112 (175 units × $257.78 weighted average cost), while the cost of goods sold valuation is $70,890 (275 units × $257.78 weighted average cost). The sum of these two amounts (less a rounding error) equals the $116,000 total actual cost of all purchases and beginning inventory.

In the preceding example, if Milagro used a perpetual inventory system to record its inventory transactions, it would have to recompute the weighted average after every purchase. The following table uses the same information in the preceding example to show the recomputations:

	Units on Hand	Purchases	Cost of Sales	Inventory Total Cost	Inventory Moving Average Unit Cost
Beginning inventory	150	$--	$--	$33,000	$220.00
Sale (125 units @ $220.00)	25	--	27,500	5,500	220.00
Purchase (200 units @ $270.00)	225	54,000	--	59,500	264.44
Sale (150 units @ $264.44)	75	--	39,666	19,834	264.44
Purchase (100 units @ $290.00)	175	29,000	--	48,834	279.05
Total			$67,166		

Note that the cost of goods sold of $67,166 and the ending inventory balance of $48,834 equal $116,000, which matches the total of the costs in the original example. Thus, the totals are the same, but the moving weighted average calculation results in slight differences in the apportionment of costs between the cost of goods sold and ending inventory.

The Specific Identification Method

The cost layering concept operates under the assumption that costs cannot be traced to specific inventory items. This assumption is largely true, since there may be hundreds of identical items in stock. However, in cases where a business only retains uniquely identifiable inventory items, it is perfectly acceptable to assign a cost to each individual unit of inventory. When an item is sold, the cost specifically linked to that item is charged to the cost of goods sold. The result is a highly accurate inventory accounting system that precisely matches inventory costs with revenues. For this system to work, it should have the following attributes:

- *Unique inventory items.* Each item in stock must be uniquely identified. This typically limits use of the specific identification method to custom-made or uniquely-configured items, such as jewelry or automobiles.
- *Cost linkage.* When goods are acquired or built, the costing system must accumulate costs at the individual unit level.
- *Expensive items.* Because of the extra cost of accumulating and tracking costs at the individual unit level, this system is only cost-effective when the items being tracked are quite expensive. Thus, it is a reasonable system for a custom watch manufacturer, but not for someone who custom-manufactures Christmas tree ornaments.

Summary

All of the costing methods described in this chapter involve varying amounts of database tracking of the individual prices paid for goods stored in inventory. This can present a massive burden for the accountant, who may need to sort through thousands of supplier invoice records to assign a proper valuation to the ending inventory asset. Much of this cost layering information is automatically compiled in an enterprise resource planning (ERP) system. However, these expensive systems are not commonly installed in smaller organizations, which must instead rely upon a disparate set of databases to compile an inventory valuation. If this is the case, consider using a standard costing system to value inventory. This concept is presented in the following Standard Costing of Inventory chapter.

Chapter 7
Standard Costing of Inventory

Introduction

Standard costing is the practice of substituting an expected cost for an actual cost in the accounting records, and then periodically recording variances that are the difference between the expected and actual costs. This approach is commonly used to derive a valuation for inventory, and is considered a simpler approach for doing so than any of the cost layering methodologies. In this chapter, we will discuss how a standard costing system functions, where it should be used, how to calculate the many variances associated with it, and how to report these variances.

Overview of Standard Costing

Standard costing involves the creation of estimated (i.e., standard) costs for inventory items. The core reason for using standard costs is that there are a number of applications where it is too time-consuming to collect actual costs, so standard costs are used as a close approximation to actual costs.

Standard costs only work within a certain range of constraints, beyond which they are no longer a close match for actual costs. For example, the cost of a purchased component may only be accurate if it is purchased in quantities of 1,000; the price would double if it were to be ordered in quantities of 100.

Since standard costs are usually slightly different from actual costs, the accountant periodically calculates variances that break out differences caused by such factors as labor rate changes and the cost of materials. The accountant may also periodically change the standard costs to bring them into closer alignment with actual costs.

How to Create a Standard Cost

At the most basic level, a standard cost is created simply by calculating the average of the most recent actual costs for the past few months. In many smaller companies, this is the extent of the analysis used. However, there are some additional factors to consider, which can significantly alter the standard cost formulation. They are:

- *Equipment age.* If a machine is nearing the end of its productive life, it may produce a higher proportion of scrap than was previously the case.
- *Equipment setup speeds.* If it takes a long time to setup equipment for a production run, the cost of the setup, as spread over the units in the production run, is expensive. If a setup reduction plan is contemplated, this can yield significantly lower overhead costs.

- *Labor efficiency changes.* If there are production process changes, such as the installation of new, automated equipment, this impacts the amount of labor required to manufacture a product.
- *Labor rate changes.* If employees are about to receive pay raises, either through a scheduled raise or as mandated by a labor union contract, incorporate it into the new standard. This may mean setting an effective date for the new standard that matches the date when the cost increase is supposed to go into effect.
- *Learning curve.* As the production staff creates an increasing volume of a product, it becomes more efficient at doing so. Thus, the standard labor cost should decrease (though at a declining rate) as production volumes increase.
- *Purchasing terms.* The purchasing department may be able to significantly alter the price of a purchased component by switching suppliers, altering contract terms, or buying in different quantities.
- *Push or pull.* The type of materials flow system used in a production facility can have a vast impact on the cost of goods produced. A pull system, such as a just-in-time system, only produces when customers place orders, while a push system, such as a material requirements planning system, produces from a forecast, irrespective of customer orders. Pull systems generally result in less expensive total costs for a product.

Any one of the additional factors noted here can have a major impact on a standard cost, which is why it may be necessary in a larger production environment to spend a significant amount of time formulating a standard cost.

The accountant is unlikely to be familiar with all of the factors just noted, which is why standard costs are more commonly derived by either the engineering or purchasing departments (or both). The primary role of the accountant is to manage the process of deriving standard costs, with inputs coming from the engineers and purchasing staff.

Historical, Attainable, and Theoretical Standards

An additional factor to consider when deriving a standard cost is whether to set it at a historical actual cost level that has been proven to be attainable, or at a rate that should be attainable, or one that can only be reached if all operations work perfectly. Here are some considerations:

- *Historical basis.* This is an average of the costs that a company has already experienced in the recent past, possibly weighted towards just the past few months. Though clearly an attainable cost, a standard based on historical results contains all of the operational inefficiencies of the existing production operation.
- *Attainable basis.* This is a cost that is more difficult to reach than a historical cost. This basis assumes some improvement in operating and purchasing efficiencies, which employees have a good chance of achieving in the short term.

- *Theoretical basis*. This is the ultimate, lowest cost that a facility can attain if it functions perfectly, with no scrap, highly efficient employees, and machines that never break down. This can be a frustrating basis to use for a standard cost, because the production facility can never attain it, and so always produces unfavorable variances.

Of the three types of standards noted here, use the attainable basis, because it gives employees a reasonable cost target to pursue. If standards are continually updated on this basis, a production facility will have an incentive to continually drive down its costs over the long term.

How to Account for Standard Costs

Standard costs are stored separately from all other accounting records, usually in a bill of materials for finished goods, and in the item master file for raw materials.

At the end of a reporting period, the following steps show how to integrate standard costs into the accounting system:

1. *Cost verification*. Review the standard cost database for errors and correct as necessary. Also, if it is time to do so, update the standard costs to more accurately reflect actual costs.
2. *Inventory valuation*. Multiply the number of units in ending inventory by their standard costs to derive the ending inventory valuation. For raw materials, this means multiplying the cost in the item master by the ending unit quantity. For finished goods, this means multiplying the bill of materials total cost by the ending unit quantity.
3. *Calculate the cost of goods sold*. Add purchases during the month to the beginning inventory and subtract the ending inventory to determine the cost of goods sold.
4. *Enter updated balances*. Create a journal entry that reduces the purchases account to zero and which also adjusts the inventory asset account balance to the ending total standard cost, with the offset to the cost of goods sold account.

EXAMPLE

Hodgson Industrial Design is using a standard costing system to calculate its inventory balances and cost of goods sold. The company conducts a month-end physical inventory count that results in a reasonably accurate set of unit quantities for all inventory items. The accountant multiplies each of these unit quantities by their standard costs to derive the ending inventory valuation. This ending balance is $2,500,000.

The beginning inventory account balance is $2,750,000 and purchases during the month were $1,000,000, so the calculation of the cost of goods sold is:

Beginning inventory	$2,750,000
+ Purchases	1,000,000
- Ending inventory	(2,500,000)
= Cost of goods sold	$1,250,000

To record the correct ending inventory balance and cost of goods sold, Hodgson records the following entry, which clears out the purchases asset account and adjusts the ending inventory balance to $2,500,000:

	Debit	Credit
Cost of goods sold	1,250,000	
Purchases		1,000,000
Inventory		250,000

The preceding approach to accounting for inventory assumes that all variances between standard and actual costs are flushed out of the balance sheet by charging them to the cost of goods sold, leaving an ending inventory balance that is comprised entirely of standard costs. This approach is fine, as long as the difference between extended standard costs and extended actual costs is immaterial. If not, there are two views regarding how to proceed:

- *Apportionment.* The variance is apportioned between the cost of goods sold and ending inventory. This approach requires extra effort by the accounting staff to develop an apportionment procedure, which introduces extra effort into the already-cluttered period-end closing process.
- *Charge off.* Variances that exceed standard costs (which is usually the case) represent an anomaly that is essentially a wasted cost. As such, they are considered period costs, and so should be charged to expense at once.

From an efficiency perspective, we recommend charging these variances to the cost of goods sold in the current period, rather than attempting to apportion them between the cost of goods sold and ending inventory. However, a sufficiently large variance will have a material impact on the income statement if it is entirely charged to expense, and so should probably be apportioned to ending inventory.

A variation on the standard costing concept is to only use it for the valuation of work-in-process and finished goods inventory. Raw materials and purchased merchandise are valued using a cost layering concept, such as FIFO or LIFO. Doing so provides the auditors with excellent evidence of raw material and merchandise costs, while still giving the company the luxury of having an efficient methodology available for valuing its more complex inventory items.

Overview of Variances

A variance is the difference between the actual cost incurred and the standard cost against which it is measured. There are two basic types of variances from a standard that can arise, which are the rate variance and the volume variance. Here is more information about both types of variances:

- *Rate variance.* A rate variance (which is also known as a *price* variance) is the difference between the actual price paid for something and the expected price, multiplied by the actual quantity purchased. The "rate" variance designation is most commonly applied to the labor rate variance, which involves the actual cost of direct labor in comparison to the standard cost of direct labor. The rate variance uses a different designation when applied to the purchase of materials, and may be called the *purchase price variance* or the *material price variance.*
- *Volume variance.* A volume variance is the difference between the actual quantity sold or consumed and the budgeted amount, multiplied by the standard price or cost per unit. If the variance relates to the use of direct materials, it is called the *material yield variance.* If the variance relates to the use of direct labor, it is called the *labor efficiency variance.* Finally, if the variance relates to the application of overhead, it is called the *overhead efficiency variance.*

Thus, variances are based on either changes in cost from the expected amount, or changes in the quantity from the expected amount. The most common variances that an accountant elects to report on are subdivided within the rate and volume variance categories for direct materials, direct labor, and overhead. The primary variances are:

Category	Rate Variance	Volume Variance
Materials	Purchase price variance	Material yield variance
Direct labor	Labor rate variance	Labor efficiency variance
Fixed overhead	Fixed overhead spending variance	Not applicable
Variable overhead	Variable overhead spending variance	Variable overhead efficiency variance

All of the variances noted in the preceding table are explained in the following sections, including examples to demonstrate how the variances are applied.

The Purchase Price Variance

The purchase price variance is the difference between the actual price paid to buy an item and its standard price, multiplied by the actual number of units purchased. The formula is:

(Actual price - Standard price) × Actual quantity = Purchase price variance

The standard price is the price that product engineers believe a company should pay for an item, given a certain quality level, purchasing quantity, and speed of delivery. Thus, the variance is really based on a standard price that was the collective opinion of several employees based on a number of assumptions that may no longer match a company's current purchasing situation.

EXAMPLE

During the development of its annual budget, the engineers and purchasing staff of Hodgson Industrial Design decide that the standard cost of a green widget should be set at $5.00, which is based on a purchasing volume of 10,000 for the upcoming year. During the subsequent year, Hodgson only buys 8,000 units, and so cannot take advantage of purchasing discounts, and ends up paying $5.50 per widget. This creates a purchase price variance of $0.50 per widget, and a variance of $4,000 for all of the 8,000 widgets that Hodgson purchased.

There are a number of possible causes of a purchase price variance. For example:
- *Layering issue.* The actual cost may have been taken from an inventory layering system, such as a first-in first-out system, where the actual cost varies from the current market price by a substantial margin.
- *Materials shortage.* There is an industry shortage of a commodity item, which is driving up the cost.
- *New supplier.* The company has changed suppliers for any number of reasons, resulting in a new cost structure that is not yet reflected in the standard.
- *Rush basis.* The company incurred excessive shipping charges to obtain materials on short notice from suppliers.
- *Volume assumption.* The standard cost of an item was derived based on a different purchasing volume than the amount at which the company now buys.

Material Yield Variance

The material yield variance is the difference between the actual amount of material used and the standard amount expected to be used, multiplied by the standard cost of the materials. The formula is:

(Actual unit usage - Standard unit usage) × Standard cost per unit

= Material yield variance

The standard unit usage is developed by the engineering staff, and is based on expected scrap rates in a production process, the quality of raw materials, losses during equipment setup, and related factors.

EXAMPLE

The engineering staff of Hodgson Industrial Design estimates that eight ounces of rubber will be required to produce a green widget. During the most recent month, the production process used 315,000 ounces of rubber to create 35,000 green widgets, which is nine ounces per product. Each ounce of rubber has a standard cost of $0.50. Its material yield variance for the month is:

(315,000 Actual unit usage - 280,000 Standard unit usage) × $0.50 Standard cost/unit

= $17,500 Material yield variance

There are a number of possible causes of a material yield variance. For example:
- *Scrap*. Unusual amounts of scrap may be generated by changes in machine setups, or because changes in acceptable tolerance levels are altering the amount of scrap produced. A change in the pattern of quality inspections can also alter the amount of scrap.
- *Material quality*. If the material quality level changes, this can alter the amount of quality rejections. If an entirely different material is substituted, this can also alter the amount of rejections.
- *Spoilage*. The amount of spoilage may change in concert with alterations in inventory handling and storage.

Labor Rate Variance

The labor rate variance is the difference between the actual labor rate paid and the standard rate, multiplied by the number of actual hours worked. The formula is:

(Actual rate - Standard rate) × Actual hours worked = Labor rate variance

The standard labor rate is developed by the human resources and industrial engineering employees, and is based on such factors as the expected mix of pay levels among the production staff, the amount of overtime likely to be incurred, the amount of new hiring at different pay rates, the number of promotions into higher pay levels, and the outcome of contract negotiations with any unions representing the production staff.

EXAMPLE

The human resources manager of Hodgson Industrial Design estimates that the average labor rate for the coming year for Hodgson's production staff will be $25/hour. This estimate is based on a standard mix of personnel at different pay rates, as well as a reasonable proportion of overtime hours worked.

During the first month of the new year, Hodgson has difficulty hiring a sufficient number of new employees, and so must have its higher-paid existing staff work overtime to complete a number of jobs. The result is an actual labor rate of $30/hour. Hodgson's production staff worked 10,000 hours during the month. Its labor rate variance for the month is:

($30/hr Actual rate - $25/hour Standard rate) × 10,000 Hours = $50,000 Labor rate variance

There are a number of possible causes of a labor rate variance. For example:
- *Incorrect standards.* The labor standard may not reflect recent changes in the rates paid to employees (which tend to occur in bulk for all staff).
- *Pay premiums.* The actual amounts paid may include extra payments for shift differentials or overtime.
- *Staffing variances.* A labor standard may assume that a certain job classification will perform a designated task, when in fact a different position with a different pay rate may be performing the work.

Labor Efficiency Variance

The labor efficiency variance is the difference between the actual labor hours used to produce an item and the standard amount that should have been used, multiplied by the standard labor rate. The formula is:

(Actual hours - Standard hours) × Standard rate = Labor efficiency variance

The standard number of hours represents the best estimate of the industrial engineers regarding the optimal speed at which the production staff can manufacture goods. This figure can vary considerably, based on assumptions regarding the setup time of a production run, the availability of materials and machine capacity, employee skill levels, the duration of a production run, and other factors. Thus, the multitude of variables involved makes it especially difficult to create a standard that can be meaningfully compared to actual results.

EXAMPLE

During the development of its annual budget, the industrial engineers of Hodgson Industrial Design decide that the standard amount of time required to produce a green widget should be 30 minutes, which is based on certain assumptions about the efficiency of Hodgson's production staff, the availability of materials, capacity availability, and so forth. During the month, widget materials were in short supply, so Hodgson had to pay production staff even when there was no material to work on, resulting in an average production time per unit of 45 minutes. The company produced 1,000 widgets during the month. The standard cost per labor hour is $20, so the calculation of its labor efficiency variance is:

(750 Actual hours - 500 Standard hours) × $20 Standard rate
= $5,000 Labor efficiency variance

There are a number of possible causes of a labor efficiency variance. For example:

- *Instructions.* The employees may not have received written work instructions.
- *Mix.* The standard assumes a certain mix of employees involving different skill levels, which does not match the actual staffing.
- *Training.* The standard may be based on an assumption of a minimum amount of training that employees have not received.
- *Work station configuration.* A work center may have been reconfigured since the standard was created, so the standard is now incorrect.

Variable Overhead Spending Variance

The variable overhead spending variance is the difference between the actual and budgeted rates of spending on variable overhead. The formula is:

Actual hours worked × (Actual overhead rate - Standard overhead rate)

= Variable overhead spending variance

The variable overhead spending variance is a compilation of production expense information submitted by the production department, and the projected labor hours to be worked, as estimated by the industrial engineering and production scheduling staffs, based on historical and projected efficiency and equipment capacity levels.

EXAMPLE

The accounting staff of Hodgson Industrial Design calculates, based on historical and projected cost patterns, that the company should experience a variable overhead rate of $20 per labor hour worked, and builds this figure into the budget. In April, the actual variable overhead rate turns out to be $22 per labor hour. During that month, production employees work 18,000 hours. The variable overhead spending variance is:

18,000 Actual hours worked × ($22 Actual variable overhead rate
- $20 Standard overhead rate)

= $36,000 Variable overhead spending variance

There are a number of possible causes of a variable overhead spending variance. For example:

- *Account misclassification.* The variable overhead category includes a number of accounts, some of which may have been incorrectly classified and so do not appear as part of variable overhead (or vice versa).
- *Outsourcing.* Some activities that had been sourced in-house have now been shifted to a supplier, or vice versa.

- *Supplier pricing.* Suppliers have changed their prices, which have not yet been reflected in updated standards.

Variable Overhead Efficiency Variance

The variable overhead efficiency variance is the difference between the actual and budgeted hours worked, which are then applied to the standard variable overhead rate per hour. The formula is:

$$\text{Standard overhead rate} \times (\text{Actual hours - Standard hours})$$

$$= \text{Variable overhead efficiency variance}$$

The variable overhead efficiency variance is a compilation of production expense information submitted by the production department, and the projected labor hours to be worked, as estimated by the industrial engineering and production scheduling staffs, based on historical and projected efficiency and equipment capacity levels.

EXAMPLE

The accounting staff of Hodgson Industrial Design calculates, based on historical and projected labor patterns, that the company's production staff should work 20,000 hours per month and incur $400,000 of variable overhead costs per month, so it establishes a variable overhead rate of $20 per hour. In May, Hodgson installs a new materials handling system that significantly improves production efficiency and drops the hours worked during the month to 19,000. The variable overhead efficiency variance is:

$$\$20 \text{ Standard overhead rate/hour} \times (19,000 \text{ Hours worked - } 20,000 \text{ Standard hours})$$

$$= \$20,000 \text{ Variable overhead efficiency variance}$$

Fixed Overhead Spending Variance

The fixed overhead spending variance is the difference between the actual fixed overhead expense incurred and the budgeted fixed overhead expense. An unfavorable variance means that actual overhead expenditures were greater than planned. The formula is:

$$\text{Actual fixed overhead - Budgeted fixed overhead} = \text{Fixed overhead spending variance}$$

The amount of expense related to fixed overhead should (as the name implies) be relatively fixed, and so the fixed overhead spending variance should not theoretically vary much from the budget. However, if the manufacturing process reaches a step cost trigger point, where a whole new expense must be incurred (such as adding a new production line), this can cause a significant unfavorable variance.

Also, there may be some seasonality in fixed overhead expenditures, which may cause both favorable and unfavorable variances in individual months of a year, but which cancel each other out over the full year.

EXAMPLE

The production manager of Hodgson Industrial Design estimates that fixed overhead should be $700,000 during the upcoming year. However, since a production manager left the company and was not replaced for several months, actual expenses were lower than expected, at $672,000. This created the following favorable fixed overhead spending variance:

$672,000 Actual fixed overhead - $700,000 Budgeted fixed overhead

= -$28,000 Fixed overhead spending variance

There are a number of possible causes of a fixed overhead spending variance. For example:

- *Account misclassification.* The fixed overhead category includes a number of accounts, some of which may have been incorrectly classified and so do not appear as part of fixed overhead (or vice versa).
- *Outsourcing.* Some activities that had been sourced in-house have now been shifted to a supplier, or vice versa.
- *Supplier pricing.* Suppliers have changed their prices, which have not yet been reflected in updated standards.

Problems with Variance Analysis

There are several problems with the variances just described in this chapter, which are:

- *The use of standards.* A central issue is the use of standards as the basis for calculating variances. What is the motivation for creating a standard? Standard creation can be a political process where the amount agreed upon is designed to make a department look good, rather than setting a target that will improve the company. If standards are politically created, variance analysis becomes useless from the perspective of controlling the company.
- *Feedback loop.* The accounting department does not calculate variances until after it has closed the books and created financial statements, so there is a gap of potentially an entire month from when a variance arises and when it is reported to management. A faster feedback loop would be to eliminate variance reporting and instead create a reporting process that provides for feedback within moments of the occurrence of a triggering event.
- *Information drill down.* Many of the issues that cause variances are not stored within the accounting database. For example, the reason for excessive

material usage may be a machine setup error, while excessive labor usage may be caused by the use of an excessive amount of employee overtime. In neither case will the accounting staff discover these issues by examining their transactional data. Thus, a variance report only highlights the general areas within which problems occurred, but does not necessarily tell anyone the nature of the underlying problems.

The preceding issues do not always keep accounting managers from calculating complete sets of variances for management consumption, but they do bring the question of whether the work required to calculate variances is a good use of the accounting staff's time.

The Controllable Variance

A controllable variance refers to the "rate" portion of a variance. A variance is comprised of two primary elements, which are the volume variance and the rate variance. The volume element is that portion of the variance attributable to changes in sales volume or unit usage from a standard or budgeted amount, while the rate element is the difference between the actual price paid and a standard or budgeted price.

The controllable variance concept is usually applied to factory overhead, where the calculation of the controllable variance is:

Actual overhead expense - (Budgeted overhead per unit × Standard number of units)

Thus, the controllable variance within the total factory overhead variance is that portion not related to changes in volume.

From a practical perspective, a controllable variance may be completely uncontrollable if it is calculated from a baseline standard cost that is impossible to attain.

The Favorable or Unfavorable Variance

A favorable variance is the excess amount of a standard or budgeted amount over the actual amount incurred. Obtaining a favorable variance (or, for that matter, an unfavorable variance) does not necessarily mean much, since it is based upon a budgeted or standard amount that may not be an indicator of good performance.

Budgets and standards are frequently based on politically-derived wrangling to see who can beat their baseline standards or budgets by the largest amount. Consequently, a large favorable variance may have been manufactured by setting an excessively low budget or standard. The one time to take note of a favorable (or unfavorable) variance is when it sharply diverges from the historical trend line, and the divergence was not caused by a change in the budget or standard.

Where to Record a Variance

There are always going to be variances in a standard costing system, where the variance is the difference between actual and standard costs. How should they be recorded? There are two schools of thought, which are:

- *Variances are exceptions.* This viewpoint holds that a standard is the cost level that a company should be attaining, so any variance from that amount is an exception, and should be charged to the cost of goods sold in the current period. Thus, if a variance is an exception, only carry forward the standard cost of an item in inventory, and eliminate any other expense in the current period. This is the simplest method, since the variance calculation and subsequent charge to expense are easy.

- *Inventory is valued at actual cost.* According to generally accepted accounting principles, the inventory asset is supposed to be valued at its actual cost, which in a standard costing system is the standard cost, plus or minus all variances. Thus, this viewpoint holds that variances should be allocated between the period-end inventory asset and the cost of goods sold. Doing so requires additional allocation calculations, which can be time-consuming.

Clearly, it is easier to charge variances to the cost of goods sold. To reduce the validity of the argument that inventory should be valued at its actual cost, update standard costs with sufficient frequency to ensure that all variances from standard costs will be so small that there is no material difference between the value of the inventory at standard cost or actual cost. A useful tool for initiating these changes is the standard to actual cost comparison report, which generates an extended variance for the difference between standard and actual costs. If the report reveals a large variance, it is time to adjust a standard cost to be more closely aligned with actual costs. A sample report follows:

Sample Standard to Actual Cost Comparison Report

Item Description	Standard Cost	Actual Cost	Variance	Unit Volume	Extended Variance
Battery unit	$12.00	$12.90	-$0.90	1,000	-$900
Drill bit	1.50	1.25	0.15	5,000	750
Drill case	4.80	4.50	0.50	150	75
Drill motor	3.75	3.75	--	20,000	--
Trigger assembly	2.50	3.10	-0.60	2,500	-1,500

In the sample report, there are three items (the battery unit, drill bit, and trigger assembly) that have high extended variances between their standard and actual costs. In these situations, a change in the standard cost to more closely align with actual costs is probably in order.

Tip: Adopt a change threshold for extended variances between standard and actual costs. Standard cost adjustments are warranted above the threshold, and are not made below the threshold. Doing so reduces the labor associated with making constant standard costing adjustments.

Which Variances to Report

Many variances have been described in this chapter. Does the accounting department really need to report them all to management? Not necessarily. If management agrees with a reduced reporting structure, report on just those variances over which management has some ability to reduce costs, and which contain sufficiently large variances to be worth reporting on. The following table provides commentary on the characteristics of the various variances:

Name of Variance	Commentary
Materials	
Purchase price variance	Material costs are controllable to some extent, and comprise a large part of the cost of goods sold; possibly the most important variance
Material yield variance	Can contain large potential cost reductions driven by quality issues, production layouts, and process flow; a good opportunity for cost reductions
Labor	
Labor rate variance	Labor rates are difficult to change; do not track unless work can be shifted into lower pay grades
Labor efficiency variance	Can drive contrary behavior in favor of long production runs, when less labor efficiency in a just-in-time environment results in greater overall cost reductions; not recommended
Overhead	
Variable overhead spending variance	Caused by changes in the actual costs in the overhead cost pool, and so should be reviewed
Variable overhead efficiency variance	Caused by a change in the basis of allocation, which has no real impact on underlying costs; not recommended
Fixed overhead spending variance	Since fixed overhead costs should not vary much, a variance here is worth careful review; however, most components of fixed overhead are long-term costs that cannot be easily changed in the short term

The preceding table shows that the variances most worthy of management's attention are the purchase price variance, variable overhead spending variance, and fixed overhead spending variance. Reducing the number of reported variances is well worth the accountant's time, since reporting the entire suite of variances calls for a great deal of investigative time to track down variance causes and then configure the information into a report suitable for management consumption.

How to Report Variances

A variance is a simple number, such as an unfavorable purchase price variance of $15,000. It tells management very little, since there is not enough information on which to base any corrective action. Consequently, the accountant needs to dig down into the underlying data to determine the actual causes of each variance, and then report the causes. Doing so is one of the most important value-added activities of the accountant, since it triggers specific management action. The following table is an example of the level of variance detail that the accountant should report to management:

Variance Item	Amount*	Variance Cause
Purchase Price		
Order quantity	$500	Bought wrappers at half usual volume, and lost purchase discount
Substitute material	1,500	Used more expensive PVC piping; out of stock on regular item
Variable Overhead		
Rush order	300	Overnight charge to bring in grease for bearings
Utility surcharge	2,400	Charged extra for power usage during peak hours
Fixed Overhead		
Property taxes	3,000	Tax levy increased by 8%
Rent override	8,000	Landlord charge for proportional share of full-year expenses

* Note: All amounts shown are unfavorable variances

The preceding table can be expanded to include the names of the managers responsible for correcting each item noted.

Summary

Standard costing is a simple way to derive the cost of inventory, and avoids the annoyance of tracking cost layers. However, the resulting valuations may not closely track actual inventory costs, resulting in potentially large variances for which accounting entries must be made. To minimize the effect of these variances, we suggest that standard costs be updated on a regular basis, such as quarterly. An annual standard cost update may be too infrequent, since actual costs may substantially diverge from standard costs during such a long interval.

Chapter 8
Job Costing

Introduction

Job costing is the system for compiling those costs associated with a specific job or project. A large part of the costs included in a job are associated with inventory. Job costing is one of the most heavily used methods for tracking costs in environments where custom jobs are produced for customers. In this chapter, we give an overview of job costing and discuss the specific accounting transactions associated with it.

Overview of Job Costing

Job costing is used to accumulate costs at a small-unit level. For example, job costing is appropriate for deriving the cost of constructing a custom machine, designing a software program, or building a small batch of products. Job costing involves the following accounting activities:

- *Materials*. It accumulates the cost of components and assigns these costs to a product or project once the components are used.
- *Labor*. Employees charge their time to specific jobs, which are then assigned to the jobs based on the labor cost of the employees.
- *Overhead*. It accumulates overhead costs into cost pools, and allocates these costs to jobs.

Job costing is an excellent tool for examining the costs associated with specific jobs at a very detailed level.

EXAMPLE

Twill Machinery's primary output is milling machines. Twill has just completed job number 1003, which is for a custom-designed milling machine ordered by a long-term customer. The costs assigned to the job include an allocation of $12,000 for 200 hours of rework on burrs discovered in numerous places on the metal edges of the machine. Further investigation reveals that the burrs were caused by improper metal stamping when the component parts were originally created.

Since the customer is likely to order additional versions of the same machine, management assigns a task group to investigate and correct the metal stamping process. Twill would probably not have found this problem if the job costing system had not highlighted it.

Job costing results in discrete "buckets" of information that the accountant can review to see if costs should really be assigned to a particular job. If there are many jobs currently in progress, there is a strong chance that costs will be incorrectly assigned. Since the nature of the job costing system makes it highly auditable, these errors can be detected and corrected.

If a job is expected to run for a long period of time, the accountant can periodically compare the costs accumulated in the bucket for a job to its budget, and give management advance warning if costs appear to be running above projections. This gives management time to either get costs under control over the remainder of the project, or possibly approach the customer about a billing increase to cover some or all of the cost overrun.

Job costing demands a considerable amount of costing precision if costs are to be reimbursed by customers (as is the case in a cost-plus contract, where the customer pays all costs incurred, plus a profit). In such cases, the accountant must review the costs assigned to each job before releasing it to the billing staff, which creates a customer invoice. This can cause long hours for the accountant at the end of a job, since the company controller will want to issue an invoice as soon as possible.

When Not to Use Job Costing

As just noted, job costing is the ideal solution for discrete manufacturing situations where costs can be clearly associated with specific products or projects. There are also a number of situations where job costing is not the best alternative. Here are some examples:

- *High data entry cost.* If it is extremely difficult to collect information for the job costing system, the compiled information may be more expensive than the cost of the product. Usually, it is possible to obtain some of the required information at a lower cost, but the accountant must decide whether to pursue additional improvements in costing information at a higher marginal cost.
- *High proportion of allocated costs.* In many production environments, the overhead cost is so high that it exceeds the amount of those costs directly traceable to a job. If the basis of overhead allocation is arbitrary, does it make sense to allocate costs to jobs at all? An alternative may be to only accumulate costs that have a proven relationship to a job, and to leave all other costs in a general overhead cost pool.
- *Low cost per unit.* If a product has a minimal per-unit cost, as is the case for a downloaded electronic product, there is no point in collecting what little cost information may be available.
- *Process environment.* If a company is building vast quantities of the same product, such as in a ball bearing plant or an oil refinery, there is no way to collect information for a specific unit of production. In this case, see the Process Costing chapter for a more applicable system.

Accounting for Direct Materials in Job Costing

In a job costing environment, materials to be used on a product or project first enter the facility and are stored in the warehouse, after which they are picked from stock and issued to a specific job. If spoilage or scrap is created, normal amounts are charged to an overhead cost pool for later allocation, while abnormal amounts are charged directly to the cost of goods sold. Once work is completed on a job, the cost of the entire job is shifted from work-in-process inventory to finished goods inventory. Then, once the goods are sold, the cost of the asset is removed from the inventory account and shifted into the cost of goods sold, while the company also records a sale transaction. The following example shows how to account for these direct material movements.

EXAMPLE

Twill Machinery orders $10,000 of sheet metal, which arrives and is stored in the warehouse. Twill records this transaction with the following entry:

	Debit	Credit
Raw materials inventory	10,000	
Accounts payable		10,000

Twill's production scheduling staff creates job number 1200, which is designated to accumulate the costs associated with a laying press for an antique book bindery. The production scheduling staff authorizes the issuance of a pick list to the warehouse, which is used to pick items from stock for the construction of job 1200. The pick list includes the following items:

Item	Cost
Sheet metal	$1,500
Hardboard platen	450
Press bed	280
Adjustment wheel	150
Total cost	$2,380

Twill uses the following entry to record the transfer of raw materials to work-in-process for job 1200. Note that only a portion of the sheet metal is moved to work-in-process; the rest of the purchased amount remains in the warehouse, to be used on some other job.

	Debit	Credit
Work-in-process (Job 1200)	2,380	
Raw materials inventory		2,380

During production of the laying press, Twill experiences $300 of abnormal scrap, which it charges directly to the cost of goods sold (not to Job 1200), on the grounds that it must recognize the expense at once. The entry is:

	Debit	Credit
Cost of goods sold	300	
Work-in-process (Job 1200)		300

At the end of the month, $5,000 of normal scrap cost has accumulated in the waste overhead cost pool, which accumulates the costs of normal scrap and spoilage. The accountant determines that 10% of this amount, or $500, should be allocated to Job 1200. The entry is:

	Debit	Credit
Work-in-process (Job 1200)	500	
Waste cost pool		500

Twill completes work on the laying press and shifts all related material costs to the finished goods inventory account. The entry is:

	Debit	Credit
Finished goods (Job 1200)	2,580	
Work-in-process (Job 1200)		2,580

Please note that these entries do not yet include labor costs or an allocation for manufacturing overhead; these topics are addressed in the following sections.

Accounting for Labor in Job Costing

In a job costing environment, labor may be charged directly to individual jobs, if the labor is directly traceable to those jobs. All other manufacturing-related labor is recorded in an overhead cost pool and is then allocated to the various open jobs. The first type of labor is called direct labor, and the second type is known as indirect labor. When a job is completed, the associated cost is shifted into a finished goods inventory account. Then, once the goods are sold, the cost of the asset is removed from the inventory account and shifted into the cost of goods sold account, while the company also records a sale transaction. The following example shows how to account for these labor transactions.

EXAMPLE

This is a continuation of the preceding example, where Twill Machinery is building a laying press for an antique book bindery. Twill pays its employees at the end of each month, and records the following payroll entry for its production department:

	Debit	Credit
Work-in-process (Job 1200)	8,000	
Work-in-process (Job 1201)	16,000	
Work-in-process (Job 1202)	41,000	
Overhead cost pool	35,000	
Wages payable		100,000

At the end of the month, Twill allocates the indirect labor in the overhead cost pool to the various open jobs. Of the $35,000 of labor in the overhead cost pool, Twill allocates $4,000 to Job 1200 with the following entry:

	Debit	Credit
Work-in-process (Job 1200)	4,000	
Overhead cost pool		4,000

Twill completes work on the laying press and shifts all related labor costs to the finished goods inventory account. The entry is:

	Debit	Credit
Finished goods (Job 1200)	12,000	
Work-in-process (Job 1200)		12,000

This final entry comes from the $8,000 of direct labor that was initially charged against Job 1200 and the $4,000 of indirect labor that was allocated to it.

Accounting for Actual Overhead Costs in Job Costing

In a job costing environment, non-direct costs are accumulated into one or more overhead cost pools, from which costs are allocated to open jobs based upon some measure of cost usage. The key issues when applying overhead are to consistently charge the same types of costs to overhead in all reporting periods, and to consistently apply these costs to jobs. Otherwise, it can be extremely difficult for the accountant to explain why overhead cost allocations vary from one period to the next.

EXAMPLE

This is a continuation of the preceding example, where Twill Machinery is building a laying press for an antique book bindery. During the most recent reporting period, Twill incurred the following costs, all of which it records in an overhead cost pool:

Expense Type	Amount
Production facility rent	$60,000
Equipment repair costs	15,000
Building repair costs	9,000
Production supplies	3,000
Total	$87,000

Twill allocates overhead costs to jobs based on their use of production equipment. Job 1200 accounted for 12% of total equipment usage during the month, so Twill allocates 12% of the $87,000 in the cost pool to Job 1200 with the following entry:

	Debit	Credit
Work-in-process (Job 1200)	10,440	
Overhead cost pool		10,440

Twill completes work on the laying press and shifts all related overhead costs to the finished goods inventory account. The entry is:

	Debit	Credit
Finished goods (Job 1200)	10,440	
Work-in-process (Job 1200)		10,440

Accounting for Standard Overhead Costs in Job Costing

The accumulation of actual costs into overhead pools and their allocation to jobs, as noted in the preceding section, can be a time-consuming process that interferes with closing the books for a reporting period. To speed up the process, an alternative is to allocate standard costs that are based on historical costs. These standard costs will never be exactly the same as actual costs, but can be easily calculated and allocated.

The overhead allocation process for standard costs is to use historical cost information to arrive at a standard rate per unit of activity, and allocate this standard amount to jobs based on their units of activity. Then subtract the total amount allocated from the overhead cost pool (which contains actual overhead costs), and dispose of any remaining amount in the overhead cost pool. Use any of the following methods to dispose of the remaining overhead amount:

- *Charge to cost of goods sold.* Charge the entire variance to the cost of goods sold. This is the simplest method.

- *Allocate the variance*. Allocate the variance to the accounts for finished goods, work-in-process, and cost of goods sold, based on the ending balances in these accounts. This approach is slightly more time-consuming, but is the most theoretically correct allocation method.
- *Charge to jobs*. Allocate the variance to those jobs that were open during the reporting period. This approach is the most time-consuming. It essentially reverts a company back to an actual costing system, since the results of this method will approximate those created under an actual cost allocation system.

The allocation of an overhead cost pool is by definition inherently inaccurate, since the underlying costs cannot be directly associated with a job. Consequently, it is best to use the simplest of the above methods to dispose of any residual amounts in the overhead cost pool.

> **Tip:** If the company is billing customers under a cost-plus arrangement, customers may take a considerable interest in the allocation of costs, since they are paying for the allocation. In this case, clear the allocation method with customers before using it.

EXAMPLE

Twill Manufacturing decides to revise its cost allocation method to the standard costing system. In the past three months, the company incurred the following amounts of manufacturing overhead:

Month 1	$71,000
Month 2	82,000
Month 3	87,000
Average monthly overhead	$80,000

The manufacturing facility usually experiences 2,000 hours of machine usage per month, so Twill adopts a standard overhead allocation rate of $40 per hour of machine usage, which it derives as follows:

$80,000 Average monthly overhead ÷ 2,000 Hours of machine usage
= $40/hour allocation rate

During the most recent month, Job 1200 incurred $10,440 of actual overhead costs (see the preceding example). In that month, it used 240 hours of machine time, which at a standard application rate of $40/hour, results in an overhead allocation of $9,600. Thus, the use of a standard overhead rate that is based on an historical average amount of costs incurred results in an $840 reduction in the amount of overhead charged to Job 1200.

In Month 3, the standard $40/hour rate is charged to 2,000 of machine time used, for a total allocation of $80,000. This leaves $7,000 of actual overhead costs remaining in the overhead cost pool (since $87,000 of actual overhead costs were incurred in Month 3). Rather than go through the effort of allocating this residual to any accounts or jobs, the accountant elects to charge it directly to the cost of goods sold with the following entry:

	Debit	Credit
Cost of goods sold	7,000	
Overhead cost pool		7,000

The net effect of this adjustment is that Twill records $7,000 more expense in the current month than might otherwise have been the case. If the company had instead elected to use the allocation of actual overhead costs, the costs would have remained in the inventory account as an asset until the jobs were billed to customers.

The Importance of Closing a Job

A job is the same as an account – it is a bucket in which transactions are recorded. Once all work on a specific job is complete, close the associated job. By doing so, people can be kept from inadvertently (or deliberately) charging additional expenses to it. More particularly, the monthly overhead cost allocation may result in overhead being charged to *all* open jobs, even if there has been no activity in some of those accounts in months. Further, closing a job keeps anyone from deliberately shifting both billings and expenses in and out of the related account. This activity is used to fraudulently alter the reported profitability levels of specific jobs.

It may be several weeks or a month after a job is complete, before the job is closed. Before that time, late supplier invoices may arrive that should be charged against the job. However, once a job has been closed, it should not be reopened without documented approval from senior management. Otherwise, the accountant is continually dealing with minor account adjustments for many months into the future.

The Role of the Subsidiary Ledger in Job Costing

The preceding sections should make it clear that a job costing system causes quite a large number of accounting transactions. If a company has many jobs, this can result in a veritable blizzard of transactions, which can create a record keeping problem. There are three ways to record accounting transactions at the job level, which are:

- *In a spreadsheet.* The most primitive way to record job-level transactions is to treat the primary accounting software as though there are no jobs, and instead record the job-specific information on a separate spreadsheet for each job. Under this approach, all transactions are still recorded in the accounting system under the corporate chart of accounts, but do not identify any jobs. Using a spreadsheet greatly increases the risk that information stored on the spreadsheet will not match the information in the general ledger, but eliminates the need for separate job-level accounts in the accounting software. This method is acceptable if there are few jobs that do not involve a large number of transactions.

- *In the general ledger.* A more advanced method is to create a new account in the general ledger for each job. This approach centralizes all information in a single database, but also clutters up the general ledger with a large number of additional accounts and transactions. This method is acceptable if there are few jobs having low-to-moderate numbers of transactions.

- *In subsidiary ledgers.* The cleanest method is to record job-related transactions in a subsidiary ledger. Under this approach, a unique account can be created for each job in a subsidiary ledger, and summary totals rolled up from the subsidiary ledger to the general ledger at the end of each reporting period. This keeps a great deal of clutter out of the general ledger, though it is necessary to access the subsidiary ledger to research the details of transactions – the information will not be available in the general ledger. This method is nearly mandatory when there are many jobs and large transaction volumes.

There is an obvious progression in the record keeping methods presented here. A small operation can get by with spreadsheet-based records until it begins to have problems reconciling the information in the spreadsheets with the accounting system. It then moves to record keeping in the general ledger until the number of accounts and transactions makes the general ledger too complex, and finally shifts to subsidiary ledgers to handle more high-volume situations.

Summary

Job costing is one of the most common cost accumulation systems in existence, since it is ideally suited to storing and organizing information about the cost of a specific product or project. However, it is a time-consuming system that requires a large amount of data entry and error checking. Consequently, only use it if there is a real need for such a large amount of detailed cost information. If not, just use a set of general ledger accounts to store a moderate amount of information – and that may be enough for all management reporting needs.

Chapter 9
Process Costing

Introduction

Process costing is a costing system used when large quantities of the same item are manufactured. In these situations, it is much too inefficient to track the cost of each individual product. Instead, accumulate the cost of a large number of units produced, and allocate the entire cost over all units produced. Thus, every unit created has exactly the same cost as every other unit produced.

In this chapter, we give an overview of process costing and how it is calculated, discuss situations where it should (and should not) be used, and also address how it can be integrated into a hybrid accounting system.

Overview of Process Costing

Job costing is generally the preferred method for deriving a product's cost, since it yields highly precise information. However, there are many situations where the volume of production is so high that there is no way to track the cost of each individual product in a cost-effective manner. Also, it may be impossible to differentiate the costs associated with individual products. If either situation is the case, the usual solution is to use process costing. The classic example of a process costing situation is oil refining, where the cost of any individual gallon of fuel cannot be differentiated from another one.

In process costing, there are three methods available for generating a cost per unit. They are:

- *Weighted average costing.* This method averages all costs from multiple periods and assigns them to units. It is most applicable to simple costing environments, and where there are few cost changes from period to period. It is the simplest calculation method.
- *Standard costing.* This method assigns standard costs to production units and treats variances from actual costs separately. It is used when a company has a standard costing system in operation.
- *First in, first out (FIFO) costing.* This method assigns costs to production units based on the periods in which costs are incurred. It produces the highest degree of accuracy, and is also the most complex to calculate. The FIFO method is most useful where costs vary substantially from period to period, so that management can see product cost trends.

There is no last in, first out (LIFO) costing method used in process costing, since the underlying assumption of process costing is that the first unit produced is, in fact, the first unit used, which is the FIFO concept. Thus, the LIFO concept is invalid in a true process costing environment.

The typical manner in which costs flow in process costing is that direct material costs are added at the beginning of the process, while all other costs (both direct labor and overhead) are gradually added over the course of the production process. For example, in a food processing operation, the direct material (such as a cow) is added at the beginning of the operation, after which various rendering operations gradually convert the direct material into finished products (such as steaks).

The Weighted Average Method

The weighted average method is the simplest way to calculate process costs. To calculate the weighted average cost of a production unit, it is necessary to first derive the number of units of production, which assumes that direct materials are added at the beginning of the process. This calculation is shown in the "Production Units" section of the following example, where 500 units are completed in the reporting period, and 200 units are still in production. We assume that direct materials were added to all 700 units, but that additional conversion costs were only fully applied to the 500 completed units. In the example, we assume that the 200 units still in process are only 30% complete, so we multiply the 200 units in process by the 30% conversion estimate to arrive at an adjusted 60 production units for the purposes of applying conversion costs. This means there are 560 production units to which conversion costs can be applied.

EXAMPLE

	Direct Materials	Conversion Costs	Totals
Step 1: Production Units			
Completed units	500	500	
Units in process*	200	60	
Production unit totals	700	560	
Step 2: Cost per Unit			
Beginning cost in WIP	$4,000	$2,000	$6,000
Costs in current period	30,000	15,000	45,000
Total costs	$34,000	$17,000	$51,000
Cost per unit**	$48.571	$30.357	
Step 3: Allocate Costs			
Completed units cost	$24,286	$15,179	$39,465
Ending WIP units cost	9,714	1,821	11,535
Total costs	$34,000	$17,000	$51,000

* 30% complete at month-end
** Based on production unit totals listed above

The second step in using the weighted average method is to calculate the cost per production unit, which appears in the "Cost per Unit" section in the preceding example. The calculation steps are:

1. Enter the beginning direct materials costs for any beginning work-in-process items in the Direct Materials column, in the "Beginning cost in WIP" row.
2. Enter the beginning conversion costs for any beginning work-in-process items in the Conversion Costs column, in the "Beginning cost in WIP" row.
3. Enter all current period direct materials costs in the Direct Materials column, in the "Costs in current period" row.
4. Enter all current period conversion costs in the Conversion Costs column, in the "Costs in current period" row.
5. Total all costs in the Direct Materials column and the Conversion Costs column, and enter the total in the "Total costs" row for each column, respectively.
6. Divide the total costs in the Direct Material column by the production unit totals listed in the same column, and enter the cost per unit in the "Cost per unit" row for that column.
7. Divide the total costs in the Conversion Costs column by the production unit totals listed in the same column, and enter the cost per unit in the "Cost per unit" row for that column.

The final step in using the weighted average method is to calculate total costs to assign to the work-in-process and finished goods inventory accounts. The following calculations appear in the Allocate Costs section in the preceding example:

1. Multiply the number of completed units in the Direct Materials column (500 in the example) by the cost per unit ($48.571 in the example), and enter the total in the Direct Materials column, in the "Completed units cost" row.
2. Multiply the number of completed units in the Conversion Costs column (500 in the example) by the cost per unit ($30.357 in the example), and enter the total in the Conversion Costs column, in the "Completed units cost" row.
3. Multiply the number of units in process in the Direct Materials column (200 in the example) by the cost per unit ($48.571 in the example), and enter the total in the Direct Materials column, in the "Ending WIP units cost" row.
4. Multiply the number of units in process in the Conversion Costs column (60 in the example) by the cost per unit ($30.357 in the example), and enter the total in the Conversion Costs column, in the "Ending WIP units cost" row.

In essence, these calculations create a reduced number of units in process, based on the presumed percentage of completion, which results in a reduced allocation of conversion costs to ending work-in-process units. In contrast, direct materials are allocated to the full number of work-in-process units, because the assumption is that direct materials are added at the *beginning* of the production process.

A great deal of the effort in these calculations is directed at creating different allocations for direct costs and conversion costs. If we did not differentiate between the two types of costs, and instead assumed that *all* costs are assigned at the beginning of the production process, the amount allocated to the work-in-process account will increase, while the amount allocated to finished goods will decline. This shift in costs can have an impact on reported profits if a large part of the finished goods are sold by the end of the reporting period, since the costs that would normally be recorded as finished goods are not charged to the cost of goods sold, but are instead recorded as a work-in-process asset, and deferred from recognition until a later reporting period.

The Standard Costing Method

If a company uses a standard costing system (see the Standard Costing of Inventory chapter), the accountant is accustomed to working with predetermined costs and then calculating variances from those standards. It is possible to alter the basic process costing model to accommodate standard costs.

In the following example, we use the same general format as was just outlined for the weighted average method, with the following modifications:

- *Cost per unit.* In Step 2 in the example, we have replaced actual costs with a single standard cost for direct materials, and a single standard cost for conversion costs. These standard costs are derived by the company, and are generally close to the actual costs used in the weighted average method.
- *Allocate costs.* In Step 3 in the example, we have multiplied the production units by the standard costs noted in Step 2, rather than the actual costs that would have been used in the weighted average method.
- *Variance analysis.* The final portion of the example contains a new Step 4, which contains a compilation of the actual costs incurred during the period (taken from Step 3 of the preceding example), from which the standard costs calculated in Step 3 of this example are subtracted to derive variances. These variances are then charged to the cost of goods sold in the current period.

89

EXAMPLE

	Direct Materials	Conversion Costs	Totals
Step 1: Production Units			
Completed units	500	500	
Units in process*	200	60	
Production unit totals	700	560	
Step 2: Cost per Unit			
Standard cost per unit**	$48.500	$30.000	
Step 3: Allocate Costs			
Completed units cost	$24,250	$15,000	$39,250
Ending WIP units cost	9,700	1,800	11,500
Total costs	$33,950	$16,800	$50,750
Step 4: Variance Analysis			
Actual cost totals:			
Beginning cost in WIP	$4,000	$2,000	$6,000
Costs in current period	30,000	15,000	45,000
Total actual costs	$34,000	$17,000	$51,000
Total standard costs	$33,950	$16,800	$50,750
Cost variance	$50	$200	$250

* 30% complete at month-end
** Based on standard costs

The standard costing variation on the process costing model is slightly more difficult to derive than the weighted average model, since it adds standard costs and a variance calculation to the basic model. Still, it is not an especially difficult calculation.

The First In, First Out Method

The first in, first out (FIFO) method is more complicated than the weighted average or standard costing methods, so do not use it unless the increased accuracy of its results is of importance to corporate decision making. Generally, only use the FIFO method when there are significant cost fluctuations between consecutive reporting periods that will result in significant differences in cost allocations in each of the periods.

The key change in the FIFO calculation from the weighted average method revolves around the segregation of the work-in-process costs that had been recorded in the preceding period. The key calculation steps, using the same example from the weighted average method section, are:

1. *Separate beginning work-in-process.* In Step 1 of the example, segregate the units in beginning work-in-process from the other production units. There should be no allocation of direct materials to these units, since that allocation would have been done in a prior period. Also, the conversion factor for the beginning work-in-process units may very well differ from the conversion factor used for the ending units in process. The following example shows a conversion factor for the beginning work-in-process of 50%, and of 30% for the ending work-in-process. The result is a lower unit total in the Direct Materials column, since the FIFO method only lists units here if additional costs are to be added to the units. There is also a lower unit total in the Conversion Costs column, because the 200 beginning work-in-process units are only 50% complete, and are therefore listed as 100 units.

2. *Calculate cost per unit.* In Step 2 of the example, we no longer include the cost of beginning work-in-process, since that is dealt with in the following step. Instead, we only calculate the cost per unit for costs incurred in the current period.

3. *Allocate costs.* In Step 3 of the example, we have created a cost layer for the beginning work-in-process called the "Beginning WIP cost," which establishes a separate cost layer for beginning inventory. We then follow the usual calculation steps, excluding the beginning work-in-process cost, which are:

    a. Multiply the 100 beginning WIP units in the Conversion Costs column by the $32.609 conversion cost per unit to derive the $3,261 of conversion costs added to beginning work-in-process.

    b. Multiply the 300 completed units in the Direct Materials column by the $60.000 direct materials cost per unit to derive the $18,000 of direct materials costs added to the new completed units.

    c. Multiply the 300 completed units in the Conversion Costs column by the $32.609 conversion cost per unit to derive the $9,783 of conversion costs added to the new completed units.

    d. Multiply the 200 ending WIP units in the Direct Materials column by the $60.000 direct materials cost per unit to derive the $12,000 of direct materials costs added to the ending work-in-process units.

    e. Multiply the 60 ending WIP units in the Conversion Costs column by the $32.609 conversion cost per unit to derive the $1,956 of conversion costs added to the ending work-in-process units.

EXAMPLE

	Direct Materials	Conversion Costs	Totals
Step 1: Production Units			
Beginning WIP units*	--	100	
Completed units	300	300	
Ending WIP units**	200	60	
Production unit totals	500	460	
Step 2: Cost per Unit			
Costs in current period	$30,000	$15,000	$45,000
Cost per unit***	$60.000	$32.609	
Step 3: Allocate Costs			
Beginning WIP cost	$4,000	$2,000	$6,000
Costs added to beginning WIP	--	3,261	3,261
Costs added to new completed units	18,000	9,783	27,783
Costs added to ending WIP	12,000	1,956	13,956
Total costs	$34,000	$17,000	$51,000

* 50% complete at the beginning of the month
** 30% complete at the end of the month
*** Based on production unit totals listed above

The end result is an allocation of the same amount of costs used in the original weighted average cost example, but with different proportions of costs being divided between the finished goods and ending work-in-process accounts.

The Hybrid Costing System

A hybrid costing system is an accounting system that includes features of both a job costing and process costing system. It is also known as an operation costing system.

A hybrid costing system is useful when a production facility handles groups of products in batches and charges the cost of materials to those batches (see the Job Costing chapter), while also accumulating labor and overhead costs at the departmental or work center level and allocating these costs at the individual unit level (as is the case in a process costing environment).

Hybrid costing is most commonly used in situations where there is identical processing of a baseline product, as well as individual modifications that are made beyond the baseline level of processing. For example, this situation arises when identical products are manufactured until they reach a painting operation, after which each product receives a different coating, with each coat having a different cost.

As another example, a company produces a variety of refrigerators, all of which require essentially the same processing, but differing amounts of materials. It can use a job costing system to assign varying amounts of materials to each refrigerator, while using the process costing method to allocate the costs of labor and overhead equally across all of the refrigerators produced.

EXAMPLE

Puller Corporation uses process costing to calculate the cost of its ubiquitous plastic door knobs, which are identical in all respects, and which cost $0.25 each. Puller stores its plastic door knobs in an unfinished state and waits for customer orders before applying additional finishing operations.

The final finishing operation can involve either a chrome lamination operation, a spray-on mahogany finish, or rolling in a tumbler that simulates distressed furniture. Each of these operations results in a different cost. The cost of additional finishing in chrome is $0.15, the mahogany finish is $0.05, and the tumbler operation is $0.12. These additional costs are significantly different from each other and will be completed in small batches, depending upon the size of customer orders.

Based on the variety of possible outcomes and the smaller size of production runs for finishing operations, Puller elects to keep its process costing system for the initial creation of plastic door knobs, but to switch to a job costing system to calculate finishing costs.

The key issue in choosing to use a hybrid system is whether certain parts of the production process are more easily accounted for under a different system than the one used by the bulk of the manufacturing operation. Many companies do not realize that they are using a hybrid costing system - they have simply adapted their accounting systems to the operational requirements of their business models.

Process Costing Journal Entries

Process costing is really just a simplified version of job costing, because it treats an entire production process as a single job. That being the case, the same journal entries shown in the Job Costing chapter can be used to record process costs.

To use the weighted average process costing example used earlier in this chapter, the allocation of direct materials to production units results in $24,286 being allocated to completed units, and $9,714 to ending work-in-process units. The journal entry for this calculation is:

	Debit	Credit
Finished goods inventory	24,286	
Work-in-process inventory	9,714	
Raw materials inventory		34,000

To continue with the same example, $15,179 of conversion costs were allocated to completed units, and $1,821 to ending work-in-process units. The journal entry for this calculation is:

	Debit	Credit
Finished goods inventory	15,179	
Work-in-process inventory	1,821	
Conversion cost pool		17,000

If a standard costing variation on the process costing system were to be used, the only additional entry is to charge any variances to the cost of goods sold. To use the variances calculated earlier in the standard costing example, there is a $50 unfavorable variance for direct materials, and a $200 unfavorable variance for conversion costs. The journal entry to record these variances is:

	Debit	Credit
Cost of goods sold	250	
Raw materials inventory		50
Conversion cost pool		200

The journal entries used for the FIFO method are quite similar in structure to those used for the weighted average method, though the proportions of costs recorded between the work-in-process and finished goods accounts differ somewhat. Also, the entries do not include the amount of costs in beginning work-in-process, which were recorded in the preceding period. The journal entries to record the results of the example in the earlier FIFO section are:

	Debit	Credit
Finished goods inventory	18,000	
Work-in-process inventory	12,000	
Raw materials inventory		30,000
To allocate direct materials to finished goods and work-in-process		

	Debit	Credit
Finished goods inventory	13,044	
Work-in-process inventory	1,956	
Conversion cost pool		15,000
To allocate conversion costs to finished goods and work-in-process		

In the last journal entry, the $13,044 addition to finished goods inventory is comprised of both the $9,783 that was directly allocated to completed units in the earlier example, and the $3,261 allocated to the units in beginning work-in-process (which assumes that beginning work-in-process was converted to finished goods during the reporting period).

Problems with Process Costing

The single largest problem with the process costing concept is the use of an estimated percentage of completion of work-in-process at the end of a reporting period. This percentage is a key part of the calculation to assign costs to work-in-process inventory, and so can be used to shift costs into or out of the current period to modify reported levels of profitability.

EXAMPLE

The production manager of Colossal Furniture, Mr. Mammoth, will receive a bonus if the company records a profit of $10,000 in November. The company uses a hybrid accounting system for its production of high chairs for oversized infants. Mr. Mammoth has control over the percentage of completion for units in process in the process costing portion of the accounting system.

The actual percentage of completion for units in process is 42%, but Mr. Mammoth calculates that if he authorizes a change to 45% completion, this will cause a higher allocation of costs to work-in-process, and thereby increases profits just enough to earn him the bonus.

The accounting manager is not aware of the bonus situation, and does not complain about what appears to be a minor increase in the percentage of completion. Mr. Mammoth receives his bonus.

A simple method that avoids manipulation of the percentage of completion is to use a standard percentage that is never changed in any reporting period. This technique does eliminate the risk of management override of the percentage; however, it introduces a new risk, which is that management can initiate a large amount of new work-in-process at the end of the reporting period, to which the standard percentage of completion now applies. Thus, management could potentially shift into a new form of reporting fraud if new controls are placed elsewhere in the system.

EXAMPLE

The internal audit staff of Colossal Furniture recommends to senior management that the percentage of completion used in its process costing calculation be fixed at 50%, thereby eliminating the type of manipulation described in the preceding example.

In December, the production manager (still Mr. Mammoth, despite his earlier manipulations) can earn yet another bonus if the company records a profit of $20,000. Near the end of the month, it appears that the company will be $5,000 short of its profit goal. To meet his target, Mr. Mammoth releases a large amount of work into the production area on December 31. No work is actually performed on any of these new projects, but because they are now categorized as work-in-process, the accountant must apply the standard percentage of completion to them.

The accountant allocates $5,000 of conversion costs to the new work-in-process items, which shifts these costs into the balance sheet as assets, thereby reducing the cost of goods sold by $5,000. Mr. Mammoth again earns his bonus.

Summary

Process costing is a common method for calculating the cost of standardized products that are produced in large quantities. It results in reasonably accurate results, so long as all of the products for which costs are being derived are actually the same in all respects. If not, it is better to incorporate some aspects of a job costing system into the process costing system, resulting in a hybrid system that yields a higher level of inventory costing accuracy.

Chapter 10
Overhead Allocation

Introduction

When inventory is recorded in the balance sheet, an appropriate amount of manufacturing overhead costs must be allocated to the inventory. In this chapter, we list the types of costs that can be included in an overhead allocation, and how overhead can be allocated in an efficient manner.

> **Related Podcast Episode:** Episode 119 of the Accounting Best Practices Podcast discusses overhead allocation. It is available at: **accountingtools.com/podcasts** or **iTunes**

Overhead Allocation

A key tenet of Generally Accepted Accounting Principles is that overhead costs must be applied to inventory for financial reporting purposes. In many businesses, the cost of overhead is substantially greater than direct costs, so the accounting staff must expend considerable attention on the proper method of allocating overhead to inventory.

There are two types of overhead, which are administrative overhead and manufacturing overhead. Administrative overhead includes those costs not involved in the development or production of goods or services, such as the costs of front office administration and sales; this is essentially all overhead that is *not* included in manufacturing overhead. Manufacturing overhead is all of the costs that a factory incurs, other than direct costs.

The costs of manufacturing overhead are to be allocated to any inventory items that are classified as work-in-process or finished goods. Overhead is not allocated to raw materials inventory, since the operations giving rise to overhead costs only impact work-in-process and finished goods inventory. Administrative overhead is charged to expense as incurred; it is not allocated to inventory.

The following items are usually included in manufacturing overhead:

Depreciation of factory equipment	Quality control and inspection
Factory administration expenses	Rent, facility and equipment
Indirect labor and production supervisory wages	Repair expenses
Indirect materials and supplies	Rework labor, scrap and spoilage
Maintenance, factory and production equipment	Taxes related to production assets
Officer salaries related to production	Uncapitalized tools and equipment
Production employees' benefits	Utilities

When there are inordinate amounts of costs related to rework, scrap, and spoilage, the excess amounts should be charged to expense in the current period, rather than being included in overhead. The amount that is "excess" can be estimated based on an analysis of historical trends of costs incurred, or by determining which specific transactions were clearly greater than normal.

Tip: Create an accounting policy that clearly states which costs are to be included in manufacturing overhead. By following this policy, overhead costs can be more consistently formulated across multiple reporting periods.

The typical procedure for allocating overhead is to accumulate all manufacturing overhead costs into one or more cost pools, and to then use an activity measure to apportion the overhead costs in the cost pools to the inventory produced in the period. Thus, the overhead allocation formula is:

Cost pool ÷ Total activity measure = Overhead allocation per unit

Tip: Where possible, use a single cost pool to aggregate manufacturing overhead costs, since this reduces the amount of accounting effort required to allocate overhead.

EXAMPLE

Mulligan Imports has a small production operation for an in-house line of golf clubs. During April, it incurs costs for the following items:

Cost Type	Amount
Building rent	$65,000
Building utilities	12,000
Factory equipment depreciation	8,000
Production equipment maintenance	7,000
Total	$92,000

All of these items are classified as manufacturing overhead, so Mulligan creates the following journal entry to shift these costs into an overhead cost pool:

	Debit	Credit
Overhead cost pool	92,000	
Depreciation expense		8,000
Maintenance expense		7,000
Rent expense		65,000
Utilities expense		12,000

The activity measure used should be something that is already being measured, since this lightens the work load of the accounting staff. Thus, if an allocation based on machine hours is slightly more relevant but will require the creation of a new tracking system, consider an alternative measure for which a tracking system is already in place.

Overhead costs can be allocated by any reasonable measure, as long as it is consistently applied across reporting periods. Common bases of allocation are direct labor hours charged against a product, or the amount of machine hours used during the production of a product. The amount of allocation charged per unit is known as the *overhead rate*.

The overhead rate can be expressed as a proportion, if both the numerator and denominator are in dollars. For example, Armadillo Industries has total indirect costs of $100,000 and it decides to use the cost of its direct labor as the allocation measure. Armadillo incurs $50,000 of direct labor costs, so the overhead rate is calculated as:

$$\frac{\$100{,}000 \text{ Indirect costs}}{\$50{,}000 \text{ Direct labor}}$$

The result is an overhead rate of 2.0.

Alternatively, if the denominator is not in dollars, the overhead rate is expressed as a cost per allocation unit. For example, Armadillo decides to change its allocation measure to hours of machine time used. The company has 10,000 hours of machine time usage, so the overhead rate is now calculated as:

$$\frac{\$100{,}000 \text{ Indirect costs}}{10{,}000 \text{ Machine hours}}$$

The result is an overhead rate of $10.00 per machine hour.

EXAMPLE

Mulligan Imports has a small golf shaft production line, which manufactures a titanium shaft and an aluminum shaft. Considerable machining is required for both shafts, so Mulligan concludes that it should allocate overhead to these products based on the total hours of machine time used. In May, production of the titanium shaft requires 5,400 hours of machine time, while the aluminum shaft needs 2,600 hours. Thus, 67.5% of the overhead cost pool is allocated to the titanium shafts and 32.5% to the aluminum shafts.

In May, Mulligan accumulates $100,000 of costs in its overhead cost pool, and allocates it between the two product lines with the following journal entry:

	Debit	Credit
Finished goods – Titanium shafts	67,500	
Finished goods – Aluminum shafts	32,500	
Overhead cost pool		100,000

This entry clears out the balance in the overhead cost pool, readying it to accumulate overhead costs in the next reporting period.

The preceding example that transfers all overhead costs into finished goods inventory is not entirely correct. If any of these finished goods were sold during the reporting period, the amount of overhead apportioned to them must be charged to the cost of goods sold. A common approach for doing so is to compile the number of units remaining in stock at the end of the period and to assign overhead to these items based on the overhead rate. All overhead accumulated during the period that exceeds this amount is charged to the cost of goods sold.

EXAMPLE

The controller of Dude Skis finds that the company has accumulated $50,000 of manufacturing overhead during its most recent reporting period, for which the allocation rate per pair of skis is $20. Of the skis produced during the reporting period, 1,500 are still in stock at the end of the period. Based on the allocation rate, $30,000 of overhead can be assigned to ending inventory, leaving $20,000 to be charged to the cost of goods sold. The associated journal entry is:

	Debit	Credit
Finished goods inventory	30,000	
Cost of goods sold	20,000	
Overhead cost pool		50,000

Tip: A common error when closing the books is to forget to charge off accumulated overhead costs to the cost of goods sold. To ensure compliance, include a specific step in the closing procedure that addresses this issue.

If the basis of allocation does not appear correct for certain types of overhead costs, it may make more sense to split the overhead into two or more overhead cost pools, and allocate each cost pool using a different basis of allocation. For example, if warehouse costs are more appropriately allocated based on the square footage consumed by various products, store warehouse costs in a warehouse overhead cost pool, and allocate these costs based on square footage used.

Thus far, we have assumed that only actual overhead costs incurred are allocated. However, it is also possible to set up a standard overhead rate that can be used for multiple reporting periods, based on long-term expectations regarding how much overhead will be incurred and how many units will be produced. If the difference between actual overhead costs incurred and overhead allocated is small, charge the difference to the cost of goods sold. If the amount is material, apportion the difference between the cost of goods sold and inventory.

EXAMPLE

Mulligan Imports incurs overhead of $93,000, which it stores in an overhead cost pool. Mulligan uses a standard overhead rate of $20 per unit, which approximates its long-term experience with the relationship between overhead costs and production volumes. In September, it produces 4,500 golf club shafts, to which it allocates $90,000 (allocation rate of $20 × 4,500 units). This leaves a difference between overhead incurred and overhead absorbed of $3,000. Given the small size of the variance, Mulligan charges the $3,000 difference to the cost of goods sold, thereby clearing out the overhead cost pool.

Averaging of Overhead Rates

An accounting manager that is interested in closing the books quickly may resist the accumulation and allocation of actual overhead costs on a monthly basis. This is because the accounts payable and payroll functions must be closed before overhead aggregation can even be started, which means that overhead allocation is a key bottleneck in the production of financial statements. To avoid this problem, a standard overhead allocation rate can be compiled from a historical average, and applied to the goods produced in each period. However, doing so creates a disparity between the standard amount of overhead applied and the actual amount of overhead incurred. This variance may be acceptable during periods when financial statements are not being issued outside of the company.

In cases where the financial statements are to be audited or reviewed, the controller should allow a longer closing period in order to compile actual overhead cost information. Doing so gives the accounting department time to flush out any variances between standard and actual overhead costs that may have accumulated in the ending inventory account.

Summary

A key issue is that overhead allocation is not a precisely-defined science – there is plenty of latitude in how a business can go about allocating overhead. The amount of allowable diversity in practice can result in slipshod accounting, so be sure to use a standardized and well-documented method to allocate overhead using the same calculation in every reporting period. This allows for great consistency, which auditors appreciate when they validate the calculations supporting overhead allocations.

Chapter 11
Obsolete Inventory

Introduction

If a company maintains any inventory, it is likely that some portion of the inventory will never be used. If so, these items will either be scrapped at a complete loss, or dispositioned at a discounted price. In either case, the company must recognize a loss on the obsolete inventory. In this chapter, we discuss three alternative approaches to accounting for obsolete inventory, as well as the circumstances under which each approach is most appropriate. We end on the topic of how various issues within a business can impact the timing and amount of loss recognition related to obsolete inventory.

Related Podcast Episode: Episode 66 of the Accounting Best Practices Podcast discusses obsolete inventory. It is available at: **accountingtools.com/podcasts** or **iTunes**

Expected Dispositions Method

A materials review board (MRB) should be used to locate obsolete inventory items. This group reviews inventory usage reports or physically examines the inventory to determine which items should be disposed of. The MRB should meet regularly to investigate obsolete inventory, perhaps on a monthly or quarterly basis. Following these meetings, the group releases a listing of obsolete inventory items. Once the report is released, the accountant follows these steps:

1. Take the obsolete inventory report to the purchasing manager, and ask for a best estimate of the amount the company can obtain by disposing of each item on the list.
2. Subtract the disposition price from the book value of each item on the report. The difference is the amount of expense that should be recognized for the obsolete inventory.
3. Create a reserve for the amount of the obsolete inventory. The debit is to either the cost of goods sold or a separate obsolete inventory expense account. The credit is to a contra account that is paired with and offsets the inventory account on the balance sheet. This means that the full amount of the loss associated with obsolete inventory is charged to expense as soon as the accountant becomes aware of the loss. The loss is not spread over multiple periods.

4. When an inventory item is actually disposed of, there are three variations on how to treat the disposal, which are:

- *Disposition matches estimate.* If the amount received from inventory disposition exactly matches the estimated amount, simply debit the reserve account and credit the inventory account. There is no impact on the income statement.
- *Disposition is higher than estimate.* If the amount received from disposition is higher than expected, debit the reserve account for the expected disposal amount, credit the cost of goods sold for the extra disposition income, and credit the inventory account for the full amount of the loss.
- *Disposition is lower than estimate.* If the amount received from disposition is lower than expected, debit the reserve account for the expected disposal amount, debit the cost of goods sold for the additional loss, and credit the inventory account for the full amount of the loss.

EXAMPLE

Milagro Corporation has $100,000 of excess home coffee roasters it cannot sell. However, it believes there is a market for the roasters through a reseller in China, but only at a sale price of $20,000. Accordingly, the controller recognizes a reserve of $80,000 with the following journal entry:

	Debit	Credit
Cost of goods sold	80,000	
Reserve for obsolete inventory		80,000

After finalizing the arrangement with the Chinese reseller, the actual sale price is only $19,000, so the controller completes the transaction with the following entry, recognizing an additional $1,000 of expense:

	Debit	Credit
Reserve for obsolete inventory	80,000	
Cost of goods sold	1,000	
Inventory		81,000

EXAMPLE

Use the same facts from the last example, except now the Chinese reseller is willing to pay $25,000 for the excess coffee roasters. This is an extra $5,000 over the amount that was initially expected to be received, and results in the following entry:

	Debit	Credit
Reserve for obsolete inventory	80,000	
Cost of goods sold		5,000
Inventory		75,000

In this case, the net reduction in the inventory asset is $75,000.

This approach to accounting for obsolete inventory requires that the accountant have an exact list of which inventory items are obsolete, as well as access to information about disposal prices. When tracked properly, the result should be a reserve account for which there is a supporting spreadsheet that lists the expected losses to be taken on specific inventory items. For example, the detailed supporting spreadsheet for a reserve account might contain the following information:

Reserve Account Supporting Spreadsheet

Item Number	Item Name	Book Value	Estimated Disposition	Estimated Loss
GR-0042	Green widget	$10,740	$2,000	$8,740
BL-0047	Blue widget	21,050	14,000	7,050
BK-1039	Black widget	32,700	6,500	26,200
CL-0013	Clear widget	9,300	1,500	7,800
	Totals	$73,790	$24,000	$49,790

In the sample spreadsheet, the $49,790 total estimated loss should match the account total for the reserve for obsolete inventory account.

Clearly, a large amount of work is required to maintain such a detailed level of support for the reserve account. If the volume of obsolete inventory is quite high, the expected dispositions method may not be a cost-effective option. Instead, consider using the reserve method that is outlined in the following section.

Reserve Method

The expected dispositions method just described relies upon the precise determination of exactly which inventory items are obsolete, as well as careful tracking of the amounts for which they are eventually sold. This level of inventory tracking can be burdensome for the accountant, and is likely to be impossible where there are a large number of inventory items constantly being dispositioned.

An alternative approach that is much simpler is the reserve method, where an estimate is made of the amount of obsolete inventory on hand. This estimate is typically based on a comparison of historical obsolescence levels to the inventory investment, adjusted for any expected changes to the obsolescence level. The estimate is used as the basis for creating a reserve account that is offset against the inventory account. The balance in the reserve is then reduced by any actual reductions in the book value of inventory as obsolete items are dispositioned. In each successive period, the remaining reserve balance is compared to a re-calculation of the probable amount of obsolete inventory, and adjusted accordingly. The following example illustrates the concept.

EXAMPLE

Kelvin Corporation maintains a massive stock of antique-style and more modern thermometers for home and commercial use. Given the large number of product options maintained in stock, it is no surprise that a number of finished goods versions are declared obsolete on a regular basis, and sold off to third-party discounters at a substantial loss.

Kelvin's controller uses the reserve method to account for this obsolete inventory. To determine whether the reserve is adequate, the controller compares the annual actual obsolete inventory write-off to the average ending inventory balance on a rolling 12-month basis. For the last 12 months, this proportion was 4% of the average inventory valuation. At the end of the current month, the total inventory balance is $1,000,000. Based on the historical proportion, the reserve for obsolete inventory should contain $40,000. At month end, the actual balance in the account is only $32,000, so the controller funds the account with the following entry:

	Debit	Credit
Cost of goods sold	8,000	
Reserve for obsolete inventory		8,000

Later in the next month, $5,000 of obsolete inventory is removed from stock and scrapped. The controller records this transaction with the following entry, which reduces the reserve account:

	Debit	Credit
Reserve for obsolete inventory	5,000	
Inventory		5,000

The only impact on the income statement occurs when the reserve account is funded, not when inventory is actually dispositioned.

The reserve method does not require precise tracking of exactly which inventory items are considered to be obsolete, which makes this a much more efficient alternative for the accountant. However, the method suffers from the following problems:

- *Estimation basis.* The balance in the reserve account is based on an estimate that is largely derived from historical experience. If there is a sudden change in the salability of inventory, this may not be reflected in the reserve, which means that the full amount of obsolete inventory is not being recognized.
- *Justification requirement.* Since the reserve is based on an estimate, expect to argue with the company's auditors about the amount of the year-end reserve, especially if the company is taking a position that the amount of the reserve should be reduced below the historical level. Auditors are typically not amenable to such a reduction when there is no historical basis for doing so.

- *Possible manipulation.* The reserve is typically replenished following a charge against the account to reflect the write-off of specific inventory items. Therefore, if someone were to refrain from such write-offs for a period of time, the reserve would incorrectly appear to be fully funded.

Tip: Monitor the amount of actual inventory write-offs in each accounting period, and follow up with the MRB if it appears that write-offs have been halted or severely curtailed.

Expensing Method

The preceding discussion of setting up an obsolescence reserve is the most appropriate way to deal with obsolete inventory. However, that approach is moderately complex. If the inventory investment is minor, a simpler approach is to charge obsolete items to expense as they are discovered. Doing so is acceptable, as long as the amount charged to expense in any period is immaterial. The danger of using the expensing method is that the accounting staff will not address obsolete inventory until the end of the year, and then discover that a much larger amount of inventory cost must be charged to expense than had been expected.

Tip: When using the expensing method for obsolete inventory, the assumption is that the amount charged to expense is so small that it is not worth tracking in a separate account. Instead, charge the expense to the cost of goods sold account.

Another concern with the expensing method is that it tends to delay expense recognition, since no entry is made until inventory is actually disposed of. The earlier two methods record an expense as soon as there is an *expectation* of a loss. The expense recognition timing difference between the methods could amount to several months.

EXAMPLE

Finchley Fireworks has a just-in-time production system, and so rarely has much of an investment in fireworks in its warehouse. Instead, fireworks are manufactured based on actual customer orders. Given the circumstances, the controller is comfortable using the expensing method to charge obsolete inventory to expense. For example, in the most recent month, a small shipment of fireworks is rejected by a customer, and must be written off. The entry is:

	Debit	Credit
Cost of goods sold	100	
Inventory		100

A group of outside investors purchase Finchley, with plans to greatly expand the company's market share. They want to do so by creating a vast stockpile of fireworks, and then advertising one-hour turnaround on all customer orders. The controller expects that this will increase the on-hand inventory investment from essentially zero to $5,000,000. Given the larger investment, the controller believes it is now necessary to switch to the reserve method, since a material amount of inventory is likely to become obsolete each year.

Issues with Obsolete Inventory Recognition

There are several issues with the recognition of obsolete inventory, which relate to the management of reported earnings and the diligence with which obsolete inventory is examined. The main concerns are:

- *Timing.* Someone can improperly alter a company's reported financial results by altering the timing of the actual dispositions of obsolete inventory. For example, if a supervisor knows that he can receive a higher-than-estimated price on the disposition of obsolete inventory, he can either accelerate or delay the sale in order to shift gains into whichever reporting period needs the extra profit. This can be a particular concern when the amount of reported profit can impact a corporate bonus plan, since there will be pressure to delay extra expenses or accelerate profits to maximize bonuses.
- *Expense recognition.* Management may be reluctant to suddenly drop a large expense reserve into the financial statements, preferring instead to recognize small incremental amounts which make inventory obsolescence appear to be a minor problem. Since GAAP mandates immediate recognition of any obsolescence as soon as it is detected, the accountant may have a struggle enforcing immediate recognition over the objections of management. A reasonable solution is to use the reserve method, which is less likely to result in sudden spikes in expense recognition.

Tip: Include a hefty obsolete inventory reserve in the annual budget. Management is much less likely to question a large write-off when the amount is relatively close to the budgeted level.

- *Optimism.* The MRB may feel that it can find a use for certain inventory items, even though there is not currently any usage planned in the production schedule, and no special deals are being offered to customers. If so, the result can be a gradual buildup in inventory balances that really should have been flagged for disposal at an earlier date, followed by a sudden write-down once the MRB finally realizes that full-price dispositions cannot be achieved.

Tip: Have an accountant attend MRB meetings, in order to discern which inventory items are not being designated as obsolete, despite evidence to the contrary.

- *Timely reviews.* Inventory obsolescence is a minor issue as long as management reviews inventory on a regular basis, so that the incremental amount of obsolescence detected is small in any given period. However, if management does not conduct a review for a long time, this allows obsolete inventory to build up to quite impressive proportions, along with an equally impressive amount of expense recognition. To avoid this issue, conduct frequent obsolescence reviews, and use the reserve method to maintain a reserve based on historical or expected obsolescence, even if specific inventory items have not yet been identified as being obsolete.

Tip: Have a senior manager take responsibility for the MRB, and ask that the group be scheduled for monthly review meetings. If senior management takes this level of interest in obsolete inventory, periodic reviews are much more likely to be performed.

EXAMPLE

Milagro Corporation sets aside an obsolescence reserve of $20,000 for obsolete coffee roasters. However, in January the purchasing manager knows that the resale price for obsolete roasters has plummeted, so the real reserve should be closer to $30,000, which would call for the immediate recognition of an additional $10,000 of expense. Since this would result in an overall reported loss in Milagro's financial results in January, he waits until May, when Milagro has a very profitable month, and completes the sale at that time, thereby incorrectly delaying the additional obsolescence loss until the later date.

Summary

There is no perfect way to handle the accounting for obsolete inventory. The expected dispositions method requires an inordinate amount of detailed accounting work, the reserve method can be inaccurate, and the expensing method tends to delay expense recognition. Of the methods presented here, we suggest using the reserve method. The basis for creating the reserve is easy to compile, so the accounting is cost-effective. The calculation basis should be consistently followed, which makes it easier to justify the balance in the account to the company's auditors. However, be aware that a sudden change in inventory usage patterns could make the reserve balance inaccurate.

Chapter 12
Lower of Cost or Market Rule

Introduction

One of the oldest accounting rules is the lower of cost or market rule, which was set forth in the old Accounting Research Bulletin No. 43. This rule requires a business to write down the recorded cost of an inventory item when its market value is lower than its cost, subject to certain conditions. In this chapter, we explain the concept and how to mitigate the labor required to comply with the rule.

> **Related Podcast Episode:** Episode 200 of the Accounting Best Practices Podcast discusses the revised lower of cost or market rule. It is available at: **accounting-tools.com/podcasts** or **iTunes**

Lower of Cost or Market Rule

The lower of cost or market rule (LCM) is required by generally accepted accounting principles, and essentially states that the cost of inventory is recorded at whichever cost is lower – the original cost or its current market price (hence the name of the rule). More specifically, the rule mandates that the recognized cost of an inventory item should be reduced to a level that does not exceed its replacement cost as derived in an open market. This replacement cost is subject to the following two conditions:

- The recognized cost cannot be greater than the likely selling price minus costs of disposal (known as net realizable value).
- The recognized cost cannot be lower than the net realizable value minus a normal profit percentage.

This situation typically arises when inventory has deteriorated, or has become obsolete, or market prices have declined. The following example illustrates the concept.

EXAMPLE

Mulligan Imports resells five major brands of golf clubs, which are noted in the following table. At the end of its reporting year, Mulligan calculates the upper and lower price boundaries of the LCM rule for each of the products, as noted in the table:

Product	Selling Price	-	Completion/ Selling Cost	=	Upper Price Boundary	-	Normal Profit	=	Lower Price Boundary
Free Swing	$250		$25		$225		$75		$150
Golf Elite	190		19		171		57		114
Hi-Flight	150		15		135		45		90
Iridescent	1,000		100		900		300		600
Titanium	700		70		630		210		420

The normal profit associated with these products is a 30% margin on the original selling price.

The information in the preceding table for the upper and lower price boundaries is then included in the following table, which completes the LCM calculation:

Product	Upper Price Boundary	Lower Price Boundary	Existing Recognized Cost	Replacement Cost*	Market Value**	Lower of Cost or Market
Free Swing	$225	$150	$140	$260	$225	$140
Golf Elite	171	114	180	175	171	171
Hi-Flight	135	90	125	110	110	110
Iridescent	900	600	850	550	600	600
Titanium	630	420	450	390	420	420

* The cost at which the item could be acquired on the open market
** The replacement cost, as limited by the upper and lower pricing boundaries

The LCM decisions noted in the last table are explained as follows:
- *Free Swing clubs.* It would cost Mulligan $260 to replace these clubs, which is above the upper price boundary of $225. This means the market value for the purposes of this calculation is $225. Since the market price is higher than the existing recognized cost, the LCM decision is to leave the recognized cost at $140 each.
- *Golf Elite clubs.* The replacement cost of these clubs has declined to a level below the existing recognized cost, so the LCM decision is to revise the recognized cost to $171. This amount is a small reduction from the unadjusted replacement cost of $175 to the upper price boundary of $171.
- *Hi-Flight clubs.* The replacement cost is less than the recognized cost, and is between the price boundaries. Consequently, there is no need to revise the replacement cost. The LCM decision is to revise the recognized cost to $110.

- *Iridescent clubs.* The replacement cost of these clubs is below the existing recognized cost, but is below the lower price boundary. Thus, the LCM decision is to set the market price at the lower price boundary, which will be the revised cost of the clubs.
- *Titanium clubs.* The replacement cost is much less than the existing recognized cost, but also well below the lower price boundary. The LCM decision is therefore to set the market price at the lower price boundary, which is also the new product cost.

A variation on the LCM rule simplifies matters somewhat, but only if a business is *not* using the last in, first out method or the retail method. The variation states that the measurement can be restricted to just the lower of cost and net realizable value.

If the amount of a write-down caused by the LCM analysis is minor, charge the expense to the cost of goods sold, since there is no reason to separately track the information. If the loss is material, track it in a separate account (especially if such losses are recurring), such as "Loss on LCM adjustment." A sample journal entry for a large adjustment is:

	Debit	Credit
Loss on LCM adjustment	147,000	
Finished goods inventory		147,000

Additional factors to consider when applying the LCM rule are:
- *Analysis by category.* The LCM rule is normally applied to a specific inventory item, but it can be applied to entire inventory categories. In the latter case, an LCM adjustment can be avoided if there is a balance within an inventory category of items having market below cost and in excess of cost.
- *Hedges.* If inventory is being hedged by a fair value hedge, add the effects of the hedge to the cost of the inventory, which frequently eliminates the need for an LCM adjustment.
- *Last in, first out layer recovery.* A write-down to the lower of cost or market can be avoided in an interim period if there is substantial evidence that inventory amounts will be restored by year end, thereby avoiding recognition of an earlier inventory layer.
- *Raw materials.* Do not write down the cost of raw materials if the finished goods in which they are used are expected to sell either at or above their costs.
- *Recovery.* A write-down to the lower of cost or market can be avoided if there is substantial evidence that market prices will increase before the inventory is sold.
- *Sales incentives.* If there are unexpired sales incentives that will result in a loss on the sale of a specific item, this is a strong indicator that there may be an LCM problem with that item.

> **Tip:** When there is an LCM adjustment, it must be taken at once – the expense cannot be recognized over multiple reporting periods.

Inventory Translation Adjustment

A special situation can arise when inventory is being carried on the books of a subsidiary in a currency that is not the functional currency of the subsidiary (the functional currency is the currency in which a business conducts the majority of its transactions). If this is the case, the inventory must first be remeasured into the designated functional currency, using historical exchange rates. These historical costs are then compared with the market prices of the inventory as stated in the functional currency. This step can result in application of the LCM rule, where an inventory write-down is required in the functional currency, even though no such write-down is called for in the books of the subsidiary (which use an alternative currency).

The reverse situation can also arise. A business might have recognized an LCM write-down in its books of record, using a currency that is not the designated functional currency. Once the currency has been converted to the functional currency, it is possible that the market price now exceeds the adjusted historical cost, in which case the LCM write-down can be reversed.

EXAMPLE

Monique Ponto produces high-end women's watches. The company has a subsidiary that operates in the independent republic of Ralston, located in the Caribbean. The subsidiary maintains its books of record in Ralston Pounds. However, the parent company has designated the functional currency of the subsidiary to be U.S. dollars. The exchange rate between the two currencies was 2 RP = 1 USD when the subsidiary bought a gold watch casing for 1,000 RP. Or, as measured in the functional currency, the watch casing cost 500 USD. As of the balance sheet date of the subsidiary, the exchange rate had changed to 2.2 RP = 1 USD.

Scenario 1: The current replacement cost of the watch casing is 1,050 RP, which is higher than its original cost of 1,000 RP. However, when translated into USD at the current exchange rate of 2.2 RP to 1 USD, the current replacement cost in USD has declined to $477 from its original cost of $500. This calls for an inventory write-down of $23 in the functional currency financial statements.

Scenario 2: The current replacement cost of the watch casing is 1,200 RP, which is higher than its original cost of 1,000 RP. When translated into USD at the current exchange rate of 2.2 RP to 1 USD, the current replacement cost in USD has increased to $545 from its original cost of $500. No inventory write-down is required, since the market price now exceeds historical cost.

Practical Application

The LCM concept can be a painful one to apply if management is determined to examine every item in stock. Doing so requires that market prices be obtained for every item, along with the estimated costs of completion and disposal. If there are many inventory items in stock, this can be a major undertaking. To reduce the effort involved, consider a combination of the following actions:

- *Timing.* Only conduct an LCM examination at the longest possible intervals. For a private company that only issues annual audited financial statements, conducting the examination at year-end may be sufficient. For a publicly-held company that issues quarterly financial statements, a quarterly review may be needed. There are few situations where a monthly examination should be conducted.

- *Work-in-process.* It is inordinately difficult to compile the costs of completion for each individual item that is currently in production at the end of a reporting period. Unless work-in-process inventory is a large number, consider adopting a corporate policy that only raw materials and finished goods inventory will be reviewed. This is a reasonable policy in cases where goods cycle through production relatively quickly.

- *80/20 rule.* The bulk of all inventory items have a low cost, and so even a catastrophic decline in their value will have little impact on the overall inventory valuation. Consequently, exclude these items from the examination, and concentrate instead on the 20% of all inventory items that make up 80% of the total inventory valuation. This approach can massively reduce the amount of inventory items under examination.

In addition to these concepts, be sure to have an ongoing system of reviews to detect obsolete inventory. If these items are withdrawn from the inventory records on a regular basis, there should be few remaining items that are in danger of triggering an LCM adjustment.

Summary

Though the conservative intent of the lower of cost or market rule is a good one, it is an unmitigated pain for the accountant to conduct an ongoing LCM investigation. Consequently, consider using the concepts noted earlier in the Practical Application section to concentrate LCM efforts on the smallest possible number of inventory items, and to conduct the review at long intervals.

Chapter 13
Inventory Spoilage, Rework, and Scrap

Introduction

The typical manufacturing facility generates a significant amount of waste – in some cases, an extraordinary amount of inventory is lost that represents a major reduction of corporate profits. Given the significance of the amount of waste, the accountant should make a major effort to properly record and report it, so that management can take action to control the underlying issues. In this chapter, we review the three types of inventory waste (spoilage, rework, and scrap), as well as how to account for them.

Definition of Spoilage

Spoilage is produced goods that are defective. A defective product is one that does not meet a predetermined acceptance criterion.

EXAMPLE

The Atlas Machining Company produces a widget that is judged acceptable if its actual thickness is within 5% of the predetermined specification. Therefore all widgets it produces that are more than 5% of this specification are considered spoilage, and are thrown out.

Across the street, the Billabong Machining Company produces a similar widget that it considers to be acceptable if its actual thickness is within 2% of the predetermined specification. All widgets outside of this range are thrown out.

Thus, based on the criteria that Atlas and Billabong have settled upon in advance, different quantities of the same product are designated as spoilage.

Spoilage frequently arises at the initiation of a production run, when the production staff is initially setting up equipment and manufactures a few products that are outside of the range of acceptable tolerances. Such spoilage may be significant without good setup controls.

Spoilage usually cannot be reworked without spending an inordinate amount on labor, so it is usually scrapped and sold off for a very low price. Spoilage is not normally sold off as finished goods, since it is by definition out of specification, and therefore may not work properly, or could even be dangerous to the user.

Accounting for Normal Spoilage

If the amount of spoilage occurring is within the normal range of expectations for spoilage in a manufacturing process, include it in the cost of the product.

EXAMPLE

Henderson Industrial manufactures plastic cartons for local dairies. The historical amount of spoilage that it experiences is 1% of all production. Each spoiled carton consumes plastic resin having a cost of $0.25. Henderson's accountant includes the cost of this resin in the carton bill of materials. The line items in the bill of materials are:

Line Item	Cost
Resin	$0.2500
Plastic cap	0.0200
Label	0.0150
Spoilage	0.0025
Total cost	$0.2875

The spoilage line item in the bill of materials is calculated as:

1% Probability of occurrence × $0.25 Cost per unit

Henderson then multiplies the total cost in the bill of materials by the number of units produced in the period to calculate its cost of goods sold, thereby incorporating the cost of spoilage into its cost of goods.

An alternative method of accounting for normal spoilage is to accumulate its cost during the reporting period, add this cost to the manufacturing overhead cost pool at the end of the month, and then allocate it to the goods produced during the month.

EXAMPLE

To continue with the preceding example, Henderson Industrial decides to stop recording normal spoilage in its bills of material, and instead records the actual cost of spoilage in a manufacturing overhead cost pool. It calculates this cost by adding up the number of spoiled cartons and multiplying by the component cost of each one. In May, the calculation is:

1,500 Spoiled cartons × $0.25/unit resin cost = $375

Henderson's accountant includes this cost in the manufacturing overhead cost pool, which is comprised of the following costs in May:

Manufacturing Overhead Line Item	Amount
Manufacturing supervisor salaries	$140,000
Building rent	50,000
Utilities	15,000
Spoilage	375
Total	$205,375

During May, Henderson manufactured 10,000,000 cartons. The amount of the overhead cost pool allocated to each carton is:

$$\$205,375 \div 10,000,000 \text{ Cartons} = \$0.021/\text{carton}$$

Accounting for Abnormal Spoilage

What happens when there is an abnormal amount of spoilage? The preceding method of including it in the bill of materials cannot be used, since that method only works if there is a consistent and reliable amount of spoilage that does not vary significantly from period to period. Instead, charge the amount of abnormal spoilage to the cost of goods sold expense in the period in which it occurs. If the amount is of sufficient size to warrant it, consider recording the abnormal spoilage in a separate account.

EXAMPLE

Quest Clothiers, makers of rugged outdoor wear, experiences abnormal spoilage when it uses substandard thread on some of its outerwear, resulting in burst seams. The cost of the spoilage is $20,000, which it records as follows:

	Debit	Credit
Abnormal spoilage expense	20,000	
Inventory		20,000

Accounting for the Sale of Spoilage

If a company is able to sell its spoiled stock, there are two ways to record it. The first approach is to record it as revenue (usually within a unique revenue account). This alternative is most useful when the revenue is large enough to warrant separate treatment for sales that are expected to continue in the future. However, the amount of revenue from the sale of spoiled stock is usually too minor to make this approach worthwhile.

The more common alternative is to net any proceeds against the recorded cost of the spoilage. This gives management a good idea of the true cost of spoilage, though it does not reveal the amount of any lost profits.

EXAMPLE

To continue with the preceding example, Quest Clothiers sells a group of garments that were subject to abnormal spoilage, in the amount of $2,000. Quest rarely experiences abnormal spoilage, and so prefers to account for the sale as a one-time event, electing to net it against the cost of spoilage with the following entry:

	Debit	Credit
Cash	2,000	
Abnormal spoilage expense		2,000

Cost Allocation to Spoilage

Normally, overhead costs are allocated to manufactured goods. Should this be done for goods that are spoiled? Common practice is to do so, though only through the point in the production process that a product reaches before it is recognized as spoiled and withdrawn. However, this can be time-consuming for the accountant to track, especially when spoilage is rare and can occur in a number of areas within the production facility. Consequently, it may be necessary to apply overhead to spoiled goods as though they completed the entire production process, as long as the effect of this change in comparison to a more precise level of cost allocation is minimal.

EXAMPLE

Quest Clothiers discovers spoilage at all stages of its production process, usually in small amounts. Quest does not calculate cost allocations for discrete segments of its production process; instead, it only allocates costs for the entire process from a single cost pool. Quest calculates the amount of overhead that would be applied to the average amount of monthly spoilage, versus applying no overhead to it at all, and finds that the differential is only $10,000, in comparison to its monthly cost of goods sold of $2,000,000. Given the immateriality of the overhead application decision, Quest elects to apply overhead to spoilage as though it had completed the entire production process, and documents its findings in case the auditors wish to review it.

Definition of Rework

Rework is any product that is initially found to be faulty, and which is then repaired and sold; the sale price may be at a reduction from the standard price for a similar product that does not require rework.

The production managers of many companies do not like to deal with rework, since it frequently requires the efforts of the more skilled production staff to repair;

also, the lower prices of rework items yield a lower gross margin than would a product that does not require rework. Consequently, given the low level of profitability associated with rework, there is a tendency to let it build up in inventory, which also presents a risk of obsolescence.

Reporting Rework

As just noted, there is an inordinately high risk that goods requiring rework will become obsolete, so the accountant should monitor the amount on hand and the amount of estimated effort needed to prepare it for sale, and share this information with management. A sample report that could be used is shown in the following exhibit, which reveals the amount of estimated effort required by each of a company's work centers to rework inventory, as well as the current recorded cost of this inventory. The report is useful not only for showing the production planners how much time to schedule at each work center, but also to get a general idea of a company's working capital investment in rework inventory.

Sample Rework Status Report

| Product | Rework Hours Required | | | | ($) |
	Bending	Curing	Painting	Assembly	Valuation
Product Alpha	12	82	6	24	$3,500
Product Beta	14	86	7	28	4,200
Product Charlie	23	100	12	46	8,000
Totals	49	268	25	98	$15,700

An alternative reporting format is shown in the following exhibit, which assigns a job number to each product or group of products that require rework. This report is more specific, itemizing the exact repair steps required to complete a rework item. Production managers prefer this higher level of detail, which gives them sufficient information to properly schedule rework. It is also useful for determining which products can be reworked for the minimum amount of effort, which is useful for clearing rework items from inventory quickly.

Sample Detailed Rework Report

Product	Batch Number	Rework Description	Rework Cost	Estimated Completion
Product Alpha	4003	Re-bend drain corners	$129	May 14
Product Beta	4011	Extend curing time by five hours	340	May 17
Product Charlie	4017	Strip paint and apply new layer	72	May 21
Product Delta	4025	Repackage in undamaged boxes	415	May 27

119

Accounting for Rework

It takes a great deal of effort to account for the work required to bring rework items back into sellable condition. This accounting requires special tracking codes, and may involve work centers located throughout a production facility. The staff of each work center must record its labor hours and any new materials used to rework an item, after which the information must be input into a rework database. The accountant periodically extracts this information from the database and reports on rework costs to management.

If the amount of rework that a company normally deals with is minor, there is no need to account for it separately in the general ledger at all. It is more cost-effective to allow the production accounting systems to record rework as a normal part of doing business. The only downside is that the company has no idea of the exact amount of costs it is expending on rework.

The reverse situation may also arise, where a company is operating under the burden of a great deal of rework. Since this may have a major negative impact on profits, the accountant must have a system for recording the cost of rework, if only so that management has a good feedback system for how well it subsequently reduces the amount of rework.

Definition of Scrap

Scrap is the amount of unused material that remains after a product has been manufactured. The classic example of scrap is in a metal stamping operation, where there is always some scrap remaining after a number of parts have been punched from a metal sheet.

Accounting for Scrap

The accounting for scrap is essentially the same as for spoilage, as described earlier in this chapter. Scrap can be accounted for in one of three ways:

- *Include scrap in the bill of materials.* This approach only works if a standard costing system is in place that uses the bill of materials to calculate the cost of goods sold.
- *Include in a cost pool.* This approach is a reasonable alternative to including the information in the bill of materials, and is somewhat easier to calculate.
- *Charge to the cost of goods sold.* This approach matches the treatment for abnormal scrap, and has the singular advantage of requiring no accounting transactions at all. Though it provides no method for determining the cost of scrap, the amount of scrap may be so small that management is comfortable with the arrangement.

The preceding steps were all noted earlier for spoilage accounting. Another alternative is to precisely track the cost of scrap and charge it to specific jobs (see the Job Costing chapter). This approach requires considerable effort to accumulate costs, but is useful in a cost reimbursement situation where the customer will reimburse the company for all costs that it can document.

Scrap, by definition, has little residual value, so it rarely makes sense to record its sale in a separate revenue account. Instead, it is most commonly recorded net of the cost of goods sold, thereby reducing a company's cost of goods sold.

EXAMPLE

Micron Metallic runs a large metal stamping machine that creates parts for washing machines. In the June reporting period, it recorded $80,000 of scrap from its stamping operations. Since this amount usually represents about 5% of Micron's cost of goods sold, which is a material amount, the controller always records scrap in a separate account. At the end of each month, a scrap hauler takes away the scrap metal and pays Micron based on the weight of the metal removed. The June payment from the scrap hauler is $800, which the controller records with the following entry:

	Debit	Credit
Cash	800	
Scrap expense		800

If a company elects to allow its scrap to accumulate for some time before selling it to a third party, the value of the scrap may be sufficiently material to call for a journal entry at the end of each reporting period to account for the gain in assets. For example, if there were a $10,000 gain in scrap during a month, the entry would be recorded as:

	Debit	Credit
Inventory - scrap	10,000	
Cost of goods sold		10,000

This entry reduces expenses during the month and creates an asset that is an estimate of the market value of the scrap. Then, when the scrap is eventually sold, eliminate the inventory asset and adjust for any differences between the actual and estimated amounts of the market value. To continue with the example, the scrap is sold early in the following month, for $9,750. There is a residual loss of $250, which is so small that it is not worth recording in a separate account. Instead, it is charged to the cost of goods sold with the following entry:

	Debit	Credit
Cash	9,750	
Cost of goods sold	250	
Inventory - scrap		10,000

Summary

The typical manufacturing operation creates a significant amount of inventory waste throughout its operations. Not only does this waste have a large negative impact on profits, but it also results in incorrectly high inventory balances. The accountant must have recording systems in place that track the amount of waste, its cost, the cost to rework it, and any amounts received from the sale of waste. Depending upon the materiality of waste, it may be necessary to create separate accounts in which to track it. If there is little waste, it may be acceptable to record it within the cost of goods sold, without attempting to break out the information.

Chapter 14
Joint and By-Product Costing

Introduction

In some industries, a number of products may be derived from a single production process, such as when a meat packing facility cuts up an animal carcass into a number of different finished goods. In these industries, it is not possible to accurately ascribe certain production costs to specific products, if these costs were incurred prior to the point in the production process when individual finished goods are identifiable. These are known as joint costs. A joint cost is a cost which benefits more than one product, and for which it may not be possible to separate its contribution to each product.

Several cost allocation methods have been created to deal with joint costs and a similar issue known as by-products. In this chapter, we will describe these issues, and how well (or not) the various allocation methods perform.

Split-Off Points and By-Products

A company needs to use joint costing or by-product costing if it has a production process where it cannot determine the final product until later in the process. The point at which it can finally determine the final product is called the split-off point. There may even be several split-off points; at each one, another product can be clearly identified, and is (literally) split off from the production process, possibly to be further refined into a finished product. If the company has incurred any manufacturing costs prior to the split-off point, it must use some method for allocating these costs to the final products. If it incurs any costs after the split-off point, the costs are likely associated with a specific product, and can be more readily assigned to them.

EXAMPLE

California Chardonnay Corporation operates several wineries that press their own grapes. During this process, there is a split-off point that produces an abundant amount of grape seed oil. The company may then sell the grape seed oil to various cooking oil manufacturers, or it may engage in several straining operations to further refine the grape seed oil into a more pure form that it can then sell to cosmetics manufacturers as the primary ingredient in skin moisturizers; alternatively, the company can add a stabilizer to the purified oil and sell it to a shaving cream manufacturer as a face shaving lubricant.

California Chardonnay has two split-off points – one where the grape seed oil is separated, and another where the purified oil is split off for sale as a skin moisturizer ingredient.

Besides the split-off point, there may also be one or more by-products. A by-product is a product that arises from a manufacturing process, but whose sales are minor in comparison to the sales of the primary products generated by the manufacturing process.

EXAMPLE

Latham Lumber operates a sawmill, which routinely produces large quantities of planks. As part of the milling process, Latham produces a significant amount of sawdust as a by-product, which has little value. The company sells the sawdust to a third party that converts it into "scatter," which is used to simulate the effect of ground cover in dioramas.

Why We Allocate Joint Costs

If a company incurs costs prior to a split-off point, it must allocate them to products, under the dictates of generally accepted accounting principles. If these costs were not allocated to products, they would have to be treated as period costs, and charged to expense in the current period. This may be an incorrect treatment of the cost if the associated products were not sold until sometime in the future, since the company would be charging a portion of the product cost to expense before realizing the offsetting sale transaction.

Allocating joint costs does not help management, since the resulting information is based on essentially arbitrary allocations. Consequently, the best allocation method does not have to be especially accurate, but it should be easy to calculate, and be readily defensible if it is reviewed by an auditor.

Joint Cost Allocation

There are two common methods for allocating joint costs. One allocates costs based on the sales value of the resulting products, while the other is based on the estimated final gross margins of the resulting products. The calculation methods follow:

1. *Allocate based on sales value.* Add up all production costs through the split-off point, then determine the sales value of all joint products as of the same split-off point, and then assign the costs based on the sales values. If there are any by-products, do not allocate any costs to them; instead, charge the proceeds from their sale against the cost of goods sold. This is the simpler of the two methods.
2. *Allocate based on gross margin.* Add up the amount of all processing costs that each joint product incurs after the split-off point, and subtract this amount from the total revenue that each product will eventually earn. This approach requires additional cost accumulation work, but may be the only viable alternative if it is not possible to determine the sale price of each product as of the split-off point (as was the case with the preceding calculation method).

EXAMPLE

Allocation based on sales value: Hassle Corporation generates three products from a joint manufacturing process that incurs $90 of costs through the split-off point. It allocates costs to these products based on their sales value at the split-off point. The calculation follows:

Product Name	Type	Revenue at Split-Off	Percent of Total Revenue	Cost Allocation
Product Alpha	Joint	$100	67%	$60
Product Beta	Joint	50	33%	30
Product Charlie	By-product	0	0%	0
		$150	100%	$90

Under this method, Hassle Corporation designates Product Charlie as a by-product, so it does not share in the allocation of costs. If the company eventually sells any of Product Charlie, it will net the resulting revenues against the costs assigned to Products Alpha and Beta.

Allocation based on gross margin: Hassle Corporation's controller decides to assign joint costs based on the gross margins of the products after the split-off point. His calculation follows:

Product Name	Final Revenue	Costs Following Split-Off	Margin Following Split-Off	Proportion of Total Margins	Cost Allocation
Product Alpha	$200	$125	$75	53%	$48
Product Beta	100	60	40	29%	26
Product Charlie	25	0	25	18%	16
	$325	$185	$140	100%	$90

The cost allocations are entirely different between the two allocation methods, since the first calculation is based on revenue at the split-off point, and the second is largely based on costs incurred after the split-off point.

Joint Product and By-Product Pricing

The costs allocated to joint products and by-products should have no bearing on the pricing of these products, since the costs have no relationship to the value of the items sold. Prior to the split-off point, all costs incurred are sunk costs, and as such have no bearing on any future decisions – such as the price of a product.

The situation is quite different for any costs incurred from the split-off point onward. Since these costs can be attributed to specific products, never set a product price to be at or below the total costs incurred after the split-off point. Otherwise, the company will lose money on every product sold.

If the floor for a product's price is only the total costs incurred *after* the split-off point, this brings up the odd scenario of potentially charging prices that are lower than the total cost incurred (including the costs incurred *before* the split-off point). Clearly, charging such low prices is not a viable alternative over the long term, since a company will continually operate at a loss. This brings up two pricing alternatives:

- *Short-term pricing.* Over the short term, it may be necessary to allow extremely low product pricing, even near the total of costs incurred after the split-off point, if market prices do not allow pricing to be increased to a long-term sustainable level.

- *Long-term pricing.* Over the long term, a company must set prices to achieve revenue levels above its total cost of production, or risk bankruptcy.

In short, if a company is unable to set individual product prices sufficiently high to more than offset its production costs, and customers are unwilling to accept higher prices, it should cancel production – irrespective of how costs are allocated to various joint products and by-products.

Special Concerns with By-Product Costing

By-products are, by definition, minor items, but they can cause variations in a company's financial results. The following problems can arise:

- *Definition of a by-product.* If a company defines a product of a production process as a by-product, it can validly assign no cost to that by-product (if it is allocating costs based on sales value). If the company then holds a significant amount of the by-product in inventory and sells it in a batch, it will record a large amount of revenue with no offsetting cost of goods sold, resulting in an inordinate profit. The solution is to have a corporate policy that limits the by-product designation to those products having a small historical percentage of company sales.

- *Batch sales of by-products.* A company may let its by-products build up for several months and then sell them all in a large batch (which may be mandated by the buyer). If this happens, the company then subtracts all sale proceeds from the cost of goods sold in the month when the sale occurs, which can cause sudden increases in the gross margin. This result may be unavoidable, though a possible solution is to not designate *any* items as by-products.

- *Sale price variation.* By-products are frequently commodities, and so are unusually subject to the supply and demand forces in the marketplace. The result may be significant fluctuations in by-product revenues. Since these revenues are then netted against the cost of joint products (if the allocation is based on sales value), the result may be continual fluctuation in the reported costs of the joint products. To completely avoid this issue, do not designate *any* items as by-products.

Summary

The key point to remember about the cost allocations associated with joint products and by-products is that the allocation is simply a formula – it has no bearing on the value of the product to which it assigns a cost. The only reason we use these allocations is to achieve valid cost of goods sold amounts and inventory valuations under the requirements of the various accounting standards.

Chapter 15
Inventory Disclosures

Introduction

There are surprisingly few disclosures related to the inventory asset. In this chapter, we note each disclosure required by generally accepted accounting principles, along with examples of how the required information could be disclosed in the financial statements.

Inventory Disclosures

The following information should be disclosed about a company's inventory practices in its financial statements:

- *Basis*. Note the basis on which inventories are stated. If there is a significant change in the basis of accounting, the nature of the change and the effect on income (if material) shall be stated.

EXAMPLE

Inventories are valued at the lower of cost or market value. Product-related inventories are primarily maintained on the first-in, first-out method. Minor amounts of product inventories, including certain cosmetics and commodities, are maintained on the last-in, first-out method. The cost of spare part inventories is maintained using the average-cost method.

During the period, the company changed from the last-in, first-out method to the first-in, first-out method. The effect of this change was an increase in before-tax income of $2,500,000.

- *Lower of cost or market losses*. If there are substantial and unusual losses caused by the lower of cost or market rule, disclose this amount separately in the income statement. This is not a requirement.

EXAMPLE

During the year, certain stockpiled ore was written down to its net realizable value, resulting in a charge of $7,500,000.

- *Goods above cost*. Disclose the particulars concerning any inventory items that have been stated above cost.

- *Goods at sales prices*. Disclose the particulars concerning any inventory items that have been stated at their sales prices.

EXAMPLE

The company's gold production is typically sold immediately upon completion of the refining process, leaving minimal on-hand stocks. These residual stocks are recorded at the quoted market bid price as of 12/31/X4, less the estimated cost of expenditures expected to be incurred in the sale process.

- *Firm purchase commitments*. Separately state in the income statement the amounts of any net losses that have been accrued on firm purchase commitments.

EXAMPLE

The company is party to a firm purchase commitment contract to purchase 100,000 barrels of heating oil from a major supplier in each of the next three years, at a price of $120 per barrel. Given current market prices, we have accrued a loss of $3,600,000 on this contract.

- *Estimate*. Disclose any significant estimates related to inventory.

EXAMPLE

The company has recorded an obsolescence reserve against its inventory of $500,000. The amount is based on an estimate of 10% of product returns related to failures detected in the company's baby changer product line. This estimate is derived from an analysis of recent returns related to similar issues in other products.

Summary

There are few disclosures required for inventory – surprisingly, the number of disclosures likely to actually be made is even smaller. Barring unusual circumstances, a business will, in all likelihood, only need to disclose its basis of accounting for inventory. This particular item will require some expansion if there is a change in the basis of accounting. Otherwise, the disclosure of inventory-related information is notably brief.

Chapter 16
Inventory Transactions

Introduction

This chapter addresses a variety of journal entries associated with inventory transactions. The chapter begins with the initial recognition of inventory cost, and then proceeds in alphabetical order through a variety of other transactions. Sample journal entries are noted, where applicable, arranged in the debit and credit order most likely to be found in practice. We also point out those situations in which journal entries may be automated.

Initial Cost Recognition

The initial recognition of the cost of inventory typically includes the following items:
- The base cost of the inventory
- Any shipping and handling charges incurred to have the inventory transported to the company's premises
- Any customs and related fees incurred to bring inventory across borders to the company's premises

There is no need to separately categorize these expenditures in different accounts. Instead, they can be clustered into a single inventory account (if the perpetual inventory system is used) or a single purchases account (if the periodic inventory system is used). Sample entries for both inventory systems are:

	Debit	Credit
Raw materials inventory	xxx	
Merchandise inventory	xxx	
Accounts payable		xxx
To record the purchased cost of goods in a perpetual inventory system		

	Debit	Credit
Purchases	xxx	
Accounts payable		xxx
To record the purchased cost of goods in a periodic inventory system		

Here are a few additional considerations related to the initial recognition of inventory cost:
- *Cash discounts.* When a company buys inventory on credit and takes an early payment discount, the amount of the discount is most commonly rec-

orded separately and not offset against the cost of inventory, since early payment is a financing decision.

- *Foreign currency payment.* If an inventory purchase is paid for in a foreign currency, record the transaction at the exchange rate in effect on the date of purchase.
- *Settlement gains.* If an inventory purchase is made on credit and the company subsequently settles the amount due with a reduced payment, the gain is not offset against the cost of the inventory. Instead, the gain is recorded separately.

Acquired Inventory Transactions

When a company acquires another business entity, it should record the assets and liabilities acquired at their fair values. This rule includes inventory. From a practical perspective, it is inordinately difficult to determine the fair value of thousands of inventory items. Instead, consider recording the bulk of all acquired inventory items at the amounts at which the acquiree recorded them, and only reviewing the most expensive items for fair value adjustments. A sample entry to record an acquisition where the payment was in cash is:

	Debit	Credit
Accounts receivable	xxx	
Inventory	xxx	
Fixed assets	xxx	
Goodwill	xxx	
Accounts payable		xxx
Cash		xxx

If an acquirer instead engages in an asset purchase, it is only buying specific assets and liabilities from an acquiree. When cash is paid for assets, recognize the assets at the amount of cash paid for them. If noncash assets are used in payment, measure the assets acquired at the fair value of the consideration paid or the fair value of the assets acquired, whichever is more reliably measurable. If assets and liabilities are acquired in a group, allocate the cost of the entire group to the individual components of that group based on their relative fair values.

Backflushing Transactions

In a backflushing arrangement, the relieving of raw materials is performed automatically by the computer system. The production staff adds up the number of units produced and enters this information into the inventory tracking system. The system then multiplies this unit count by the associated bills of material to determine the standard amount of raw materials that should have been used. The system then relieves these amounts from the raw materials inventory, and creates new units in finished goods. If the accounting staff were to perform this transaction manually (which they do not), the entry at a highly aggregated level would be:

	Debit	Credit
Finished goods inventory	xxx	
Raw materials inventory		xxx

The system would actually record the new finished goods at a higher cost than just the associated raw materials, since there would also be adjustments for allocated overhead costs and direct labor.

Bill and Hold Transactions

In a bill and hold transaction, the seller is allowed to recognize revenue in situations where it continues to hold the goods sold to a buyer, but only if all of the following conditions are met:

- The risks of ownership have passed to the buyer;
- The buyer has committed to purchase the goods;
- The buyer requests that the seller continue to hold the goods;
- There is a fixed delivery schedule;
- There are no further performance obligations by the seller;
- The goods are segregated and not for use to fill other customer orders; and
- The goods are complete and ready for shipment.

From a transactional perspective, the key concern in a bill and hold arrangement is to ensure that inventory is relieved by the amount of the goods that are being billed to a customer. This is not so simple, since the normal triggering mechanism for this entry is the shipment of goods. In the absence of a shipment event, there should instead be a bill and hold procedure included in the period-end closing process that requires a search for bill and hold items, and a requirement to remove the cost of these items from stock. A sample entry is:

	Debit	Credit
Cost of goods sold	xxx	
Finished goods inventory		xxx

Consider making this transaction a reversing entry, so that the entry is automatically reversed at the beginning of the next reporting period. By doing so, a normal inventory relieving transaction can be accomplished when the inventory is eventually shipped to the customer. The reversing entry and relieving transaction will then net against each other, so there is no net change in the inventory account or the cost of goods sold in the later period.

Consignment Transactions

Consignment occurs when goods are sent by their owner (the consignor) to an agent (the consignee), who undertakes to sell the goods. The consignor continues to own the goods until they are sold, so the goods appear as inventory in the accounting records of the consignor, not the consignee.

When the consignor sends goods to the consignee, there is no need to create an accounting entry related to the physical movement of goods. It is usually sufficient to record the change in location within the inventory record keeping system of the consignor.

From the consignee's perspective, there is no need to record the consigned inventory, since it is owned by the consignor. It may be useful to keep a separate record of all consigned inventory, for reconciliation and insurance purposes.

When the consignee eventually sells the consigned goods, it pays the consignor a pre-arranged sale amount, which is treated as a standard sale transaction (see the Sale Transactions section).

Cross Docking Transactions

In a cross docking arrangement, inventory is received and immediately shifted to the shipping side of the warehouse. The goods are then broken down and reconfigured for immediate delivery to customers. The end result of this process flow is a very short interval between the recordation of a receipt and a sale. There is no need for a special accounting transaction in this situation – just record the normal receipt transaction and the normal sale transaction. However, there should be a system in place for recording receipts at the point of receipt, perhaps with a bar code scanning system. Otherwise, it is possible that a sale transaction will be recorded prior to the recognized receipt of goods, which will yield a negative inventory condition.

Drop Shipping Transactions

In a drop shipping transaction, a company arranges for a supplier to ship goods directly to a customer. The goods do not transfer through the company's warehouse at all. In this case, there is no inventory transaction, since the company never has ownership of the inventory. Instead, the company records a cost of goods sold directly from the supplier's invoice, and issues an invoice to the customer at the same time (if the arrangement is on credit; otherwise, an invoice would have been issued earlier). Thus, the inventory-related portion of the transaction is recorded with the following entry:

	Debit	Credit
Cost of goods sold	xxx	
Accounts payable		xxx

The usual payables transaction flow for inventory is to first debit the inventory account and later charge the goods to expense when they are sold. In this case, since the inventory is never retained, the transaction instead becomes an immediate charge to the cost of goods sold.

Engineering Change Order Transactions

From time to time, the engineering staff may issue an engineering change order (ECO). The ECO typically reconfigures some element of a product, such as by swapping out one component and inserting another. If so, the cost of the product is likely to change. Though there is a cost change, this event does not directly impact the accountant. Instead, the engineering staff alters the bill of materials for the product to reflect the change. The altered bill of materials is then multiplied by the ending number of finished goods units, which will impact the ending inventory valuation.

Goods in Transit Transactions

Goods in transit are merchandise and other types of inventory that have left the shipping dock of the seller, but not yet reached the receiving dock of the buyer. Ideally, either the seller or the buyer should record goods in transit in its accounting records. The rule for doing so is based on the shipping terms associated with the goods, which are:

- *FOB shipping point*. If the shipment is designated as freight on board (FOB) shipping point, ownership transfers to the buyer as soon as the shipment departs the seller.
- *FOB destination*. If the shipment is designated as freight on board (FOB) destination, ownership transfers to the buyer as soon as the shipment arrives at the buyer.

From a practical perspective, the buyer may not have a procedure in place to record inventory until it arrives at the receiving dock. This causes a problem under FOB shipping point terms, because the shipping entity records the transaction at the point of shipment, and the receiving company does not record receipt until the transaction is recorded at its receiving dock - thus, no one records the inventory while it is in transit.

Kitting Transactions

Kitting is the process of removing raw materials inventory from storage and consolidating them for a production job. Once a kit is complete, it is moved to the production floor. If the production process is quite rapid, a possible accounting method is to continue to leave the kitted items in raw materials inventory; once they have been converted into finished goods, the transaction is to eliminate raw materials inventory and transfer the goods to finished goods inventory, as follows:

	Debit	Credit
Finished goods inventory	xxx	
Raw materials inventory		xxx

Alternatively, the production process may be a lengthy one. If so, relieve raw materials inventory and shift the goods into work-in-process inventory, as follows:

	Debit	Credit
Work-in-process inventory	xxx	
Raw materials inventory		xxx

In the latter case, the goods will be shifted from work-in-process inventory to finished goods inventory once the production process is complete.

If raw materials are being kitted for a specific job, they can instead be charged to that job number within the work-in-process account, thereby segregating the cost for more detailed cost accounting compilations.

Lower of Cost or Market Adjustments

Under the lower of cost or market rule, the carrying amount of inventory is reduced when the market price of inventory items decline below their book values. A sample entry to record this reduction is:

	Debit	Credit
Loss on LCM adjustment	xxx	
Finished goods inventory		xxx

See the Lower of Cost or Market Rule chapter for more information.

Obsolete Inventory Adjustments

If there are obsolete inventory items in stock, their carrying amounts should be reduced down to the amounts at which they can be dispositioned to third parties. There are several ways to record these adjustments. Under the expected dispositions method and the reserve method, the amount of an expected carrying amount reduction is charged to a reserve account, which is later used to reduce the inventory accounts when specific reductions are completed. A sample of the two entries follows:

	Debit	Credit
Cost of goods sold	xxx	
Reserve for obsolete inventory		xxx
To record reserve for obsolete inventory		

	Debit	Credit
Reserve for obsolete inventory	xxx	
Inventory		xxx
To reduce the carrying amounts of specific inventory items		

Under the expensing method, the cost of obsolete inventory reductions is only charged to expense when specific inventory items are dispositioned. A sample entry is:

	Debit	Credit
Cost of goods sold	xxx	
Inventory		xxx

For more information, see the Obsolete Inventory chapter.

Overhead Allocation Transactions

There are two transactions associated with the allocation of overhead to inventory. One is the accumulation of expenses into an overhead cost pool, followed by the allocation of the cost pool amount to the various inventory classifications. In the first case, we transfer the ending balances in the designated expense accounts with credits, and debit the overhead cost pool. A sample entry (not showing all possible source accounts) is:

	Debit	Credit
Overhead cost pool	xxx	
Benefits – manufacturing		xxx
Depreciation – equipment		xxx
Indirect labor – manufacturing		xxx
Rent – manufacturing		xxx
Utilities – manufacturing		xxx

Once the expenses have been shifted into the overhead cost pool, they are then allocated between the cost of goods sold and the various inventory accounts. A sample entry is:

	Debit	Credit
Cost of goods sold	xxx	
Finished goods inventory	xxx	
Work-in-process inventory	xxx	
Overhead cost pool		xxx

This topic is discussed in greater detail in the Overhead Allocation chapter.

Physical Count Adjustments

A physical count will likely encounter some differences between on-hand unit counts and the inventory records. If so, the changes are recorded in the inventory records. When unit costs are multiplied by the revised unit counts in the inventory records, the result will be an alteration in the ending inventory balance, for which the offsetting change is to the cost of goods sold. Thus, if a physical count adjustment reduces the amount of ending inventory, the offset will be to the cost of goods sold account, for which the expense will increase. For example:

	Debit	Credit
Cost of goods sold	xxx	
Raw materials inventory		xxx

Conversely, a physical count adjustment that *increases* the raw materials inventory would have the reverse effect.

Receiving Transactions

When goods are received at the receiving dock, the warehouse staff forwards receiving documentation to the accounting department, which matches this documentation against the supplier's invoice and the authorizing purchase order (known as three-way matching). A sample of the accounting entry is:

	Debit	Credit
Inventory	xxx	
Accounts payable		xxx

There can be a substantial delay between the date of receipt and the date of recordation, especially if a supplier is dilatory in issuing an invoice. In the meantime, the warehouse staff has likely already logged the receipt into the warehouse management system (WMS), and may have even shipped the goods back out, either as a sale transaction or as an issuance to the manufacturing area for a production job. To avoid this receiving recordation delay, give the receiving staff access to an on-line purchase order database, on which they can check off orders as having been received. The accounting system can then automatically log in the related payable without waiting for a supplier invoice.

Sale Transactions

When goods are sold to a third party on credit, there are two linked transactions. One records the sale and associated account receivable, while the other entry records the transfer of the related amount of inventory asset to the cost of goods sold expense account. This double transaction ensures that revenues are properly matched with the associated amount of expense. Sample entries are:

	Debit	Credit
Accounts receivable	xxx	
Sales		xxx

	Debit	Credit
Cost of goods sold	xxx	
Inventory		xxx

Scrap and Spoilage Adjustments

When the production process generates an unusual amount of scrap or spoilage, these amounts should be written off as incurred. A sample entry is:

Cost of goods sold	xxx	
Work-in-process inventory		xxx

If inventory is being stored in a work-in-process account, this is assumed to be the offset to the scrap or spoilage entry, since the loss typically occurs in the midst of the production process. If scrap or spoilage is instead identified within the raw materials or finished goods areas, offset the expense against these accounts.

If there is a normal amount of scrap or spoilage being incurred, it is customary to instead charge this cost to the overhead cost pool, from which the cost is later allocated between the cost of goods sold and ending inventory. A sample entry is:

Overhead cost pool	xxx	
Work-in-process inventory		xxx

The effect of recording scrap and spoilage in the overhead cost pool is that recognition of the expense will be deferred until such time as the inventory items to which the overhead is allocated are sold.

Summary

There are not really as many journal entries to be recorded as may be implied by this chapter. If a company has a warehouse management system that is closely integrated with the accounting system, the warehouse staff will create many of these transactions through system templates. The system will then automatically create the underlying journal entries, which are essentially invisible to the user. If there is a separate accounting system that does not link to any inventory records, the accounting staff will indeed be required to record many of the transactions described in this chapter. If so, it is best to aggregate transactions and record a smaller number of entries. For example, there may be a single spoilage entry for the month. By aggregating entries, the accounting staff can cut down on a large amount of clerical work, and also concentrate its efforts on creating a smaller number of highly-accurate entries.

Chapter 17
Internal Revenue Code for Inventory

Introduction

The discussion of inventory accounting elsewhere in this book has been based on generally accepted accounting principles and a great deal of standard practice regarding how inventory is to be recorded. Another source of regulatory requirements for inventory is the Internal Revenue Service, which has issued a number of rules in its Internal Revenue Code (IRC) regarding how inventory is to be treated for tax purposes. In this chapter, we state a selection of the relevant text from the Internal Revenue Code and precede each section with a brief summary.

IRC Section 471 – General Rule for Inventories

Section 471(a) presents the justification of the IRS for creating its own rules related to inventory. The text is:

(a) General rule
Whenever in the opinion of the Secretary the use of inventories is necessary in order clearly to determine the income of any taxpayer, inventories shall be taken by such taxpayer on such basis as the Secretary may prescribe as conforming as nearly as may be to the best accounting practice in the trade or business and as most clearly reflecting the income.

Section 471(b) allows for the use of inventory shrinkage estimates in the reporting of taxable income, rather than only allowing actual shrinkage to be counted. However, this calls for the presence of an adequate system of inventory counts.

(b) Estimates of inventory shrinkage permitted
A method of determining inventories shall not be treated as failing to clearly reflect income solely because it utilizes estimates of inventory shrinkage that are confirmed by a physical count only after the last day of the taxable year if—
(1) the taxpayer normally does a physical count of inventories at each location on a regular and consistent basis, and
(2) the taxpayer makes proper adjustments to such inventories and to its estimating methods to the extent such estimates are greater than or less than the actual shrinkage.

IRC Section 472 – Last In, First Out Inventories

Section 472(a) allows a business to use the LIFO method of accounting for inventory, as long as IRS rules are followed.

(a) Authorization

A taxpayer may use the method provided in subsection (b) in inventorying goods specified in an application to use such method filed at such time and in such manner as the Secretary may prescribe. The change to, and the use of, such method shall be in accordance with such regulations as the Secretary may prescribe as necessary in order that the use of such method may clearly reflect income.

Section 472(b) describes a cost layering method for inventory, and also mandates that these layers be valued at cost.

(b) Method applicable

In inventorying goods specified in the application described in subsection (a), the taxpayer shall:

(1) Treat those remaining on hand at the close of the taxable year as being: First, those included in the opening inventory of the taxable year (in the order of acquisition) to the extent thereof; and second, those acquired in the taxable year;

(2) Inventory them at cost; and

(3) Treat those included in the opening inventory of the taxable year in which such method is first used as having been acquired at the same time and determine their cost by the average cost method.

Section 472(c) requires any entity using the LIFO method for tax reporting purposes to also use it for financial reporting purposes.

(c) Condition

Subsection (a) shall apply only if the taxpayer establishes to the satisfaction of the Secretary that the taxpayer has used no procedure other than that specified in paragraphs (1) and (3) of subsection (b) in inventorying such goods to ascertain the income, profit, or loss of the first taxable year for which the method described in subsection (b) is to be used, for the purpose of a report or statement covering such taxable year—

(1) to shareholders, partners, or other proprietors, or to beneficiaries, or

(2) for credit purposes.

Section 472(d) outlines the costing methodology to be used in LIFO calculations.

(d) 3-year averaging for increases in inventory value

The beginning inventory for the first taxable year for which the method described in subsection (b) is used shall be valued at cost. Any change in the inventory amount resulting from the application of the preceding sentence shall be taken into account ratably in each of the three taxable years beginning with the first taxable year for which the method described in subsection (b) is first used.

Section 472(e) requires the permission of the IRS before a company currently using the LIFO method can switch to an alternative costing methodology.

(e) Subsequent inventories

If a taxpayer, having complied with subsection (a), uses the method described in subsection (b) for any taxable year, then such method shall be used in all subsequent taxable years unless—

(1) with the approval of the Secretary a change to a different method is authorized; or,

(2) the Secretary determines that the taxpayer has used for any such subsequent taxable year some procedure other than that specified in paragraph (1) of subsection (b) in inventorying the goods specified in the application to ascertain the income, profit, or loss of such subsequent taxable year for the purpose of a report or statement covering such taxable year

(A) to shareholders, partners, or other proprietors, or beneficiaries, or

(B) for credit purposes; and requires a change to a method different from that prescribed in subsection (b) beginning with such subsequent taxable year or any taxable year thereafter. If paragraph (1) or (2) of this subsection applies, the change to, and the use of, the different method shall be in accordance with such regulations as the Secretary may prescribe as necessary in order that the use of such method may clearly reflect income.

Section 472(f) allows a taxpayer to use a government-generated price index to create its inventory valuation.

(f) Use of government price indexes in pricing inventory

The Secretary shall prescribe regulations permitting the use of suitable published governmental indexes in such manner and circumstances as determined by the Secretary for purposes of the method described in subsection (b).

Section 472(g) requires that, if one entity in a consolidated group uses the LIFO method for tax reporting, then all of the other entities in the group must also do so. The reference to "Section 1504" is the definition of an affiliated group, which is covered in a later section in this chapter, entitled "IRC Section 1504(a) – Affiliated Group."

(g) Conformity rules applied on controlled group basis

(1) In general

Except as otherwise provided in regulations, all members of the same group of financially related corporations shall be treated as one taxpayer for purposes of subsections (c) and (e)(2).

(2) Group of financially related corporations

For purposes of paragraph (1), the term "group of financially related corporations" means—

(A) any affiliated group as defined in section 1504 determined by substituting "50 percent" for "80 percent" each place it appears in section 1504(a) ..., and

(B) any other group of corporations which consolidate or combine for purposes of financial statements.

IRC Section 473 – Qualified Liquidations of LIFO Inventories

Section 473(a) notes that, once a cost layer has been liquidated, a business cannot replace the layer with goods that have been subsequently acquired.

(a) General rule
If, for any liquidation year—
(1) there is a qualified liquidation of goods which the taxpayer inventories under the LIFO method, and
(2) the taxpayer elects to have the provisions of this section apply with respect to such liquidation, then the gross income of the taxpayer for such taxable year shall be adjusted as provided in subsection (b).

Section 473(b) mandates that the cost of any liquidated inventory layers must be included in the determination of current taxable income.

(b) Adjustment for replacements
If the liquidated goods are replaced (in whole or in part) during any replacement year and such replacement is reflected in the closing inventory for such year, then the gross income for the liquidation year shall be—
(1) decreased by an amount equal to the excess of—
(A) the aggregate replacement cost of the liquidated goods so replaced during such year, over
(B) the aggregate cost of such goods reflected in the opening inventory of the liquidation year, or
(2) increased by an amount equal to the excess of—
(A) the aggregate cost reflected in such opening inventory of the liquidated goods so replaced during such year, over
(B) such aggregate replacement cost.

Section 473(c) allows for the liquidation and subsequent reinstatement of a LIFO cost layer if the liquidation is triggered by a request from the Department of Energy or is caused by a certain type of interruption in foreign trade.

(c) Qualified liquidation defined
For purposes of this section—
(1) In general
The term "qualified liquidation" means—
(A) a decrease in the closing inventory of the liquidation year from the opening inventory of such year, but only if
(B) the taxpayer establishes to the satisfaction of the Secretary that such decrease is directly and primarily attributable to a qualified inventory interruption.
(2) Qualified inventory interruption defined
(A) In general
The term "qualified inventory interruption" means a regulation, request, or interruption described in subparagraph (B) but only to the extent provided in the notice published pursuant to subparagraph (B).
(B) Determination by Secretary

Whenever the Secretary, after consultation with the appropriate Federal officers, determines—

    (i) that—

        (I) any Department of Energy regulation or request with respect to energy supplies, or

        (II) any embargo, international boycott, or other major foreign trade interruption, has made difficult or impossible the replacement during the liquidation year of any class of goods for any class of taxpayers, and

    (ii) that the application of this section to that class of goods and taxpayers is necessary to carry out the purposes of this section, he shall publish a notice of such determinations in the Federal Register, together with the period to be affected by such notice.

Section 473(d) defines a number of the terms used in the IRC related to inventory.

(d) Other definitions and special rules

For purposes of this section—

(1) Liquidation year

The term "liquidation year" means the taxable year in which occurs the qualified liquidation to which this section applies.

(2) Replacement year

The term "replacement year" means any taxable year in the replacement period; except that such term shall not include any taxable year after the taxable year in which replacement of the liquidated goods is completed.

(3) Replacement period

The term "replacement period" means the shorter of—

    (A) the period of the three taxable years following the liquidation year, or

    (B) the period specified by the Secretary in a notice published in the Federal Register with respect to that qualified inventory interruption.

(4) LIFO method

The term "LIFO method" means the method of inventorying goods described in section 472.

(5) Election

(A) In general

An election under subsection (a) shall be made subject to such conditions, and in such manner and form and at such time, as the Secretary may prescribe by regulation.

(B) Irrevocable election

An election under this section shall be irrevocable and shall be binding for the liquidation year and for all determinations for prior and subsequent taxable years insofar as such determinations are affected by the adjustments under this section.

Section 473(e) discusses the treatment of any inventory that is acquired after a LIFO cost layer has been eliminated.

(e) Replacement; inventory basis

For purposes of this chapter—

(1) Replacements

If the closing inventory of the taxpayer for any replacement year reflects an increase over the opening inventory of such goods for such year, the goods reflecting such increase shall be considered, in the order of their acquisition, as having been acquired in replacement of the goods most recently liquidated (whether or not in a qualified liquidation) and not previously replaced.

(2) Amount at which replacement goods taken into account

In the case of any qualified liquidation, any goods considered under paragraph (1) as having been acquired in replacement of the goods liquidated in such liquidation shall be taken into purchases and included in the closing inventory of the taxpayer for the replacement year at the inventory cost basis of the goods replaced.

Section 473(f) notes the time period within which tax assessments and credits can be applied to an adjustment of a cost layer.

(f) Special rules for application of adjustments

(1) Period of limitations

If—

(A) an adjustment is required under this section for any taxable year by reason of the replacement of liquidated goods during any replacement year, and

(B) the assessment of a deficiency, or the allowance of a credit or refund of an overpayment of tax attributable to such adjustment, for any taxable year, is otherwise prevented by the operation of any law or rule of law, then such deficiency may be assessed, or credit or refund allowed, within the period prescribed for assessing a deficiency or allowing a credit or refund for the replacement year if a notice for deficiency is mailed, or claim for refund is filed, within such period.

(2) Interest

Solely for purposes of determining interest on any overpayment or underpayment attributable to an adjustment made under this section, such overpayment or underpayment shall be treated as an overpayment or underpayment (as the case may be) for the replacement year.

IRC Section 474 – Simplified Dollar-Value LIFO Method

Section 474(a) presents the simplified dollar-value LIFO method as an inventory valuation technique for a smaller business.

(a) General rule

An eligible small business may elect to use the simplified dollar-value method of pricing inventories for purposes of the LIFO method.

Section 474(b) states how government price indexes are used in the simplified dollar-value LIFO method, and defines a price index.

(b) Simplified dollar-value method of pricing inventories
For purposes of this section—

(1) In general
The simplified dollar-value method of pricing inventories is a dollar-value method of pricing inventories under which—

(A) the taxpayer maintains a separate inventory pool for items in each major category in the applicable Government price index, and

(B) the adjustment for each such separate pool is based on the change from the preceding taxable year in the component of such index for the major category.

(2) Applicable Government price index
The term "applicable Government price index" means—

(A) except as provided in subparagraph (B), the Producer Price Index published by the Bureau of Labor Statistics, or

(B) in the case of a retailer using the retail method, the Consumer Price Index published by the Bureau of Labor Statistics.

(3) Major category
The term "major category" means—

(A) in the case of the Producer Price Index, any of the two-digit standard industrial classifications in the Producer Prices Data Report, or

(B) in the case of the Consumer Price Index, any of the general expenditure categories in the Consumer Price Index Detailed Report.

Section 474(c) defines a business that would be eligible for using the simplified dollar-value LIFO method.

(c) Eligible small business
For purposes of this section, a taxpayer is an eligible small business for any taxable year if the average annual gross receipts of the taxpayer for the three preceding taxable years do not exceed $5,000,000. For purposes of the preceding sentence, rules similar to the rules of section 448(c)(3) shall apply. [Note: the reference to section 448(c)(3) follows]

Section 448(c)(3)

(A) Not in existence for entire 3-year period
If the entity was not in existence for the entire 3-year period... such paragraph shall be applied on the basis of the period during which such entity (or trade or business) was in existence.

(B) Short taxable years
Gross receipts for any taxable year of less than 12 months shall be annualized by multiplying the gross receipts for the short period by 12 and dividing the result by the number of months in the short period.

(C) Gross receipts
Gross receipts for any taxable year shall be reduced by returns and allowances made during such year.

(D) Treatment of predecessors
Any reference in this subsection to an entity shall include a reference to any predecessor of such entity.

Section 474(d) addresses several special rules related to the use of the simplified dollar-value LIFO method, such as how to transition to the method.

(d) Special rules

For purposes of this section—

(1) Controlled groups

(A) In general

In the case of a taxpayer which is a member of a controlled group, all persons which are component members of such group shall be treated as one taxpayer for purposes of determining the gross receipts of the taxpayer.

(B) Controlled group defined

For purposes of subparagraph (A), persons shall be treated as being component members of a controlled group if such persons would be treated as a single employer.

(2) Election

(A) In general

The election under this section may be made without the consent of the Secretary.

(B) Period to which election applies

The election under this section shall apply—

(i) to the taxable year for which it is made, and

(ii) to all subsequent taxable years for which the taxpayer is an eligible small business, unless the taxpayer secures the consent of the Secretary to the revocation of such election.

(3) LIFO method

The term "LIFO method" means the method provided by section 472(b).

(4) Transitional rules

(A) In general

In the case of a year of change under this section—

(i) the inventory pools shall—

(I) in the case of the first taxable year to which such an election applies, be established in accordance with the major categories in the applicable Government price index, or

(II) in the case of the first taxable year after such election ceases to apply, be established in the manner provided by regulations under section 472;

(ii) the aggregate dollar amount of the taxpayer's inventory as of the beginning of the year of change shall be the same as the aggregate dollar value as of the close of the taxable year preceding the year of change, and

(iii) the year of change shall be treated as a new base year in accordance with procedures provided by regulations under section 472.

(B) Year of change

For purposes of this paragraph, the year of change under this section is—

(i) the first taxable year to which an election under this section applies, or

(ii) in the case of a cessation of such an election, the first taxable year after such election ceases to apply.

IRC Section 1504(a) – Affiliated Group

Section 1504(a) defines every possible variation on an affiliated group, which was referenced in section 472(f).

(a) Affiliated group defined
For purposes of this subtitle—
(1) In general
The term "affiliated group" means—
(A) one or more chains of includible corporations connected through stock ownership with a common parent corporation which is an includible corporation, but only if—
(B)
(i) the common parent owns directly stock meeting the requirements of paragraph (2) in at least one of the other includible corporations, and
(ii) stock meeting the requirements of paragraph (2) in each of the includible corporations (except the common parent) is owned directly by one or more of the other includible corporations.
(2) 80-percent voting and value test
The ownership of stock of any corporation meets the requirements of this paragraph if it—
(A) possesses at least 80 percent of the total voting power of the stock of such corporation, and
(B) has a value equal to at least 80 percent of the total value of the stock of such corporation.

[Note: Section 472(f) reduced this percentage to 50%]

(3) 5 years must elapse before reconsolidation
(A) In general
If—
(i) a corporation is included (or required to be included) in a consolidated return filed by an affiliated group for a taxable year which includes any period after December 31, 1984, and
(ii) such corporation ceases to be a member of such group in a taxable year beginning after December 31, 1984,
with respect to periods after such cessation, such corporation (and any successor of such corporation) may not be included in any consolidated return filed by the affiliated group (or by another affiliated group with the same common parent or a successor of such common parent) before the 61st month beginning after its first taxable year in which it ceased to be a member of such affiliated group.
(B) Secretary may waive application of subparagraph (A)
The Secretary may waive the application of subparagraph (A) to any corporation for any period subject to such conditions as the Secretary may prescribe.
(4) Stock not to include certain preferred stock
For purposes of this subsection, the term "stock" does not include any stock which—

(A) is not entitled to vote,

(B) is limited and preferred as to dividends and does not participate in corporate growth to any significant extent,

(C) has redemption and liquidation rights which do not exceed the issue price of such stock (except for a reasonable redemption or liquidation premium), and

(D) is not convertible into another class of stock.

Summary

The bulk of the text relevant to inventory from the Internal Revenue Code has been presented in this chapter. To access the complete text, go to the Internal Revenue Code and drill down through the following section headings to locate the relevant information:

Title 26 – Internal Revenue Code
    Subtitle A – Income Taxes
        Chapter 1 – Normal Taxes and Surtaxes
            Subchapter E – Accounting Periods and Methods of Accounting
            Part II – Methods of Accounting
                Subpart D – Inventories
                    Section 471 – General Rule for Inventories
                    Section 472 – Last in, First Out Inventories
                    Section 473 – Qualified Liquidations of LIFO Inventories
                    Section 474 – Simplified Dollar-Value LIFO Method for Certain Small Businesses

If a business elects to use LIFO for income tax reporting purposes, it must file Form 970 with the IRS. Go to www.irs.gov for a copy of the form. This is a detailed filing; obtain the assistance of a qualified tax professional before submitting the form.

Chapter 18
Inventory Transfer Pricing

Introduction

Some companies have chosen to become vertically integrated, which means that one subsidiary creates a component that is used by another subsidiary in its products. Companies do this either to have an assured source of components, or because suppliers are earning an inordinate profit on the components.

Vertical integration is important to the accountant, because a company must sell these components from one subsidiary to another, and it does so with a transfer price, which the accountant assists in creating. This chapter addresses the importance of the transfer price and a number of methods for creating it.

Overview of Transfer Pricing

Transfer pricing is important, because it strongly impacts the behavior of the subsidiaries that use it as the basis for transferring components to each other. Here are the key issues:

- *Revenue basis.* The manager of a subsidiary treats it in the same manner that he would the price of a product sold outside of the company. It forms part of the revenue of his subsidiary, and is therefore crucial to the financial performance on which he is judged.
- *Preferred customers.* If the manager of a subsidiary is given the choice of selling either to a downstream subsidiary or to outside customers, an excessively low transfer price will lead the manager to sell exclusively to outside customers, and to refuse orders originating from the downstream subsidiary.
- *Preferred suppliers.* If the manager of a downstream subsidiary is given the choice of buying either from an upstream subsidiary or an outside supplier, an excessively high transfer price will cause the manager to buy exclusively from outside suppliers. As a result, the upstream subsidiary may have too much unused capacity, and will have to cut back on its expenses in order to remain profitable.

Conversely, these issues are not important if corporate headquarters uses a central production planning system, and *requires* upstream subsidiaries to ship components to downstream subsidiaries, irrespective of the transfer price.

An additional topic that impacts the overall level of corporate profitability is the total amount of income taxes paid. If a company has subsidiaries located in different tax jurisdictions, it can use transfer prices to adjust the reported profit level of each subsidiary. Ideally, the corporate parent wants to recognize the most taxable income in those tax jurisdictions where corporate income taxes are lowest. It can achieve this by lowering the transfer prices of components going into the subsidiaries located in those tax jurisdictions having the lowest tax rates.

A company should adopt those transfer prices that result in the highest total profit for the consolidated results of the entire entity. Almost always, this means that the company sets the transfer price to be the market price of the component, subject to the issue just noted regarding the recognition of income taxes. By doing so, subsidiaries can earn more money for the company as a whole by having the option to sell to outside entities, as well as in-house. This gives subsidiaries an incentive to expand their production capacity to take on additional business.

EXAMPLE

Entwhistle Electric makes compact batteries for a variety of mobile applications. It was recently purchased by Razor Holdings, which also owns Green Lawn Care, maker of low-emission lawn mowers. The reason for Razor's purchase of Entwhistle was to give Green an assured supply of batteries for Green's new line of all-electric lawn mowers. Razor's corporate planning staff mandates that Entwhistle set a transfer price for batteries shipped to Green that equals its cost, and also requires that Entwhistle fulfill all of Green's needs before it can sell to any other customers. Green's orders are highly seasonal, so Entwhistle finds that it cannot fulfill orders from its other customers at all during the high point of Green's production season. Also, because the transfer price is set at cost, Entwhistle's management finds that it no longer has a reason to drive down its costs, and so its production efficiencies stagnate.

After a year, Razor's corporate staff realizes that Entwhistle has lost 80% of its previous customer base, and is now essentially relying upon its sales to Green to stay operational. Entwhistle's profit margin has vanished, since it can only sell at cost, and its original management team, faced with a contracting business, has left to work for competitors.

Transfer prices do not have to match the market price to achieve optimal results. There are cases where there is no market price at all, so a company needs to create a price in order to spur management behavior that is favorable to the company as a whole.

EXAMPLE

Entwhistle Electric creates five tons per year of black plastic shavings as part of its production of battery casings. Since there is no market for black plastic scrap, the company has traditionally thrown it into the trash. The annual trash haulage and environmental disposal fees associated with this scrap are about $1,000.

Entwhistle's fellow corporate subsidiary, Green Lawn Care, learns of the black plastic scrap situation, and offers to buy it from Entwhistle for a token $10 a ton, as well as haul it away for free. Green can melt down this scrap and use it in the black plastic trim on its electric lawn mowers.

Entwhistle agrees to the deal, not only because of the minor $50 in annual revenues, but also because of the eliminated disposal fees and the mitigated risk of having any environmental issues related to the scrap.

In short, transfer prices can have a significant impact on how the managers of subsidiaries run their operations, and on how much a company as a whole pays in income taxes. Though we have pointed out that market prices are the best basis for developing transfer prices, there are a number of pricing methods available. We will explore both market pricing and these other methods next.

Market Price Basis for Transfer Pricing

The simplest and most elegant transfer price is to use the market price. By doing so, the upstream subsidiary can sell either internally or externally and earn the same profit with either option. It can also earn the highest possible profit, rather than being subject to the odd profit vagaries that can occur under mandated pricing schemes. Downstream subsidiaries will also be indifferent to the source of their components, since the price is the same from all suppliers. If the price is simple to obtain, such as through industry trade journals or price sheets, there is also little reason for buying and selling subsidiaries to argue over the price.

However, market-based prices are not always available. Here are several areas of concern:

- *Product differentiation.* The most common problem is that the products being sold in the market are differentiated from each other by a variety of unique features, so there is no standard market price.
- *Quality differentiation.* Product features may be the same, but quality differences between products cause significant pricing disparities.
- *Specialty products.* The components in question may be of such a highly specialized nature that there is no market for them at all.
- *Internal costs.* The cost of selling internally to another subsidiary is somewhat lower than the cost of selling to an external customer, since there are fewer selling costs and bad debts associated with an internal sale; this means that comparing potential sales based just on the market price is not entirely correct.
- *Corporate planning.* If there is a centralized planning staff, they may not want the subsidiaries to make decisions based on the market price, because they want all components routed to internal subsidiaries to relieve supply shortages. This is not necessarily a problem, as long as the internal sales are conducted at the market price.

In short, market-based pricing is highly recommended, but it does not apply in many situations. If market pricing cannot be used, consider employing one of the alternative methods outlined in the following sections.

Adjusted Market Price Basis for Transfer Pricing

If it is not possible to use the market pricing technique just noted, consider using the general concept, but incorporating some adjustments to the price. For example, reduce the market price to account for the presumed absence of bad debts, since corporate management will likely intervene and force a payment if there is a risk of non-payment. Also, reduce the market price to account for the absence of any sales staff in transactions, since these internal sales should not require any sales effort to complete – a sale is reduced to some paperwork between the purchasing and planning staffs of the two subsidiaries.

If these bad debt and selling costs are actually eliminated from the selling subsidiary and the buying subsidiary can make purchases at lower prices, both entities benefit from the price reductions. The result may be a tendency to prefer selling within the company rather than to outside parties, which is what corporate managers want to see.

The main problem with adjusted market prices will be arguments between the subsidiaries over the size of the downward adjustments. There should be a procedure in place for how the adjustments are determined. If not, the subsidiary manager with the better negotiating ability will win, which may result in the other subsidiary taking its business elsewhere. The corporate staff should monitor these negotiations and intervene as necessary.

Negotiated Basis for Transfer Pricing

It may be necessary to negotiate a transfer price between subsidiaries, without using any market price as a baseline. This situation arises when there is no discernible market price because the market is very small or the goods are highly customized.

Negotiated prices can vary wildly, depending on the negotiating skills of the participants. The variable cost of production for the selling subsidiary should be used as the minimum possible price, so that it does not lose money. The resulting price usually gives both participants some ability to earn a profit. However, there are some issues with it:

- *Unfairness*. If the negotiated price excessively favors one subsidiary, the other subsidiary will likely search outside of the company for better deals.
- *Negotiation time*. If a component represents a large amount of revenue for the selling subsidiary, or a large cost for the buying subsidiary, they may spend an inordinate amount of time negotiating the price.

For the reasons noted here, negotiated prices are considered to be a suboptimal solution, and so should only be used in a minority of transfer pricing situations for items representing a small proportion of total business activity.

... **Pricing**

... ve a transfer price, an alternative
... bution margin. To do so, follow

... duct will sell to an outside entity
... finished their processing of the

... lished product. This is revenues
... product.

... the various subsidiaries that
... subsidiary's share of the total

This ... an allocation of the contribution margin to the subsidiaries. However, it also suffers from the following problems:

- *Allocation methodology*. Since the allocation of contribution margin is based on each subsidiary's share of the total cost, a subsidiary can increase its share if it *increases* its costs. Also, if a subsidiary reduces its costs, the cost savings is essentially apportioned among all of the subsidiaries, which gives a subsidiary little reason to reduce its costs. Thus, the allocation method drives subsidiaries to engage in behavior that does not benefit the company as a whole.

- *Complicated allocation*. If a company has many subsidiaries, there may be so many transfers of parts associated with a specific product that it is difficult to determine which subsidiaries should be credited with the contribution margin, or the amount of the allocation. This also requires a large amount of accounting staff time, as well as an allocation procedure that is rigidly adhered to; otherwise, the subsidiaries will bicker over how much contribution margin they receive.

Despite the problems noted here, the contribution margin approach can be a workable alternative to using market prices to develop transfer prices.

Cost Plus Basis for Transfer Pricing

If there is no market price at all on which to base a transfer price, consider using a system that creates a transfer price based on the cost of the components being transferred. The best way to do this is to add a margin onto the cost, where the standard cost of a component is compiled, a standard profit margin is added, and the result is the transfer price. While this method is useful, be aware of two flaws that can cause problems:

- *Cost basis*. When the pricing system is based on adding a margin to the underlying cost, there is no incentive to reduce the underlying cost. If anything, subsidiary managers will be tempted to alter their cost accounting systems to shift more costs *into* those components being sold to another subsidiary, thereby dumping costs onto a different entity.

- *Standard margin.* The margin added to the cost may not relate to the margin that a subsidiary earns on its sales to outside customers. If it is too low, subsidiary managers have no incentive to manufacture the component. If the margin is too high, and this margin is incorporated into the final product price, the subsidiary selling the completed product may find that its cost is too high to earn a profit.

Despite the issues noted here, the cost plus method can still work, as long as corporate management mandates ongoing cost reductions throughout the company, and also verifies whether the margins added to costs are reasonable. Also, it may work if there are so few transfers that the economic benefits to be gained from rigging the system are minimal.

Cost Anomalies in a Cost-Based Transfer Price

Of the transfer pricing methods described here, the contribution margin basis and the cost plus basis both involve cost inputs. When collecting the cost information used to derive transfer prices, be aware of several issues that can impact costs, and which may result in a great deal of variability in the transfer price. These issues are:

- *Cost allocations.* When a selling subsidiary can shift its costs to a buying subsidiary, there is a tendency to shift more overhead costs into the components being sold to the buying subsidiary.
- *Cost reduction incentive.* When the manager of a selling subsidiary knows he can sell products to a buying subsidiary and cover his costs, there is no incentive to reduce those costs. It would be egregious to let costs increase, but there is no longer any incentive to decrease costs. This problem is less critical if the selling subsidiary still sells most of its products to outside entities, since it must still maintain control over its costs in order to be competitive.
- *Volume changes.* If the unit volume ordered by a buying subsidiary changes substantially over time, the selling subsidiary will have to manufacture parts in varying batch sizes, which may result in very different costs, depending on the volume produced. If the transfer price is fixed for a relatively long-term period, the selling subsidiary may find itself either benefiting from these volume changes or experiencing very low profits that are caused by small batch sizes.

A partial solution to several of these problems is to agree on a standard cost at the beginning of the year, and review it periodically. Corporate management should be involved in this process, both to impose cost reduction goals and to verify whether any shifting of overhead costs to downstream subsidiaries is being attempted. Using a standard cost allows buying subsidiaries to plan for costs with considerable certainty, while selling subsidiaries can improve their profits if they reduce costs to below the agreed-upon standard costs.

Pricing Problems Caused by Transfer Pricing

Transfer pricing between subsidiaries causes a problem for the marketing department of whichever subsidiary is selling the final product to outside customers, because it does not know which part of the transferred-in price is comprised of variable costs, and which is fixed costs. If the marketing department is developing long-term sustainable costs, it knows the price needs to be higher than both types of costs combined, in order to assure long-term sustainable profitability. However, this is not the case for short-term pricing situations where a customer may be asking for a pricing discount in exchange for a large order. In the latter situation, the costing system needs to clearly differentiate which product costs are variable, and which are not.

Another issue with price setting arises when several subsidiaries in a row add as many costs as they can to the transfer price, as well as a profit margin. By the time the final product arrives at the subsidiary that sells it to an outside customer, the cost may be so high that the last subsidiary cannot possibly earn a profit on the sale. The following example illustrates the problem.

EXAMPLE

Razor Holdings adopts a transfer pricing policy under which each of its subsidiaries can add a 30% margin to the additional costs transferred to buying subsidiaries. In the following scenario, its Lead Supply subsidiary sends lead components to Entwhistle Electric, which incorporates the lead into its batteries. Entwhistle sends the batteries to Green Lawn Care, which includes the batteries in its electric lawn shears.

	Lead Supply	Entwhistle Electric	Green Lawn Care
Transferred cost	$0	$5.85	13.98
Additional cost	4.50	6.25	15.00
30% markup	1.35	1.88	1.02
Transfer price	$5.85	$13.98	$30.00

Unfortunately, the market price for electric lawn shears is $30, so the Green Lawn Care subsidiary will only earn a profit of $1.02, or 3%, on each sale. However, the company as a whole will earn a profit of $4.25 ($1.35 for Lead Supply + $1.88 for Entwhistle + $1.02 for Green), or 14%.

Thus, Green Lawn Care likely questions why it is bothering to sell electric lawn shears, while corporate management is somewhat more pleased with the overall result.

Possible solutions are to allow the furthest downstream subsidiary to buy its components elsewhere, or to have corporate management reduce the margins allowed to upstream subsidiaries.

The Tax Impact of Transfer Prices

We have discussed various methods for developing transfer prices in most of the preceding sections, but they may all be overridden by corporate management if it wants to achieve the lowest possible amount of income taxes paid. This is a major area of corporate planning, because it causes a permanent reduction in income taxes paid, not just a deferral of tax payments to a later period.

The essential tax management concept is to set a high transfer price for buying subsidiaries located in tax jurisdictions that have a high income tax rate, so they report a high cost of goods sold, and therefore pay the minimum amount of high-percentage income tax. Conversely, the transfer price should be as low as possible for those buying subsidiaries located in tax jurisdictions that have a low income tax rate, so they report a low cost of goods sold, and therefore pay the maximum amount of low-percentage income tax. The overall impact for the corporate parent should be a reduction in income taxes paid.

EXAMPLE

Razor Holdings owns Entwhistle Electric, which is located in the United States, and Green Lawn Care, which is located in Ireland. The corporate tax rate in the United States is 35%, and the rate in Ireland is 12.5%. Because of the disparity in tax rates, Razor wants Entwhistle to sell all of its components to Green at a low price. By doing so, Entwhistle earns a minimal profit on these inter-company sales and therefore has minimal income on which to pay taxes, while Green has a very low cost of goods sold and a correspondingly high net profit, on which it pays the reduced Irish income tax. Razor implements this strategy for the current fiscal year, with the following results:

	Entwhistle Subsidiary (United States)	Green Lawn Care (Ireland)
Revenue	$10,000,000	$35,000,000
Cost of goods sold and administrative expenses	8,000,000	21,000,000
Profit	$2,000,000	$14,000,000
Profit %	20%	40%
Income tax rate	35%	12.5%
Income tax	$700,000	$1,750,000

If Entwhistle had sold its products to other customers, rather than internally, it would have realized a profit of an additional $1,000,000, which would have called for an additional $350,000 income tax payment to the United States government. However, the transfer pricing strategy essentially shifted the additional $1,000,000 of profit to the Ireland tax jurisdiction, which was then taxed at only 12.5%. Thus, Razor created a permanent tax savings of $225,000 through its transfer pricing strategy, which is calculated as:

(35% United States tax rate – 12.5% Ireland tax rate) × $1,000,000 Taxable profit

---

The practices just noted could lead a company to adopt outrageous transfer pricing practices that shift virtually all profits to whichever tax jurisdictions have the lowest tax rates. To keep such egregious behavior from occurring, the Internal Revenue Service has issued guidelines in Section 482 of the Internal Revenue Code that specify how transfer prices can be formulated. Section 482 contains multiple alternative formulations, with the preferred practice being to use market rates as the transfer price, followed by variations on the cost plus profit methodology. These formulations allow for the inclusion of a variety of adjustments, which can alter a transfer price significantly. A company usually takes advantage of the Section 482 guidelines to the greatest extent possible in order to achieve the lowest possible consolidated tax payment. The IRS prefers to have companies use transfer prices that are largely based on market prices, leaving the minimum amount of additional adjustments for a company's accountants to manipulate.

There is always a chance that auditors from a taxing jurisdiction will take issue with the transfer pricing methods used by a company, which may lead to substantial fines and penalties. This is a particular problem when a company is being audited by multiple tax jurisdictions, with each one trying to maximize its tax receipts at the expense of the other jurisdictions.

To avoid these audit costs, larger companies frequently enter into an advance pricing agreement (APA) with multiple tax jurisdictions, which is known as a *bilateral APA*. The APA outlines in advance the procedure that a company will take to establish its transfer prices. An APA application involves a presentation by the company of why it plans to use a certain transfer pricing method, why alternate methods were not chosen, and a description of the transactions to which the transfer pricing method will be applied. Having an APA in place means that a company will be much less likely to incur penalties and fines, though it may still be subject to audits, to ensure that it is complying with the terms of the APA.

In short, transfer pricing can have a major impact on the amount of income tax payments that a company must make, by shifting reported net income amongst subsidiaries located in various tax jurisdictions. The transfer prices used to create these tax reductions are subject to regulation by the various tax jurisdictions, which can lead to an ongoing series of audits. To avoid the aggravation of audits and any resulting additional payments, consider entering into bilateral advance pricing agreements.

Summary

The key point to remember about all of the transfer pricing systems noted in this chapter is that no one system is likely to work perfectly in all situations. Instead, it may be necessary to use several systems at once to most closely align pricing with the circumstances surrounding various transfers. In general, it is best to adopt market-based prices as the default transfer pricing system, and to incorporate modifications to market prices as needed.

Also, incorporate a well-documented procedure into the transfer pricing system, in order to minimize bickering between the various subsidiaries regarding which transfer prices to use. Otherwise, subsidiary managers will spend an inordinate amount of time negotiating prices, instead of improving the sales and operations of their companies.

Chapter 19
Inventory Controls

Introduction

Inventory is undoubtedly the single most difficult asset area to control. There may be thousands of different inventory items, stored in many locations throughout a company, and handled by large numbers of employees. In a manufacturing environment, the situation is further complicated by tracking the status of materials as they progress through the production process. In addition, there are special sub-processes for handling scrapped and reworked goods, as well as the disposition of obsolete inventory. If not properly controlled, the result of this vast range of activities is a derived inventory valuation that diverges widely from the actual valuation.

A proper system of control over this level of complexity requires the use of specific control points in several key processes, as well as many independent review activities to spot additional problems. In this chapter, we examine the controls that are incorporated into the inventory purchasing, receiving, and shipping functions, as well as other controls associated with inventory valuation, warehousing, and the production area.

> **Related Podcast Episode:** Episode 8 of the Accounting Best Practices Podcast discusses inventory controls. It is available at: **accountingtools.com/podcasts** or **iTunes**

Purchasing Process Overview

The purchasing of inventory involves as many as three primary activities, each of which may require controls, depending on the circumstances. The maximum range of activities can include:
1. Bidding
2. Order derivation
3. Order monitoring

All of these purchasing activities are only needed when a company uses an entirely manual purchasing system. A narrative description of these activities follows.

1. Bidding

If a prospective inventory purchase is for a large enough amount of money, the purchasing staff goes out for bid in order to obtain the best deal. This is an increasingly rare circumstance, as more businesses are trying to reduce the number of suppliers they use and accelerate the purchasing process. Still, it is sometimes used, especially in government purchasing. If a company engages in bidding, there will likely be a bidding packet assembled that documents who was contacted, the resulting bids, and why the winner was selected.

2. Order derivation

Once a supplier has been selected, the purchasing staff creates a multi-part purchase order that authorizes a purchase. One copy goes to the supplier, one is retained in the purchasing department and matched to the original requisition form, and other copies go to the receiving and accounting departments. The receiving department needs to refer to the purchase order when the goods arrive, and the accounting department needs it to verify that the amounts billed on supplier invoices were authorized. If the purchase is for a small enough amount, a procurement card may instead be used to acquire inventory.

3. Order monitoring

The purchasing staff monitors open purchase orders to ensure that suppliers complete them by the required due date, and then close out any residual balances on orders that have been mostly filled. The department may extend its order monitoring to a more formal rating system for suppliers, which it uses to determine its preferred list of suppliers.

The general flow of these three purchasing steps, including the associated paperwork, is noted in the following flowchart.

Purchasing Process Flow

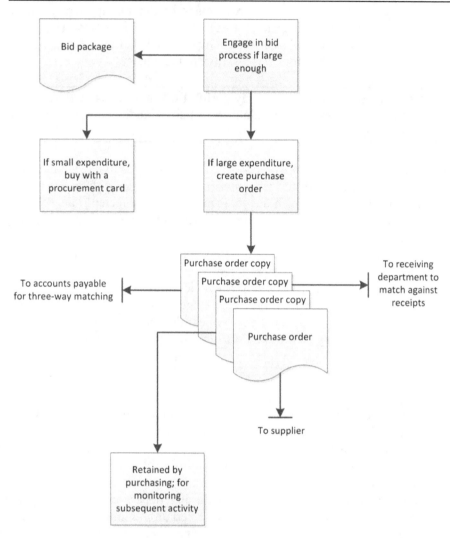

In-Process Purchasing Controls

In this section, we cover the controls that can be imposed on the core inventory purchasing processes.

1. Bidding

If the size of a purchase mandates that competitive bidding should be used, there need to be controls over the process to ensure that it is completed fairly. In addition, these larger purchases may involve supplier contracts, which require review to ensure that the contract terms are reasonable. The controls are:

- *Create bidding data trail.* There should be evidence that the purchasing staff engaged in bidding, thereby providing a barrier to suppliers giving kick-backs to the purchasing staff in exchange for their orders. This data trail should include a list of who was contacted, copies of their bids, and the reason why a purchase order was awarded to the winner.

Tip: Creating a bidding data trail is only useful if the purchasing staff knows it will be examined by someone, so schedule the internal audit team to review these documents on a regular basis.

- *Require legal review of contracts.* If the company is to engage in a contract with a supplier, have the legal staff review it to see if there are any short-comings or risks to which the company may be subjected. This control usually only applies to larger contracts; otherwise, the legal department may be buried with reviews.
- *Use a contract checklist.* The legal staff should use a standard review checklist when examining proposed contracts with suppliers. This checklist is particularly important if contract reviews are handled by the purchasing staff, since they have less legal knowledge. Sample review items include the expiration date of the contract, prices, discounts, delivery dates, quality specifications, payment terms, warranty terms, and termination notification provisions.

2. Order Derivation

The purchase order itself is the best control point in the purchasing process, since it documents exactly what is being purchased and the terms under which the company agrees to make a purchase. It is also used in the receiving and accounting departments for additional controls. The controls related to the derivation of purchase orders are:

- *Generate purchase order.* The purchasing department issues a purchase order for every purchase made above a certain minimum dollar amount. By doing so, the purchasing staff is, in essence, approving all expenditures before they have been made, which may prevent some expenditures from ever occurring. This control may be strong enough to eliminate the need for a check signer.

Tip: In practice, it will be inordinately expensive to enforce the use of purchase orders for everything. Instead, this control is more enforceable for larger purchases, with an automatic exemption for all purchases below a minimum dollar amount.

- *Obtain purchasing manager approval.* If a purchase order relates to a very expensive inventory purchase, it may be useful to involve the purchasing manager by requiring his or her signature on the purchasing authorization. This step is only going to help the control environment if the intent is to go back to the person requesting the item to make absolutely certain that they want to make the purchase.

3. Order Monitoring

An unfilled purchase order represents a future liability of the company, and so should be monitored closely. The following controls are used to ensure that this monitoring is conducted:

- *Retain a purchase order copy.* If the company does not store its purchase orders in a database, the purchasing department should retain a copy of each purchase order. This is useful for monitoring open purchase orders, as well as for tracking down orders that may have been lost by suppliers.
- *Review open purchase orders.* A major control is to tightly monitor the status of open purchase orders. This involves matching purchase orders against receiving reports to ascertain which orders are overdue, and following up on them. Though this is not a control over money, it *is* a control over operations, since missing materials can shut down a business.

Tip: Be particularly careful to track the company's orders under a blanket purchase agreement, since the company may have agreed to a minimum purchase volume in exchange for a lower price. The company should be made aware of an impending penalty payment to a supplier.

- *Close residual purchase orders.* The purchasing staff should periodically review the list of open purchase orders to see if any have been largely filled, with just a few residual units not shipped. Depending on the circumstances, it may make sense to close these purchase orders, thereby reducing the number of open items to monitor.

Additional Purchasing Controls – Fraud Related

There is a reasonable chance that fraud will occur in the purchasing area, since it involves the creation of a document that is a legal authorization to buy from a supplier. If someone can gain access to a company's purchase orders, they could order goods for which the company would be liable to pay suppliers. Accordingly, consider implementing the following controls to prevent or at least detect fraud:

- *Prenumber purchase orders.* If a company prepares purchase orders by hand and uses them as the primary authorization to pay suppliers, the purchase order document itself becomes quite valuable. Someone could fraudulently use a purchase order to order goods for themselves. To avoid this issue, prenumber all purchase orders and lock them up.

> **Tip:** In practice, the purchasing manager will probably assign a block of purchase orders to each purchasing staff person, who is then responsible for his or her forms. If so, the manager should track which purchase order numbers were assigned to each staff person. Then, if a purchase order is used improperly, the source of the offending purchase order will be readily apparent.

- *Password-protect purchasing software.* If the company creates purchase orders on-line and uses them as the primary authorization to pay suppliers, someone accessing the purchase order database can fraudulently order goods. To prevent this, use passwords to restrict access to the purchasing software.
- *Password-protect the vendor master file.* A supplier could offer a kickback to an employee for altering the terms of payment listed in the vendor master file, or an employee could create a fake supplier and use it to pay himself. These problems can be mitigated by using passwords to restrict access to the vendor master file.
- *Review the vendor master file change log.* There are a number of ways that the vendor master file can be altered for fraudulent purposes, such as changing a payment address to that of an employee, and then changing it back. To detect these alterations, review the change log on a regular basis. Change logs are usually only available in higher-end purchasing software.
- *Review expense trends.* There may be an unusual blip in a cost of goods sold expense line item in a particular month that was not caught by any of the in-process controls. Once investigated, the system can be modified to catch similar offending transactions in the future.

> **Tip:** Formulate a trailing 12-month income statement that shows the monthly results for each of the preceding 12 months for every cost of goods sold expense account. This is the best source of information for conducting an expense trend analysis.

- *Audit materials pricing.* It is possible that a purchasing agent could engage in fraud by agreeing to obtain goods from a supplier at an inflated price, with the supplier providing a kickback payment to the purchasing agent. This arrangement is difficult to detect, especially when the prices paid are only slightly higher than the average rate. Still, an audit of materials pricing may detect a pattern of supplier overbilling that can be traced back to a particular staff person.
- *Verify scrap payments.* The purchasing staff typically sells off scrap to a scrap dealer, for which the dealer pays a small amount. If these payments are made in cash, the person responsible for the scrap deliveries could pocket the cash. To avoid this situation, require all scrap dealers to pay with a check, and compare a selection of dealer payments to the company's records of scrap pickups. Also, track scrap payments on a trend line to see if there

were any periods when payments were unusually low or nonexistent. These actions can prevent and/or detect the fraudulent diversion of scrap payments.

- *Verify inventory dispositions.* When inventory is classified as obsolete, the purchasing department is tasked with the disposition of these items at the best possible price. This situation brings up the same concerns just noted for the sale of scrapped items; the purchasing staff could intercept cash payments for dispositioned items. The prevention measures are the same as for scrap – require check payments, and verify payments made. Also, consider matching the amounts received to any original estimates of the prices at which obsolete goods should sell, to see if there are pricing shortfalls or no records of any receipts.

Additional Purchasing Controls – Periodic Actions

The following controls are useful for ensuring that purchase orders are used, that they are created correctly, and that the records supporting the purchasing system are properly maintained. They are not necessarily part of a specific process; instead, the purchasing staff schedules them as separate tasks. These controls are:

- *Reject deliveries without a purchase order.* In every business, there is always someone who places orders without going through the purchasing department. A possible control over this behavior is to require the receiving department to reject all deliveries made for which there is no authorizing purchase order.
- *Review automated orders.* In many manufacturing operations, a materials planning system automatically generates purchase orders for raw materials, based on on-hand quantities and the production plan. The purchasing staff can review these automated orders before they are released, to ensure that record errors are not triggering orders that the company does not really need.

Tip: The review of automated orders is absolutely necessary when inventory record accuracy is low, since the basis for the orders may be incorrect. As record accuracy improves, the purchasing staff can confine itself to reviewing only the larger-value orders.

- *Consolidate the vendor master file.* In a larger business, it is entirely likely that multiple vendor files will be opened for a single supplier. This makes it difficult to assemble consolidated information for a single supplier, which is needed for spend management analysis. Consequently, the purchasing staff should engage in a periodic examination of the vendor master file to see if any records can be consolidated.
- *Certify suppliers.* If a company has a quality program, it may engage in a periodic supplier certification review. This can encompass such factors as testing products against contract specifications, examining delivery dates, and visiting supplier facilities. There may also be a comparative ranking

system, whereby low-scoring suppliers receive warnings, and may be replaced.

Receiving Process Overview

There are two entirely different types of receiving. Most of the time, inventory items are arriving from suppliers after they were ordered by the company's purchasing department. In a few cases, the company's own products are being returned to it by customers, after the returns were authorized by the order entry or customer service department. Despite the differences in origination and authorization, both types of deliveries are handled by the receiving department. Separate narrative descriptions of these two activities follow:

1. Receive Ordered Goods

When a delivery arrives, the receiving staff examines it to see if it was authorized, and if the product type and quantity is as specified by the company's purchasing department. If the delivery is acceptable, the receiving staff fills out a receiving report and sends a copy to the accounts payable clerk, who uses it to verify receipt before paying any related supplier invoices. The receiving staff staples a copy of the packing slip to its own copy of the receiving report for filing within the department, and forwards the delivery to the warehouse, where it is logged into the inventory tracking system and stored.

If the company has a computerized procurement system, the receiving staff can enter the purchase order associated with a delivery into the computer system, along with the quantity received. The system automatically makes this information available to the accounts payable clerk, so there is no need to forward any documents to that person. The system automatically generates a receiving report, if anyone finds it necessary to print out this information. The system may also log the received items into inventory, though no warehouse location code can be assigned until it is moved into the warehouse.

2. Receive Returned Goods

When deliveries arrive that are for returned products, the receiving staff logs them into a returns database and forwards them to the warehouse staff for evaluation. These goods may no longer be in sellable condition, or may require repackaging or other refurbishing, and so should be tracked separately from normal inventory items. The receiving staff completes a return merchandise authorization (RMA) notification form and forwards a copy to the billing clerk, who uses it to issue a credit to the customer.

The general flow of these receiving activities, including the associated paperwork, is noted in the following flowchart.

Receiving Process Flow

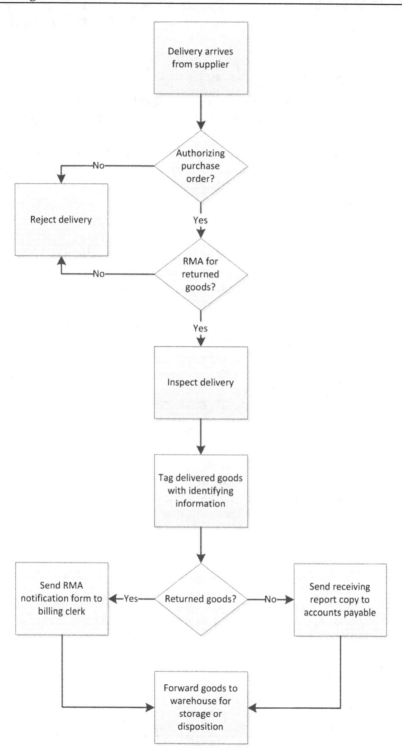

In-Process Receiving Controls

In this section, we cover the controls that can be imposed on the two types of receiving processes.

1. Receive Ordered Goods

The controls related to the receipt of ordered goods begin with testing them for various issues, and then recording them in a format that can be used by the rest of the company. The controls are:

- *Only accept deliveries for which there is a purchase order.* If a company has a policy of issuing purchase orders for all major purchases, the receiving staff should reject deliveries that are not authorized with a purchase order. This forces employees to work through the purchasing department to order goods.

Tip: This is a very difficult control to enforce, since other valid purchases may have been made with procurement cards, and so have no purchase order assigned to them. One way to avoid a debacle is to automatically accept deliveries from certified suppliers, on the grounds that they would not ship without a valid order. Also, if an item is clearly related to the cost of goods sold, the receiving department may be authorized to accept it irrespective of a missing purchase order, since it may be a rush order that is needed right now. Another option is to assign the same purchase order number to all items bought with procurement cards, just so that they will be accepted at the receiving dock.

- *Fully inspect all deliveries.* The general rule is to inspect all deliveries for quantity delivered, the product numbers delivered, and any damage.
- *Test count received items.* On a random basis, the receiving manager can open up all packaging and conduct a complete count of a delivery. This may occasionally find quantity or quality problems for which the purchasing department should be notified for further action.

Tip: Test counts can be more heavily targeted toward those suppliers with whom the company has had delivery problems in the past.

- *Reject excess material.* Suppliers sometimes run up their invoice amounts by shipping somewhat more than was authorized by the company. It is particularly important for the receiving staff to locate and reject these items when the company does not need any additional units, as is the case for short production runs.

Tip: It is not necessary to reject excess material when the company uses it on a continuing basis, as long as the overages are not excessive.

- *Flag customer-owned goods.* There are situations where a customer may send in goods that the company will modify and then send back. The receiving staff must flag these items as customer-owned, so that they are not mistakenly included in the company's ending inventory calculations.

> **Tip:** There are usually so few customer-owned items in stock that employees tend to assume that they are company-owned. The receiving staff can make this less likely by taping a brightly-colored label to these items as soon as they are received.

- *Tag all received inventory.* There should be a standard form on which the receiving staff notes the part number, description, unit of measure, and unit quantity for all received items. This makes it more efficient for the warehouse staff to identify and record items entering the warehouse.

> **Tip:** The company can require its suppliers to provide this information on a company-mandated form, preferably one that already contains the same information in a bar coded format. This simplifies the work of the receiving staff, and may allow it to scan received items directly into the inventory database.

- *Complete receiving reports.* A formal receiving report is needed to document the arrival of goods for the accounts payable staff. This control is not needed in a computerized system, where the receiving staff simply checks off received items in an on-line purchase order.
- *Maintain a receiving log.* It may be sufficient to record receipts on receiving reports for forwarding to the accounts payable staff, but a more organized approach is to also summarize them in a receiving log. The accounting staff can use this information to determine which received items arrived after the end of an accounting period, and so should be recorded in the next accounting period.

2. Receive Returned Goods

When goods are being returned to the company by its customers, the controls are similar to the testing used for received goods, except that the examination is based on a return merchandise authorization (RMA). The controls are:

- *Only accept returns for which there is a return merchandise authorization.* If the company sells in bulk to retailers and wholesalers, it is particularly likely that they will simply ship back all unsold goods if allowed to do so. To prevent this, the order entry staff issues RMA numbers when a customer provides a valid reason for a return. The receiving staff is required to reject all returns that do not have an accompanying RMA number. This can be a major control, depending on the possible volume of unauthorized returns that would otherwise be received.
- *Only accept items authorized on an RMA.* It is relatively common for retailers and wholesalers to obtain RMAs for a small number of items, and

then ship back considerably more than the amount that was authorized. Thus, the receiving staff should compare each delivery to the RMA authorization.

- *Thoroughly log all returned items.* Items being returned to the company may not be in as organized a state as when they were originally shipped to customers. Thus, it is important to identify exactly what was returned in the receiving log.

Additional Receiving Controls – Fraud Related

There is a chance that goods could be fraudulently recorded as having been received. The following controls are designed to prevent or detect this issue:

- *Password-protect receiving software.* If someone working with a supplier could access a company's receiving software and fraudulently log in a delivery as received, the company would pay for it even though it never arrived. To reduce this risk, use passwords to protect access to the receiving software.
- *Use a transaction log to record receiving transactions.* If someone accesses the receiving software to fraudulently log in a delivery as received, this can be detected with a transaction log that is attached to the receiving database. The log should record the identification of the person making the entry, as well as the nature of the entry.
- *Separation of duties.* The person who authorizes the purchase of goods should not also receive it. If this were allowed, someone could authorize a purchase, log it in as having been received (so that the company would pay for it), and then remove the inventory from the premises.

Additional Receiving Controls – Periodic Actions

The following controls are useful for keeping track of receiving reports, as well as for improving the accuracy of inventory records. They are not necessarily part of a specific process; instead, the receiving staff schedules them as separate tasks. These controls are:

- *Prenumber and track receiving reports.* If a company has a manual receiving system, prenumber the receiving forms. By doing so, the receiving manager can keep track of the form numbers, and will know when forms are missing.
- *Review receiving reports.* The receiving manager or the internal audit staff should periodically review receiving reports to see if the receiving staff did an adequate job of inspecting delivered goods.
- *Compare packing slips to inventory receipt transactions.* The warehouse staff typically counts received items again before recording them in the inventory database. The internal audit staff should periodically audit received goods to see if there are differences between the amounts stated on the pack-

ing slips that accompanied delivered goods and the quantities recorded by the warehouse staff.

Tip: It is of particular interest when this control reveals that there are disparities between the packing slip quantities and recorded quantities for the same supplier on multiple occasions. This suggests that the supplier in question is persistently issuing incorrect packing slips, which in turn suggests that it is shipping smaller quantities than it should.

- *Segregate received items during a physical inventory count.* If a company is engaged in a physical inventory count, the receiving staff should segregate all items received after a cutoff point prior to the start of the counting process. Otherwise, received items could be inadvertently included in the physical count for which there are not yet any supplier invoices in the accounting system (which would reduce the reported cost of goods sold).

Shipping Process Overview

Shipping involves three primary activities, each of which may require controls, depending on the level of automation of the order processing function. The activities are:

1. Picking
2. Shipping
3. Forward shipping information

A narrative description of these three activities follows.

1. Picking

Upon receipt of a sales order from the credit department (which verifies customer credit), the shipping manager makes a copy of it and distributes the copy to a warehouse picker. This person picks the goods listed on the sales order and brings them to the shipping area. All items picked are removed from the inventory records.

In an automated system, picking information is routed directly to hand-held computers that direct stock pickers to the locations in the warehouse where items are located, and which they use to relieve items from stock in the inventory records as soon as they are picked. Alternatively, if the computerized system does not send information to hand-held computers, it probably provides for the printing of picking tickets, which are used to pull items from stock.

If some items are not in stock, the shipping staff fills out a backorder form. One copy of the form goes to the order entry staff, which uses it to contact the customer to inform them of the backorder situation. Another copy is kept on file, and a third copy goes to the materials management staff, who must schedule it to be produced or procured. If the order processing function is computerized, the shipping staff flags the designated items in the sales order record as being on backorder, and the system handles all notifications.

2. Shipping

The shipment of goods to customers begins with the shipping manager printing the latest report from the computer system that identifies which shipments are to be delivered today, based on the required due dates listed on customer purchase orders. If the shipment system is manually operated, the shipping manager compiles this information by perusing all open sales orders for which goods have been picked.

The shipping manager then verifies that items have been picked and are ready for shipment, and contacts freight carriers to schedule pickup times. The shipping staff prepares bills of lading and packing slips for all deliveries, loads the trucks when they arrive, and completes the shipping log for the day's shipments. In a computerized system, the software prints out all of these documents and updates the shipping log.

3. Forward Shipping Information

Once shipping has been completed, the shipping department sends all shipping documents to the accounting staff, for use in creating customer invoices. If this transfer is manual, a copy of the bill of lading will be sent to accounting, possibly also with a copy of the sales order. If the system is computerized, the software will make this information available to the accounting staff automatically.

The general flow of these three shipping steps, including the associated paperwork, is noted in the following flowchart.

Shipping Process Flow

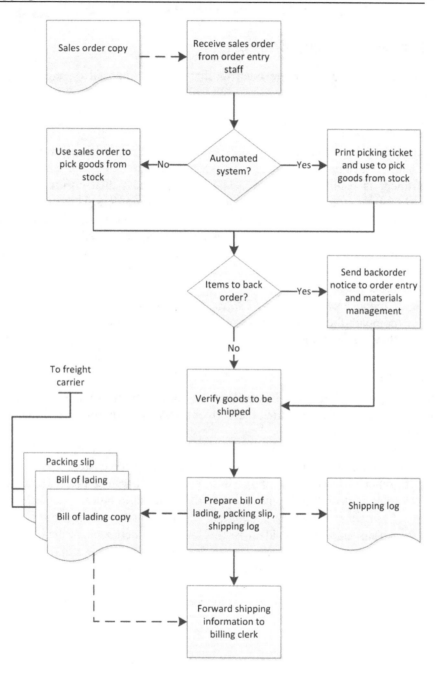

A variation on the shipping process that is less used is to direct sales orders to a supplier, who ships the goods directly to the customer (known as *drop shipping*). This involves the transmission of the sales order to the supplier, which uses it as the basis for a shipment. The supplier then transmits a copy of the bill of lading to the company, which uses it to invoice the customer.

In-Process Shipping Controls

In this section, we cover the controls that can be imposed on the core shipping process.

1. Picking

Though the job of the shipping staff essentially begins with picking products for shipment, the shipping manager must first ensure that the sales orders the department is receiving are valid. The manager must then ensure that the items picked from storage are the ones specified in the sales orders. These controls are:

- *Review for credit approval.* The shipping manager should not process any sales order unless it is either too small to require a credit approval or there is a credit approval stamp on the document. If the order processing system is computerized, there should instead be a credit approval flag on the sales order record.
- *Compare picked items to sales order.* Someone other than the picker can compare the items picked to the sales order or picking ticket, to ensure that they are the same.

2. Shipping

There should be controls to ensure that the correct items are shipped to customers, and that the company is creating the correct documentation for each shipment. These controls are:

- *Compare shipping documents to sales order.* This is the last chance for the company to ensure that what it is shipping to the customer is what the customer ordered. The comparison involves matching the part numbers and quantities on the shipping documents to the sales order.
- *Prenumber shipping documents.* In a manual shipping system, it is important to uniquely identify the shipping document associated with each delivery. Otherwise, there is no evidence that it ever shipped, and there is nothing to trigger the creation of an invoice by the accounting department. Consequently, always prenumber all shipping documents. This control does not apply in a computerized environment, since the computer automatically assigns document numbers.

3. Forward Shipping Information

Following shipment, the shipping manager is responsible for sending a copy of the shipping documents to the billing clerk in the accounting department. This is a crucial step, for unforwarded information means that invoices will not be sent to customers. The following controls are used to ensure that shipping documents are forwarded to the billing clerk:

- *Match forwarded information to shipping log.* The billing clerk should periodically compare all shipping documentation received from the shipping department with its shipping log, to verify that all shipping documentation has been delivered to the accounting department. This control is less necessary in a computerized order processing department.
- *Match supplier billings to customer billings.* If the company has a drop shipping arrangement with a supplier, the supplier is supposed to ship goods directly to the company's customers, and then notify the company that the drop shipments have been made. The company uses this notification to bill customers. If the supplier never notifies the company, there is no triggering mechanism to issue invoices to customers. A reasonable control over this issue is to compare the billings of the supplier conducting drop shipping to the company's invoices to customers. Any disparities are grounds for an investigation into why a supplier did not notify the company of a shipment.

Additional Shipping Controls – Fraud Related

Someone intent on committing fraud may try to fool the shipping manager by forwarding sales orders that have not been approved by the credit department, or by configuring sales orders to have no prices. Further, the shipping manager himself may commit fraud by backdating shipping documents to inflate revenues in a reporting period. The following controls deal with these issues:

- *Return sales orders with no authorization to the credit department.* If a sales order without a credit approval stamp is delivered to the shipping manager, the manager should forward it immediately to the credit manager. This is an excellent way to highlight sales orders that have circumvented the credit approval system.
- *Specify no-price sales orders in shipping log.* Whenever the shipping staff is given a sales order for which there is no price, it should make note of this point in the sales log. If the system is computerized, the system will automatically populate the shipping log with this information. Highlighting no-price items makes it easier for someone to later investigate deliveries for which the company is earning no revenue.

Tip: To make this control more robust, have the shipping manager notify the controller when especially large no-price sales orders are about to be shipped.

- *Verify period in which shipment is reported.* The shipping manager may be pressured by management to backdate some shipments into the preceding period, thereby increasing the amount of revenue booked in that period. This issue can be identified by comparing shipping documents from third-party shippers with the dates on which shipments are recorded in the shipping log.
- *Report on early deliveries.* Create a report that identifies deliveries made prior to the delivery date requested by the customer. This may indicate situations where employees are attempting to artificially increase revenues in the short term by issuing goods before customers want them.
- *Close the books fast.* A key problem for the accounting staff is the pressure it undergoes from the shipping department at the end of each reporting period, to allow late deliveries to be included in the period. Doing so increases the amount of revenues reported in the period. When there is a particularly large revenue shortfall, this extra shipping period may extend a day or two into the following reporting period. An excellent way to avoid this excessive pressure is to arrange for a fast close of the books, ostensibly to issue financial statements promptly. By doing so, the controller can enforce a hard close to the end of the period, after which all shipping documents will be translated into customer invoices in the following reporting period.

Additional Shipping Controls – Periodic Actions

The following controls are mostly intended to spot stray problems in the shipping process that would not necessarily be caught during the daily processing of orders. They are not usually handled as part of daily shipping activities, but rather at longer intervals. The controls are:

- *Review customer complaints.* Management should regularly review the customer complaints database to see if any complaints involve shipping the wrong goods or quantities to customers. If so, this implies that there was a breakdown somewhere in the fulfillment cycle that should be tracked down and corrected.
- *Verify that picked items are noted on sales order.* Someone other than the picker should verify that the items picked have been checked off on the sales order or picking ticket. This is particularly important in a computerized system, where the system will create a backorder transaction for all items not picked.

Tip: Verifying the data entry on every sales order can interfere with the processing of orders, so it may be more efficient to use this control on an occasional basis to see if any stock pickers are unusually bad at recording their picks on sales orders or picking tickets.

- *Conduct a periodic comparison of the products shipped to the items ordered.* The internal audit team or others outside of the fulfillment cycle should occasionally compare the products being shipped to customers to what they ordered, as stated on their purchase orders or the company's sales order that documents what they ordered. This analysis can sometimes spot issues that may call for more detailed investigation, such as backordered items for which there is no expectation of fulfillment.

- *Investigate missing shipping documents.* The shipping department should have a procedure for regularly reviewing the disposition of all shipping documents, based on their document numbers. If a shipping document is not used for whatever reason, mark it as void and record its manner of usage. By maintaining firm control over shipping documents, there is a reduced risk that shipments will not be billed. This control does not apply if the order processing function is computerized.
- *Report on unapproved items appearing in shipping report.* In a computerized order processing system, the daily picking and shipping reports should not show any sales orders that have not yet been approved by the credit department. If this information appears, the shipping manager should bring it to the attention of the credit manager.
- *Reconcile backordered items.* There should be a continual review of all backordered items to see if the company will be able to ship them in the near future, before customers cancel the ordered items. This can have a significant impact on revenues.

Intercompany Controls

If a company transfers inventory between subsidiaries or storage locations, consider installing the following controls to ensure that in-transit inventory is properly recorded:

- *Centralize inventory transactions.* A company may have multiple warehouses or subsidiaries, with inventory flowing between them. If so, the organization as a whole maintains ownership of the inventory even while it is in transit between locations. If each location were to maintain its own inventory record keeping system, it would log out inventory once goods are shipped to another location, while the receiving location will not log in the goods until received. To avoid this in-transit valuation problem, consider centralizing inventory records for all locations in a single database. If transfers are between warehouses, this functionality is provided by distribution resource planning software. If it is not possible to incur the expense of such a centralized system, at least install a procedure for notifying the receiving location of a shipment, with a requirement for the receiving location to log the inventory into an "in transit" location in its database.
- *Audit intercompany transactions.* When goods are being shipped between company locations, audit both sides of these transactions, to ensure that inventory is correctly reduced by the shipping location and increased by the receiving location.

Inventory Valuation Controls

Thus far, we have discussed controls that relate to three specific process flows – purchasing, receiving, and shipping. In addition, the accountant must be concerned with the *valuation* of inventory. Controls in this area are not related to a specific process. Instead, there are a number of possible controls that can be imposed on how inventory is recorded and valued. These controls are described in the following bullet points:

Inventory Recordation Controls

- *Restrict access to bill of material records.* Many organizations compile the value of their finished goods inventory from bills of material, which identify the exact components included in each product. If someone were to illicitly access and alter these records, the result could be a drastic change in the recorded value of inventory. The same result could arise from an inadvertent updating error. To prevent these changes, require password access to the bill of material records in the computer system, and only grant access to a few employees. Also, change the password regularly to prevent it from becoming common knowledge.
- *Audit bill of material records.* Since bills of material are used to derive the value of finished goods, it behooves the accountant to insist that these records be audited for accuracy. Ideally, someone other than the bill of material originator should compare the actual components used to construct a product to the components listed in the bill of materials. These records should be re-examined whenever there is an engineering change order, to ensure that they still reflect the actual status of a product.
- *Review checklist of off-site storage locations.* When a business stores inventory at off-site locations, these items are commonly not tracked in the main inventory database. If so, there is a risk that the off-site unit quantities will not be updated on a regular basis. To avoid the risk of incorrect quantities, maintain an updated list of all inventory locations, and ensure that updated quantity reports are received from these locations as part of the closing process.
- *Audit off-site locations.* When inventory is stored in off-site locations, do not assume that the information reported by these locations is correct. There may be errors in unit counts, units of measure, and item descriptions. A periodic audit of each location will detect these issues.

Inventory Valuation Controls

- *Audit cost layers.* If the costing system involves the use of cost layers, periodically audit the cost layer records, tracing inventory costs back to specific supplier invoices. This control is less necessary for earlier cost layers that are rarely accessed, and more necessary when cost layers are manually maintained. In cases where cost layers are manually maintained, also trace supplier invoices forward into the cost layers, to ensure that costs are being properly recorded.

- *Match standard costs to actual.* When a standard costing system is used, the difference between actual and standard costs should be relatively small. To ensure that this is the case, require that a formal review of all standard costs be conducted at least annually. Also, if there are notable differences between standard and actual costs, verify that these differences are being charged to the cost of goods sold as a variance within the correct reporting period.

- *Review journal entries.* A large number of journal entries may record transactions in the cost of goods sold and/or inventory accounts. Each of these entries represents a possibly incorrect entry that could seriously impact the inventory valuation. To ensure that these entries are reasonable, require a separate review and sign-off on each one. Also mandate that each entry must be accompanied by a document that justifies the reason for the entry, including supporting calculations.

- *Audit production setup calculations.* When there is a substantial production setup cost associated with a production run, this cost may be allocated to each unit in the production run. If the number of units actually produced varies from the amount assumed in the allocation calculation, the result can be a substantially incorrect inventory cost. For example, a setup charge of $1,000 is only $1 per unit if 1,000 units are produced, but is $100 per unit if just ten units are produced. Given this potential for enormous cost disparities, be sure to audit production setup calculations. This is of particular importance in a standard costing system where a standard setup charge may be loaded into bills of material, without any consideration of the actual number of units produced in subsequent production runs.

- *Conduct obsolete inventory review.* There should be a regular examination of the inventory by a qualified group that is focused on rooting out and dispositioning those inventory items that are obsolete. Otherwise, the inventory valuation will be inflated by the values of items that cannot be sold off at a reasonable price. A lower of cost or market examination has a similar effect. See the Obsolete Inventory chapter and Lower of Cost or Market chapter for more information.

- *Create allocation procedure.* The process of allocating overhead costs to inventory and the cost of goods sold is a manual one, and therefore subject to error. To mitigate the probability of errors, create an allocation procedure that precisely defines which costs are to be included in cost pools and how these cost pools are to be allocated.

- *Audit allocation calculations.* Conduct a periodic review of the overhead allocation calculations. The intent is to ensure that the correct costs are being included in cost pools, and that these pools are being appropriately allocated to ending inventory and the cost of goods sold based on the allowed allocation procedure.

- *Review overhead trends.* Create a report that shows the aggregated amount of overhead stored in the company's designated overhead cost pools at the

179

end of each reporting period and prior to their allocation to cost objects. When this report is presented in a trend line format for the last 12 months, any unusual spikes or declines will be immediately apparent. Further investigation of these anomalies may reveal unauthorized changes in the costs included in the cost pools.

- *Review product cost trends.* There are many ways in which the recognized cost of a product can be incorrectly compiled. To detect these issues, create and review a report that tracks the calculated cost of each inventory item on a rolling 12-month trend line. Better yet, set the report to reveal percentage changes in costs on the same trend line. A brief examination of this report will reveal unusual cost spikes or declines, which can be used as the basis for additional investigative work.

- *Review extended costs.* At the end of a reporting period, create a report that multiplies ending unit quantities by their costs to arrive at extended costs, and sort the report in declining order by extended cost. The first page of this report will reveal those inventory items that comprise the bulk of the inventory valuation. It is worthwhile to review this page to see if any inventory valuations look out of place. For example, an inadvertent change in a unit of measure could skyrocket the valuation of a lowly inventory item into the upper echelons of the inventory valuation.

Warehouse Controls

Many warehouse controls have been interspersed among the other sets of controls already noted in this chapter. In addition, we include the following controls that do not readily fall under any other category of controls:

- *Restrict warehouse access.* Build a high fence around the inventory storage area, and restrict access to a single gate. By doing so, only authorized personnel are allowed into the warehouse. This control prevents items from being stolen, and may reduce the number of cases where a visitor inadvertently moves goods from one location to another.

- *Restrict dock access.* Unauthorized visitors can enter the warehouse through any of the dock doors. This can lead to theft of goods from the storage area, as well as from the shipping and receiving areas. A general policy should be to restrict all access through the dock doors, or at least to prevent anyone from entering past a certain predetermined area adjacent to the dock doors.

- *Segregate supplier-owned inventory.* There may be an arrangement with suppliers, where they own certain raw materials until actually used within the company's production process. If so, flag these items in the inventory database as being supplier-owned, and physically segregate them in the warehouse storage area. Otherwise, they may be incorrectly recorded and valued as part of the company's own inventory.

Production Controls

The preceding discussions have addressed the bulk of all inventory controls. In addition, we note in the following bullet points a few additional controls that relate to the production area. Though few in number, these controls can have a profound impact on the amount of inventory reported in the balance sheet. They are:

- *Impose scrap reporting.* The production staff is mostly concerned with manufacturing goods, not with recording the amount of scrap that is a natural outcome of the production process. Since recording anything impedes their efficiency, they are especially unlikely to accurately report scrap levels. Nonetheless, it is imperative to do so, so that the cost of scrap can be tracked. This is of particular importance in a company that uses backflushing to relieve raw materials inventory from the inventory records. To make a scrap reporting system function properly, design the process to require the minimum possible amount of operator data entry, perhaps even by employing a production clerk to handle this chore.

- *Impose rework reporting.* In some production environments, it is possible to rework out-of-spec products and then reintroduce them into the production system for final finishing work. Rework may also arise from the return of goods by customers, where products can be resold. In either case, there must be a reporting system that notes the withdrawal of rework items from stock and their eventual return to stock, once rework activities have been completed. Otherwise, the non-reporting of rework withdrawals will tend to over-report the amount of work-in-process and finished goods on hand.

- *Review production area for excess inventory.* The production staff may squirrel away excess raw materials in the production area, for use in a future production run. If so, these inventory items are not recorded in the inventory records, so that the ending inventory valuation is too low. To prevent this issue, review the production area at regular intervals and retrieve any items that are not clearly needed for a current production job. Doing so also reduces clutter, which can lead to improved production efficiency and enhanced worker safety.

Summary

We have noted quite a large number of controls in this chapter. Each of these controls requires a certain amount of labor, and can interfere with the timely completion of more value-added activities. Consequently, there is a natural inclination to avoid implementing these controls. A middle ground used by many organizations is a reactive approach, where controls are installed to combat a situation *after* a problem has been spotted. However, this approach does not take into account *potential* issues, some of which may have much greater negative results than the concerns for which controls have already been installed. Consequently, we recommend at least an annual controls review of all activities involving inventory, preferably by a controls specialist, to see if the company is subject to any large inventory-related risks that are not being properly controlled. In addition, the same review should be conducted whenever there is a change to a process that involves inventory. And finally, we suggest a periodic review of the cost-effectiveness of controls. If a control is onerous and provides little protection, it can be eliminated in favor of a more effective and streamlined control.

Chapter 20
Fraudulent Inventory Transactions

Introduction

Inventory is a significant asset class within a business, and one which is subject to several types of fraudulent transactions, either to manipulate reported profits or simply to steal the inventory. In this chapter, we describe a selection of fraudulent inventory transactions, as well as the risk factors that make inventory fraud more likely, and how these issues can be avoided.

Those Who Commit Fraud

There are two distinctly different classes of individuals who use inventory to commit fraud. The first group is the "white collar" criminal, who is primarily concerned with the manipulation of reported financial results. These people are likely to be managers whose bonuses are at risk if the company does not report adequate financial results. In this situation, the company loses money through the bonuses that should not have been paid out. In addition, the company loses its reputation with outsiders who may be relying on the accuracy of its financial statements. In addition, the company could lose money due to lawsuit settlements brought by anyone who relied upon the incorrect financial statements.

The second group of employees who commit inventory fraud is anyone who steals the inventory. This group can also be white collar, but is more likely to be the employees who are handling inventory on a day-to-day basis. Fraud at this level tends to be small amounts of inventory that do not add up to a significant monetary total. However, a few employees can occasionally engage in industrial-grade theft and make off with astounding amounts of inventory. Also, a seemingly minor theft could involve an item that is in short supply, and which therefore has a profound effect on a company's inability to fill customer orders or complete production runs.

In short, the effect of fraud tends to be greater in the first case, where managers are altering inventory records, since reporting incorrect financial results can lead to massive settlements and bonus payments. Actual inventory theft can also have serious side-effects, but the cash loss tends to be lower. The next few sections address "white collar" fraud that inflates inventory values, followed by a briefer discussion of inventory theft.

Financial Statement Fraud – Labor Component

When deriving the cost of the inventory asset that relates to work-in-process and finished goods inventory, a key element of the cost is the labor apportioned to these inventory items. If someone wants to increase the reported level of profitability, a simple way to do so is to increase either the hourly labor cost assigned to inventory or the amount of labor time apportioned to inventory. By doing so, the ending inventory balance is increased, which reduces the amount of reported cost of goods sold, thereby increasing profits. The techniques used to engage in this type of fraud are as follows:

- *Alter the labor rate.* The simplest approach is to artificially increase the standard direct labor rate, which should be stored in a single field in the computer system for each type of labor used in the accounting records. For example, there may be a $20.00 hourly rate for a junior assembler, and a $23.00 rate for a senior assembler. Once altered, the increased cost is automatically copied through the bills of material for all inventory items, raising their costs.

- *Alter the usage rate.* A more time-consuming type of fraud is to alter the amount of labor time incorporated into each bill of material. To maximize the effect of this type of fraud, someone could determine which inventory items comprise the bulk of the finished goods inventory, and only alter the labor usage levels for these items, thereby leaving the bulk of all bills of material untouched.

- *Alter the setup assumption.* When there is a large amount of setup time involved in a production run, the engineering staff estimates the number of units that will be produced, and allocates the setup cost in the bills of material based on this assumed number of units. This allocation can be fraudulently increased simply by assuming that the setup cost will be spread across a smaller number of units. For example, $1,000 of setup labor results in an allocation of $1 per unit if 1,000 units are to be produced, but is a $10 charge per unit if the production volume is assumed to be just 100 units.

All of these types of fraud can be detected by running a comparison of the actual labor cost incurred in a period to the amount of labor cost added to inventory in the period. Another detective approach is to schedule ongoing audits of bills of material with the engineering staff, for which part of the analysis is an investigation of the labor rates and costs assigned to products. Yet another approach is to install a change log that tracks all modifications to the bill of material records in the computer system. And finally, use password protection to restrict access to the bill of material and labor rate records.

Financial Statement Fraud – Materials Component

One of the more difficult areas in which to commit financial statement fraud is in the alteration of the materials component of ending inventory. The difficulty is higher, because the purchasing department needs accurate bill of material records to order goods, and will immediately notice any improper alterations of the bills. Any changes will also be noticed by the production staff, which is using kitted goods in its production runs that are based on the bills of material. In short, there are multiple watchdogs in the company that maintain a close watch over the materials records.

Despite this built-in control system, there are still ways to commit financial statement fraud with the materials component of inventory. The goal is to increase the reported value of ending inventory, which reduces the cost of goods sold and thereby increases reported profits. The methods for doing so include the following:

- *Create all-inclusive bills.* The existing bills of material may include only higher-cost components. This approach is used when it is easier to charge off all fittings and fasteners to expense as purchased, rather than tracking them within the inventory system. A manager could mandate that the situation be reversed, and have all of these minor items recorded in the bills of material. Doing so creates a moderate increase in the valuation of ending inventory, and is perfectly legitimate – though not very efficient from the perspective of materials management.

- *Capitalize costs.* Someone could extend the preceding concept of the all-inclusive bill of material to also include all possible ancillary costs. For example, it is legitimate to include the costs of freight in, sales taxes, and customs fees in inventory, rather than charging them to expense as incurred. This approach is particularly effective when standard costs are used to value inventory, since these assumed costs will immediately be applied to the entire inventory.

- *Modify scrap adjustments.* A bill of materials may include an average amount of scrap that is expected to be incurred during the production process. If this scrap percentage is increased, so too will the total standard cost of the related inventory item, which increases ending inventory. This is a difficult form of fraud to commit, for the scrap level can only be increased a modest amount before it becomes glaringly obvious. Also, the change must be made to numerous bills of material before there is a noticeable impact on ending inventory.

- *Change the cost layering system.* If a company is operating a last in, first out cost layering system and some of the earlier layers contain inexpensive inventory costs, this represents an immediate opportunity to increase profits. A manager could advocate a switch to the first in, first out system, thereby achieving a one-time reduction in the cost of goods sold as the earlier cost layers are eliminated. There is nothing wrong with this changeover, but a manager's bonus plan should be altered to take into account the effects of this change, so that achieving a one-time bump in profits is not the sole reason for the change.

- *Adjust material costs.* If the ending inventory is valued based on standard costs, it behooves the fraudulent person to attempt to increase the standard cost of materials. However, a significant cost change may be spotted by the purchasing manager, who is usually comparing actual to standard purchasing costs. To avoid detection, one option is to increase the cost of a major commodity just prior to the period-end close, in order to maximize the aggregate inventory valuation, and then return the cost back to its original level immediately thereafter. Doing so creates a significant increase in the inventory asset in exchange for an alteration to possibly only a single commodity cost. Another option is to increase a number of costs for less-monitored materials in order to reduce the risk of detection. However, less-monitored items have attained this status because they are rarely in stock, so the net effect on the financial statements is reduced.

- *Create adjusting journal entries.* Someone could avoid making alterations to the bills of material entirely, and instead focus on entering a few modest-sized journal entries into the cost of goods sold or inventory accounts that will increase the ending inventory balance. These entries need to be below the usual detection threshold of the company's controls. Also, the entries should only be recorded in the largest cost of goods sold or inventory accounts, so that the percentage change in these accounts only causes a minor blip in the company's monitoring systems, which makes them less likely to be reviewed.

- *Ignore write downs.* A potentially large cost is the amount of inventory that is obsolete, and which should be written off. A manager could defer the recognition of this obsolescence writedown until after a bonus calculation period, thereby boosting short-term profits at the expense of having to recognize an even larger expense in a later period.

- *Double count inventory.* If management colludes with the warehouse staff, it is possible to double-count inventory balances, or create inventory balances for items that are not in stock at all. If so, these balances will increase the ending inventory asset. This type of fraud works best for inventory items that are rarely used, and which are therefore not being closely monitored by the sales or purchasing departments. However, this type of transaction must then be reversed immediately after the period-end in order to escape detection, and so tends to be a relatively short-term type of fraud. It also suffers from the level of collusion required to make it succeed.

- *Record customer and supplier-owned inventory.* Another type of fraud that requires the connivance of the warehouse staff is to record both customer-owned and supplier-owned inventory as being owned by the company. This situation can arise for customers when they forward goods for further fabrication work by the company. The situation is more common for suppliers, who may maintain stocks on-site that are only billed to the company when they are withdrawn from stock and used in the production process. If these items are not specifically tagged in the warehouse, it will not be apparent to the casual observer that they should have a zero valuation. Thus, this can be a good way to rapidly enhance the ending inventory valuation, especially if the quantities and unit values of these items are substantial. The main downside of this type of fraud is that there is no supporting purchasing documentation, which must be fabricated.

The use of all-inclusive bills is essentially a policy change involving how low-cost, high-volume items are to be tracked by a company. As such, this type of fraud can be combatted with an offsetting corporate policy, mandating that such items be charged to expense as incurred. The same policy can be used to offset the addition of freight in and other costs to the inventory valuation.

The risk of having scrap levels increased in the bills of material can be combatted in two ways. First, password-protect the bills of material to restrict access, and also monitor changes to these records with a change log. Second, conduct a comparison of estimated scrap levels to the amount of standard scrap recorded in the period; a significant difference between these amounts calls for a more detailed examination of the standard scrap rates.

Mitigating the risk of changes to materials costs involves the use of a change log and password protection. In addition, have the internal audit staff conduct periodic audits of the bills of material to review the standard costs being used, and the authorizations for any changes to these costs.

To avoid the possibility of fraud caused by improper journal entries, the best option is to password-protect access to the general ledger, and to conduct a complete analysis of all journal entries impacting inventory as part of the period-end closing process. Nonetheless, given the large number of transactions passing through these accounts, it is entirely possible that lower levels of fraud can escape detection.

Ignoring obsolete inventory can be one of the most difficult areas of fraud to avoid, since managers may have considerable control over this area. They can ensure that the materials review board does not meet, or meets at longer intervals, or chooses not to recognize the larger write downs. In egregious cases, the controller's only viable option may be to complain to the company's audit committee.

Inventory double counting is least likely in an environment where the inventory is being constantly cycle counted and audited. In this environment, the risk of detection is increased, especially if anyone wants to attempt it over a long period of time. However, a brief unit count alteration for a small number of items that is immediately corrected is difficult to spot.

The counting of customer and supplier-owned inventory as being customer-owned is not especially difficult to find, unless the persons committing fraud do an excellent job of fabricating supporting purchasing documents. Usually, there are no supporting documents at all, in which case even a cursory examination will reveal the presence of these items in the inventory valuation reports. The typical way to avoid the inclusion of these items in inventory is to segregate them in a different part of the warehouse. However, if the warehouse staff is colluding in this fraud, the goods are likely to be intermingled into the regular inventory, and so will be difficult to spot by visual inspection.

Costs can be assigned to customer or supplier-owned inventory by mistake. Someone may see a zero cost for an item, and incorrectly assume that a cost should be formulated for it. To guard against this possibility, assign unique product numbers to all inventory owned by third parties (such as beginning the product code with a "Z"), and then periodically run a report for these product codes that lists all items for which a cost has been assigned.

In summary, we must point out the risk of someone making ostensibly legitimate changes to the inventory system in order to achieve financial results that are essentially fraudulent in intent. Using all-inclusive bills of material, switching cost layering systems, and adding certain costs to inventory are all entirely legitimate activities. However, given their ability to create misleading financial statements, senior management should be unwilling to authorize the changes unless there are excellent operational reasons for doing so.

Financial Statement Fraud – Overhead Component

One of the larger components of the total cost of inventory is overhead. When this is the case, there are several ways for a person to fraudulently manipulate overhead to alter the financial statements, and without causing an excessive percentage gain in the total amount of the overhead component of ending inventory. As usual, the goal of the fraud-minded manager is to increase the reported value of ending inventory, which reduces the cost of goods sold and thereby increases reported profits. Consider the following options:

- *Produce more finished goods.* One of the simplest ways to alter financial results is to produce more goods. When additional finished goods are produced but not sold, a company is essentially deferring the recognition of overhead costs until a later period, thereby producing a short-term profit boost. This approach only works when a company uses a standard overhead allocation amount, and does not routinely adjust it to match the actual amount of overhead incurred in a reporting period. This type of fraud is especially pernicious, for it absorbs a large amount of cash in the increased inventory asset, which may not be easy to recover.

- *Alter overhead assignments.* The overhead cost pool from which costs are allocated should contain the same set of factory expenses in every period; doing so introduces a high level of consistency to the allocation of overhead. A manager could advocate the addition of other expense types to the cost pool. By doing so, costs that would normally be charged to expense as incurred are now shifted into inventory, and thereby deferred until the inventory is sold. It is entirely possible that there are a number of "gray area" expenses that could be added to the overhead cost pool, and which the company's auditors would approve. Nonetheless, pressure from a manager to add to a cost pool is a strong indicator of intent to inflate financial statement results.

- *Shift expenses into overhead expense accounts.* A variation on the last bullet point is to code more expenses into the accounts that are already being assigned to an overhead cost pool. For example, the accounts payable staff can be instructed to assign specific invoices to the production department, rather than to administrative expense. The result is an inflated overhead cost pool, which can be used to park additional expense in the inventory asset. There is no real defense against this issue, since it requires the cooperation of the accounting staff to implement, which implies that the accounting function is already corrupted.

- *Alter the standard overhead rate.* A company may calculate a standard overhead rate for the year, and only adjusts the rate at long intervals to match the actual amount of overhead that is being incurred. If so, this represents an opportunity for someone to go into the computer system and alter the standard overhead rate. The adjusted rate then automatically updates all inventory costing records, resulting in an immediate boost in the ending inventory valuation for all inventory items to which the overhead rate applies, and which can be applied for multiple months. Even more pernicious is when someone shifts the overhead rate back to its original amount as soon as the books have been closed, so there is no alteration to detect.

The fraudulent benefits to be gained from producing too many goods can be eliminated by always matching actual overhead costs incurred in a period to the amount assigned to production during the period. Doing so eliminates any possibility of gain from over allocating inventory. Another way to avoid this fraud is to also compensate managers for maintaining a low level of working capital investment, which would counteract any bonus to be gained from driving up profits.

The alteration of the expenses being compiled into the overhead cost pool is directly under the control of the controller and chief financial officer, who will hopefully be able to resist management pressure to add expenses to the pool. If not, the issue can be pointed out to the company's external auditors, who can bring the issue to the attention of the company's audit committee, or even refuse to certify the company's financial statements.

The alteration of the standard overhead rate is most easily avoided by password-protecting the field in which this information is stored. It is also useful to maintain a change log for this field, so the system records all changes, as well as the identification of the person making changes. Yet another option is to incorporate into the closing procedure a comparison of the actual overhead incurred to the amount of overhead charged to goods produced. This last item should flag any unusual overhead boosts that would be triggered by manipulation of the standard overhead rate.

Revenue Fraud

Thus far, we have defined fraud as being related to the enhancement of reported results in the financial statements, specifically by altering the cost of goods sold. In addition, chicanery can extend to the revenue reported in the income statement. In this section, we cover the impact on revenue of bill and hold transactions, job overbilling, and delaying the period-end cutoff date.

No discussion of inventory fraud would be complete without mentioning the concept of bill and hold. Someone wanting to commit fraud simply devises fake documentation that a customer is buying goods from the company, but does not want to take delivery on them yet, and so has asked the company to store them. In essence, revenues are being manufactured on goods that are still sitting in the warehouse.

Bill and hold transactions can be legitimate, but are subject to several restrictions under generally accepted accounting principles, given the obvious fraud risk. From the perspective of fraud prevention, the best bet is to simply prohibit all bill and hold transactions with a company policy.

Another way to derive revenue is to overload those jobs that are being billed on a cost reimbursement basis. The more inventory that can be charged to one of these jobs, the better, since reimbursement is essentially guaranteed, subject to customer review of the billing details. Fraud in this area can include all of the situations noted in the previous sections to increase the size of ending inventory – except now the same techniques are being applied to specific jobs. These tricks can include altering the standard overhead rate, labor rate, and scrap rate, as well as shifting administrative costs into a job and double charging for certain expenses. These activities might actually be considered standard practice in some industries, but will also earn a company a reputation for overbilling that may drive away customers.

The best way to avoid customer overbilling is to create a rigid policy regarding which costs are to be included in and excluded from jobs. Then back up the policy with continual audits of job records, along with severe actions against any employees caught boosting job costs. In essence, a company must take the position of the customer in reviewing which costs are to be applied to a job.

Yet another type of fraud that impacts revenue is delaying the closing date for a reporting period, thereby shifting revenues from the following period to the current period. In an environment where the bulk of all shipping is done in the last week of a month or quarter, the controller is usually under intense pressure to allow some shipments after midnight to be back dated into the previous day. In egregious situations, shipments for several subsequent *days* may be backdated. Back dating shipments in this manner might appear to be relatively innocuous when only a few shipments are involved. However, once the rest of the company understands that the controller will allow some leeway in this area, the number of back dated shipments will gradually increase, to the point where back dating becomes standard company practice.

Back dating deliveries is by far the most common of all types of revenue-related fraud, and is quite difficult to eradicate. The best bet for the controller is to adopt an uncompromising stance and never let *any* shipments be back dated, no matter what the circumstances may be. However, the controller will have to face down senior management over this issue from time to time, which requires considerable backbone. Another possibility is to send the internal audit staff to the shipping dock at midnight, to enforce a rigid cutoff for shipments. A less rigid approach is to release the financial statements within one day of month-end, thereby effectively shrinking the period over which back dating can be accomplished.

Inventory Theft

The more traditional view of inventory fraud is theft – in essence, the removal of goods from the premises. There are a number of ways in which this can be accomplished, of which the more common techniques are:

- *Walk out with the goods.* If the inventory storage facility is not surrounded by a fence, it is inordinately easy for someone to enter the warehouse from any direction and make off with inventory items. Alternatively, if fittings and fasteners are stored in the open in the production area, these items are also extremely easy to steal.

- *Declare a variance.* The receiving staff can remove items from a supplier delivery, and declare that the delivered quantity was lower than the amount ordered. This ploy is especially clever, since the loss is pinned on the supplier, rather than the company. The company's accounts payable staff will see that a lower quantity was received, and will take a corresponding deduction from the supplier's invoice.
- *Steal from a trailer.* When the warehouse facility is overcrowded or there is not enough receiving staff to unload trucks, trailers are stored in the yard next to the facility – sometimes for weeks. If so, and the trailers are not adequately guarded or locked, it can be exceedingly easy to steal goods from these trailers with little risk of detection.
- *Over-pick for kitting.* When materials are withdrawn from the warehouse for use in the production area, they are typically assembled into a kit and shifted in a container to the production area. A picker could collude with the production staff to remove more materials from stock than are needed, and then remove the excess amounts from the facility once they have cleared the warehouse fence.
- *Designate as scrap or rework.* Someone in the production area can designate goods in process to be scrap or rework. If so, the monitoring systems for scrap and rework inventory tend to be much more primitive than for the normal production process, which makes items easier to steal.

While it may appear simpler to engage in the theft of inventory than to modify inventory records to alter financial results, the amount physically stolen is usually not large. Despite the lesser monetary value of this type of theft, any quantities stolen can be a major problem when a company operates with only a small inventory reserve. In this case, even a slight hiccup in the on-hand inventory can cause major problems in the production process or in the timely fulfillment of customer orders. To combat these issues, here are several ways to keep inventory theft from occurring:

- *Warehouse fencing.* The most obvious control is to install a fence around the warehouse, with a gate only located at the front, which is monitored by a security camera. The fence should be high enough to prevent someone from climbing over it.
- *Monitor receiving variances.* Review the receiving shortages declared by the receiving staff, to see if there is a pattern of more variances being traceable to particular employees, or for particular types of goods.
- *Enhance yard security.* Install hefty locks on storage trailers, add guard patrols in the yard, and prominently display security cameras that monitor the area.
- *Secondary pick review.* Have a second person match picking authorizations to the amount picked, or have the production staff do the same before ac-

cepting kitted goods. However, this slows the flow of materials, and can be circumvented if employees are colluding to steal inventory.

- *Scrap trend analysis.* Monitor the amount of inventory declared to be scrap over multiple periods, to see if certain types of inventory are more likely to be declared scrap. Also enhance the systems used to subsequently monitor the disposition of scrap and rework items.

Common Fraud Risk Factors

There are a number of factors that make it more likely that inventory-related fraud will occur or is occurring in a business. These fraud risk factors include:

Nature of Items

- *Size and value.* If items that can be stolen are of high value in proportion to their size (such as diamonds), it is less risky to remove them from the premises. This is a particularly critical item if it is easy for employees to do so.
- *Ease of resale.* If there is a ready market for the resale of stolen goods (such as for most types of consumer electronics), this presents an increased temptation to engage in fraud.

Nature of Control Environment

- *Separation of duties.* The risk of fraud declines dramatically if multiple employees are involved in different phases of a transaction, since some fraud requires the collusion of at least two people. Thus, poorly-defined job descriptions and approval processes present a clear opportunity for fraud.
- *Safeguards.* When assets are physically protected, they are much less likely to be stolen. This can involve fencing around the inventory storage area, a locked bin for maintenance supplies and tools, security guard stations, an employee badge system, and similar solutions.
- *Documentation.* When there is no physical or electronic record of a transaction, employees can be reasonably assured of not being caught, and so are more likely to engage in fraud. This is also the case if there *is* documentation but records are easily modified.
- *Time off.* When a business requires its employees to take the full amount of allocated time off, this keeps them from continuing to hide ongoing cases of fraud, and so is a natural deterrent.
- *Related party transactions.* When there are numerous transactions with related parties, it is more likely that purchases and sales will be made at amounts that differ considerably from the market price.
- *Complexity.* When the nature of a company's business involves very complex transactions, and especially ones involving estimates, it is easier for employees to manipulate the results of these transactions to report better results than is really the case.

- *Dominance*. When a single individual is in a position to dominate the decisions of the management team, and especially when the board of directors is weak, this individual is more likely to engage in unsuitable behavior.
- *Turnover*. When there is a high level of turnover among the management team and among employees in general, the institutional memory regarding how transactions are processed is weakened, resulting in less attention to controls.
- *Auditing*. When there is no internal audit function, it is less likely that incorrect or inappropriate transactions will be spotted or corrected.

Pressures

- *Level of dissatisfaction*. If the work force is unhappy with the company, they will be more inclined to engage in fraud. Examples of such situations are when a layoff is imminent, benefits have been reduced, bonuses have been eliminated, promotions have been voided, and so forth.
- *Expectations*. When there is pressure from investors to report certain financial results, or by management to meet certain performance targets (perhaps to earn bonuses), or to meet balance sheet goals to qualify for debt financing, there is a high risk of financial reporting fraud.
- *Guarantees*. When the owners or members of management have guaranteed company debt, there will be strong pressure to report certain financial results in order to avoid triggering the guarantees.

Fraud Prevention Tactics

We have already noted a number of fraud prevention techniques in the earlier sections that were targeted at specific types of fraudulent transactions. In this section, we expand on the concept by addressing more generally-applicable fraud prevention tactics.

Pressures

A major fraud prevention tactic is to avoid imposing difficult stretch goals on the management team, especially when these goals are coupled with munificent bonus plans. When a person is presented with an extraordinarily difficult stretch goal, there will be a major temptation to engage in a small amount of financial tweaking to achieve the target, after which yet more tweaking will be needed to achieve a further set of outlandish goals. After a few reporting periods, a manager might find himself doing nothing but supporting a number of fraudulent activities to support a set of wildly overblown financial statements. Consequently, a key step in avoiding fraud is for senior management to pare back its expectations for the company to a reasonable level.

Another way to mitigate the pressure to engage in fraud is to adopt a conservative financing stance. This means using a higher proportion of equity to debt. By keeping the amount of debt at a conservative level, there is less pressure on management to tweak the company's results to ensure that loan covenants are met. This approach also reduces the need for any members of management to guarantee company debt.

Detection

An intelligent scammer will maintain a low level of fraud that operates below the detection thresholds that a company's controls are designed to locate. It is still possible to discern these situations through the use of random audits of all transaction sizes. However, a reasonable case can be made that these situations are not worth the trouble to locate, since the cost of detection may exceed the amount of fraud losses discovered.

A more critical detection target is to have a system in place for locating major fraud transactions, especially those that span a number of reporting periods, and which are therefore cumulatively significant. A combination of the following detection techniques should be considered:

- *Trend line analysis*. The simplest possible way to detect fraud is through a long-running analysis of financial trends. This means plotting the balances in all inventory accounts and the cost of goods sold over time, coupled with a detailed investigation of any spikes or declines in these trends. The analysis should span a long period of time, going back a number of years. By adopting a long-term review, it is more likely that the examination will spot a long-running case of fraud by revealing cost trends before the fraud began. For example, a trend line analysis could spot a decline in the ratio of obsolete inventory expense to the total inventory investment, which could be caused by a fraudulent attempt to avoid recognizing this major expense.
- *Audit committee*. Give employees easy access to the audit committee, which is comprised entirely of members of the board of directors. By keeping the company's managers out of the audit committee, employees are more likely to find a receptive audience when they report on a case of fraud, rather than reporting the information to the person committing the fraud.
- *Anonymous reporting*. Employees may be frightened of the consequences of reporting their bosses for fraudulent activity. If so, create a system for anonymous reporting to the audit committee, so that the person submitting information is not identified.

Centralization

Inventory fraud is vastly more difficult to accomplish when the underlying inventory records are stored in a place where a person cannot alter them. This can be accomplished by installing a centralized data processing system, where the corporate information technology center is physically located away from operations, and is not under the control of local managers. By taking this approach, senior corporate management is more likely to have change logs and backup databases available that can be used to track down anomalies that could be related to fraudulent transactions.

Similarly, if local employees know that evidence of their fraud is being stored elsewhere, they will be less likely to engage in it.

Summary

The main take-away from this chapter is that there are a frightening number of ways in which fraudulent inventory transactions can be introduced into a company. The usual response to these potential actions is to implement a comprehensive list of controls that can either detect or prevent fraud. However, a large set of these controls can be downright oppressive, interfering with the accounting and other functions of a business. Consequently, the need to maintain a reasonably efficient company may result in the paring back of some recommended controls. If so, at least pay attention to the presence of fraud risk factors, and create an environment where there is no need for employees to even contemplate the possibility of engaging in fraud.

Chapter 21
Inventory Policies

Introduction

It may be useful to support an inventory accounting system with a set of policies. Such policies are intended to enforce the need for certain actions at various places in the accounting system, to ensure that inventory records are properly updated and valued. In the following section, we describe a number of inventory policies and the circumstances under which they can be supportive.

Inventory Policies

In this section, we outline 15 policies that can be useful to the accountant in creating formal systems. The policies are roughly organized in order from the receipt of goods, through counting, record updates, and product sales. Not all of these policies will be applicable in all cases – for example, the policies relating to accounting standards are of no use if an organization does not employ a standard costing system.

Receiving Policy

A company may find that its purchasing practices are so loose that it is receiving more goods than were formally ordered by the purchasing department. There may also be instances where suppliers are deliberately shipping more goods than were ordered, and yet other cases where goods are fraudulently shipped on the flimsiest of excuses and then overbilled. If these issues arise regularly, a policy can be implemented that requires the receiving staff to reject all orders that are not accompanied by a valid purchase order number. For example:

> All deliveries to the company shall be rejected if they are not accompanied by an open purchase order. Also, any excess amounts delivered shall be rejected, at the discretion of the receiving department.

The receiving staff is not always happy about enforcing this policy, for it can make them unpopular figures within the company. For example, there may have been a rush order that was informally made by a department manager to deal with an emergency situation; a purchase order was not obtained for the order, so the receiving department rejects the delivery. Given this type of issue, the receiving staff is more likely to set such deliveries aside and investigate whether a valid purchase was made, rather than rejecting the deliveries at once.

Another issue with this policy is that it requires the issuance of an authorizing purchase order. Using purchase orders for every conceivable purchase is not an effective use of the purchasing department's time, and may be discouraged in favor of more streamlined techniques. If so, the receiving staff may find that this policy only functions for higher-cost deliveries.

Point of Ownership Policy

Some shipping terms state that the buyer takes title to goods as soon as they leave the seller's premises, while other shipping terms extend the seller's ownership until goods arrive at the buyer's location. The following policy variations are intended to clarify when the accounting for inventory ownership begins and ends:

> [Receiving policy] The company records ownership of goods at the receiving dock, unless the terms associated with a delivery from a supplier mandate earlier ownership.

> [Shipping policy] The company shall stop recognizing inventory and recognize revenue when goods are shipped, unless the terms associated with a delivery to a customer mandate a later transfer of ownership.

For the latter policy, the revenue recognition requirements of the accounting standards may mandate that revenue is actually recognized quite a bit later than the point of shipment, particularly if customer acceptance is involved.

Responsibility for Inventory Policy

When there is a strong intent to increase the accuracy of inventory records, there can be a problem with pinning down who is responsible for accuracy failings. Since inventory storage can span several departments and be handled by employees in several areas, there can be a "blame game" regarding how record accuracy is falling short of expectations. We advocate assigning responsibility to the materials manager, who is responsible for purchasing, materials handling, and the warehouse. The following policy locks down this responsibility:

> The materials manager is responsible for inventory record accuracy throughout the company.

Inventory Access Policy

The accuracy of the inventory records must be sacrosanct. In addition, the incidence of inventory theft must be kept to a minimum. Both goals can be achieved by instituting a standard policy of only allowing authorized persons in inventory storage areas. The concept can be extended to restrict access to the inventory records in the computer system. Sample policies are:

> Only authorized warehouse personnel are allowed access to the warehouse area. Non-authorized personnel must be accompanied by a warehouse staff person when accessing the warehouse area.

Only authorized personnel are allowed access to inventory records. Access passwords for the record-keeping system shall be changed as soon as an authorized person leaves the employment of the company.

The first policy is difficult to enforce if a large part of the raw materials are stored in bins adjacent to the production area, as is common in a just-in-time production environment. If significant and unexplained inventory shrinkage occurs in these areas, it may be necessary to shift the inventory back to the more secure warehouse area.

Inventory Owned by Third Parties Policy

When suppliers and customers store their inventory at the company's location, there is a significant risk that these items will be mixed into the company's own inventory. If so, it is entirely possible that costs will be inadvertently assigned to these items, thereby incorrectly boosting the ending inventory valuation. The following policy deals with the issue by segregating this type of inventory:

Goods owned by a third party shall be stored in a separate area and prominently labeled with the name of the rightful owner.

Consigned Inventory Identification Policy

When a company sends its inventory to third parties on a consignment basis, there is a risk that these items will be removed from the company's inventory tracking system and treated as a sale. If so, sales are inflated by the amount of the shipment, while the company also loses track of its inventory. The following policy is intended to rectify the situation:

Inventory intended for consignment shall be identified as such in the shipping log, inventory tracking system, and shipping documentation sent to the accounting department.

Physical Count Policy

When a company does not have entirely accurate inventory records, its reported results may be questionable, given the inaccuracy of the ending inventory valuation. This situation can be resolved by mandating a physical inventory count at certain intervals. The following policy states the intervals at which physical counts are required, and is useful for ensuring that these counts are scheduled and conducted.

A physical inventory count shall be conducted at the end of each fiscal quarter.

Cycle Counting Policy

Senior management may want to implement cycle counting, but finds that in practice, cycle counting is given low priority by the warehouse staff. If so, it can be useful to create the following policy, which clarifies the importance of this activity to the warehouse manager:

> A system of cycle counting reviews shall be conducted every day, with the goal of examining the entire inventory at least __ times per year.

Inventory Record Access Policy

The inventory records may be rendered inaccurate by the participation of too many unqualified employees in the recordation activity. The same concern applies to bill of material records and the item master database. This situation can be resolved by locking down access to these records and only allowing fully-qualified staff access to them. The following policy clarifies the situation:

> Only designated employees are allowed access to the inventory record database, item master, and bill of material records, for which restricted computer access is mandated.

Bill of Material Updates Policy

When standard costing is used as the basis for inventory valuation, it is of critical importance that all manufactured goods have an associated bill of materials, and that this bill be updated immediately when there are changes to the product. Otherwise, it will not be possible to assign accurate costs (if any) to products. The following policies address these concerns:

> A complete and reviewed bill of material shall be issued whenever a new or revised product is released to production.

> The associated bill of materials shall be revised at the same time an engineering change order is released, containing all revisions mandated by the change order.

> Whenever there are changes to the production process that impact the cost of a product, these changes shall be updated in the impacted bill of materials.

Standard Costing Updates Policy

If a standard costing system is used, it is of some importance to closely align these costs with actual costs, so that variances between the two are kept to a manageable minimum. The following policy is intended to mandate the maximum time interval that may pass before a formal standard costing update must be conducted. The second part of the policy is intended to require more frequent updates for those costs involved in a high proportion of the total inventory valuation.

> All standard costs shall be reviewed and updated no less than once a year. In addition, all major commodity costs shall be examined at least once a quarter, and updated as necessary.

Lower of Cost or Market Updates

There should be a regular comparison of the carrying amounts and market values of inventory items, to ensure that the lower of cost or market rule is being followed. This step can be included in the month-end closing procedure, but can also be bolstered by the following policy statement:

> A lower of cost or market analysis shall be conducted at least annually for all inventory items having material balances.

The policy clause regarding "material balances" is inserted in order to focus the analysis on only those inventory items whose adjustment will have a material impact on the financial statements.

Obsolete Inventory Updates

There should be a regular program of reviews to detect obsolete inventory, which can then be written off in the financial statements. The following policy is intended to encourage these reviews:

> The materials review board shall conduct a search for obsolete inventory on at least a quarterly basis.

Bill and Hold Policy

The management team may be tempted to offer bill and hold terms to customers, whereby the company stores goods for them in exchange for booking the related sale in the current period. Though allowed under generally accepted accounting principles under restrictive conditions, this can be an especially pernicious practice, for management will be tempted to use it to accelerate sales on a regular basis. The result can be channel stuffing, where customers are persuaded to accept goods that they would not normally purchase in exchange for unusually favorable terms. Doing so results in a short-term boost in sales, followed by a sharp decline when customers stop ordering in favor of using up their existing stocks. In general, we recommend not using the bill and hold concept at all. The following policy can be used to forbid its practice:

> The company shall not engage in bill and hold activities; that is, revenues cannot be recognized until the associated goods have been shipped to the customer.

Collections Take-Back Policy

When the collections department contacts a customer about an overdue account receivable, one collection option may be to take back goods sold to a customer, in settlement of the outstanding debt. However, this approach only works if the goods retain sufficient value to be resold at an adequate price to a third party. Consequently, it may be necessary to have a policy that either allows or restricts the take-back of goods. Allowing a take-back is most viable when the gross margin on goods sold is quite high, so that even a re-sale of the goods at a substantially reduced price will still earn back the cost of the goods. Conversely, if the margin is low, reselling at a reduced price means that the company will assuredly lose money on a take-back. A sample policy is:

> The collections staff can only authorize the take-back of inventory from customers with the concurrence of the sales manager, who must consider the resale value of the goods in question and the probability of collection from the customer.

This policy can be designed to leave some wiggle room for the collections staff, so they can still offer a take-back, but only as a last resort after all other options have been investigated. This situation occurs when the company will otherwise experience a total loss on a receivable, and can at least reduce the loss through the return of inventory.

Summary

The many inventory policies described in this chapter do not all have to be formally implemented. In many companies, the issues targeted by these policies are already being handled in a perfectly competent manner, and do not require formalization. Doing so merely clutters up the corporate policies and procedures manual and introduces an excessive amount of bureaucracy to an organization. Instead, consider rolling out one of these policies when management wants to lend particular emphasis to an initiative, or wants to point out to employees that improvement is expected in a certain area.

Chapter 22
Inventory Budgeting

Introduction

The accountant is likely to be involved in the construction of the annual budget. If so, a significant component of that budget involves the planning for inventory expenditures and ending inventory balances. The areas of the budget that incorporate some elements of inventory are the production budget, ending finished goods inventory budget, and direct materials budget. In this chapter, we describe the components of each of these budgets, as well as the issues to consider when setting inventory levels and estimating inventory costs. Issues addressed include production constraints, customer service levels, seasonality, and working capital reduction efforts.

The Production Budget

The production budget calculates the number of units of products that must be manufactured, and is derived from a combination of the sales forecast and the planned amount of finished goods inventory to have on hand (usually as safety stock to cover unexpected increases in demand). The production budget is typically presented in either a monthly or quarterly format. The basic calculation used by the production budget is:

> + Forecasted unit sales
> + Planned finished goods ending inventory balance
> = Total production required
>
> - Beginning finished goods inventory
> = Units to be manufactured

It can be very difficult to create a comprehensive production budget that incorporates a forecast for every variation on a product that a company sells, so it is customary to aggregate the forecast information into broad categories of products that have similar characteristics.

The planned amount of ending finished goods inventory can be subject to a certain amount of debate, since having too much may lead to obsolete inventory that must be disposed of at a loss, while having too little inventory can result in lost sales when customers want immediate delivery. Unless a company is planning to draw down its inventory quantities and terminate a product, there is generally a need for some ending finished goods inventory. The calculation of the production budget is illustrated in the following example.

EXAMPLE

Quest Adventure Gear plans to produce an array of plastic water bottles for the upcoming budget year. Its production needs are as follows:

	Quarter 1	Quarter 2	Quarter 3	Quarter 4
Forecast unit sales	5,500	6,000	7,000	8,000
+ Planned ending inventory units	500	500	500	500
= Total production required	6,000	6,500	7,500	8,500
- Beginning finished goods inventory	-1,000	-500	-500	-500
= Units to be manufactured	5,000	6,000	7,000	8,000

The planned ending finished goods inventory at the end of each quarter declines from an initial 1,000 units to 500 units, since the materials manager believes that the company is maintaining too much finished goods inventory. Consequently, the plan calls for a decline from 1,000 units of ending finished goods inventory at the end of the first quarter to 500 units by the end of the second quarter, despite a projection for rising sales. This may be a risky forecast, since the amount of safety stock on hand is being cut while production volume increases by over 30 percent. Given the size of the projected inventory decline, there is a fair chance that Quest will be forced to increase the amount of ending finished goods inventory later in the year.

The production budget deals entirely with unit volumes; it does not translate its production requirements into dollars. Instead, the unit requirements of the budget are shifted into other parts of the budget, such as the direct materials budget, which are then translated into dollars.

Other Production Budget Issues

So far, we have only addressed the mechanical formulation of the production budget. In addition, we must consider whether it is even *possible* to achieve the production volumes stated in this budget. As noted in this section, there are several constraints to consider, and which may require some alteration of the planned units of production.

When formulating the production budget, it is useful to consider the impact of proposed production on the capacity of any bottleneck operations in the production area. It is entirely possible that some production requirements will not be achievable given the production constraints, so the company will either have to scale back on production requirements, invest in more fixed assets, or outsource the work. The following example illustrates the issue.

EXAMPLE

Quest Adventure Gear revises the production budget described in the preceding example to incorporate the usage of a bottleneck machine in its manufacturing area. The revised format follows, beginning with the last row of information from the preceding example:

	Quarter 1	Quarter 2	Quarter 3	Quarter 4
Units to be manufactured	5,000	6,000	7,000	8,000
× Minutes of bottleneck time/unit	15	15	15	15
= Planned bottleneck usage (minutes)	75,000	90,000	105,000	120,000
- Available bottleneck time (minutes)*	110,160	110,160	110,160	110,160
= Remaining available time (minutes)	35,160	20,160	5,160	-9,840

* Calculated as 90 days × 24 hours × 60 minutes × 85% up time = 110,160 minutes

The table reveals that there is not enough bottleneck time available to meet the planned production level in the fourth quarter. However, Quest can increase production in earlier quarters to make up the shortfall, since there is adequate capacity available at the bottleneck in the earlier periods.

Note in the preceding example that the amount of available bottleneck time was set at 85 percent of the maximum possible amount of time available. We make such assumptions because of the inevitable amount of downtime associated with equipment maintenance, unavailable raw materials, scrapped production, and so forth. The 85 percent figure is only an example – the real amount may be somewhat higher or substantially lower.

One should also determine the impact of the production budget on the need for skilled production labor. This is a particular problem in custom-manufacturing environments, where it may take years of training before a person is fully qualified to engage in certain types of production. This issue can seriously constrain a company's production plans. One can model the need for additional production staff using the same model just used for a bottleneck machine, simply by assuming that the bottleneck is staff time, rather than a machine.

The availability of raw materials may keep a business from attaining the production level stated in the production budget. This can be an issue where there are few suppliers, or where supplies are located in areas where political issues or customs controls restrict the availability of supplies. If so, the procurement staff may need to stockpile the necessary materials or find alternative suppliers, or the engineering staff can redesign products that use other materials. Otherwise, raw material constraints will interfere with the production budget.

Yet another issue impacting the production budget is the need to incur step costs when production exceeds a certain volume level. For example, a company may need to open a new production facility, production line, or work shift to accommodate any additional increase in production past a certain amount of volume. It may be possible to adjust the production schedule to accelerate production in slow periods in order to stockpile inventory and avoid such step costs in later periods.

A less common problem is when the planned amount of ending inventory increases to the point where a business must invest an inordinate amount of working capital in the additional inventory. Once management realizes the amount of the extra investment involved, it may elect to plan for less ending inventory than it might consider ideal. This problem may not arise during the initial formulation of the production budget, since financing requirements are compiled later in the budgeting process. If it eventually becomes apparent that there is a problem, it will be necessary to adjust the ending finished goods inventory budget (as noted later in this chapter), which feeds into the production budget, to reduce the amount of ending inventory.

All of the factors noted in this section are major concerns, and should be considered when evaluating the viability of a production budget.

Budgeting for Multiple Products

The production budget shown thus far has centered on the manufacture of a single product. How can a production budget be created if there are multiple products? The worst solution is to attempt to re-create in the budget a variation on the production schedule for the entire budget period – the level of detail required to do so would be inordinately high. Instead, consider one of the following alternatives:

- *Bottleneck focus*. Rather than focusing on the production of a variety of products, only budget for the amount of time that they require at the bottleneck operation. For example, rather than focusing on the need to manufacture every aspect of 20 different products, focus on the time that each product needs at a single production operation. If there are multiple production lines or facilities, only budget for usage of the bottleneck at each location.
- *Product line focus*. In many cases, there are only modest differences in the production activities needed to create any product within a product line. If there are such production commonalities, consider treating the entire production line as a single product with common production requirements.
- *80/20 rule*. It is likely that only a small number of products comprise most of a company's production volume. If this is case, consider detailed budgeting for the production of the 20 percent of all products that typically comprise 80 percent of all sales, and a vastly reduced (and aggregated) amount of budgeting for the remaining products.
- *MRP II planning*. If a company uses a manufacturing requirements planning (MRP II) system, the software may contain a planning module that allows for the inputting of production requirement estimates, which then generates detailed requirements for machine usage, direct labor, and direct materials. If so, input the totals from this module into the budget without also copying in all of the supporting details.

None of the preceding suggestions for multi-product budgeting is perfect (with the possible exception of the MRP II planning module), but one of them or a variation on them should be sufficient to yield a reasonable version of a production budget.

Ending Inventory Concepts

A line item in the preceding production budget required the input of "planned ending inventory units." This is the amount of inventory that management wants to have on hand at the end of each budgeted period. This planned figure can be a simple calculation of beginning inventory levels, plus production, minus sales. However, there are a number of conceptual issues that should be considered that may result in a budgeted ending inventory figure that is substantially different from this simple calculation. Consider the following items:

- *Customer service.* If management wants to improve customer service, one way to do so is to increase the amount of ending inventory, which allows the company to fulfill customer orders more quickly and avoid backorder situations. This can be accomplished by either a gradual or more forced increase in the planned amount of ending inventory.
- *Inventory record accuracy.* If the inventory record keeping system is inaccurate, it is necessary to maintain additional amounts of inventory on hand, both of raw materials and finished goods, to ensure that customer orders are fulfilled on time. If the level of inventory accuracy can be upgraded, there is less need to keep additional stocks on hand.
- *Manufacturing planning.* If a manufacturing resources planning (MRP II) system is being used, then the company is producing in accordance with a sales and production plan, which requires a certain amount of both raw materials and finished goods inventory. If there is a change to the just-in-time (JIT) manufacturing planning system, then the business is only producing to specific customer requirements, which tends to reduce the need for inventory. Thus, a switch from an MRP II to a JIT system can result in lower inventory levels.
- *Product life cycles.* If there are certain products or even entire product lines that a company is planning to terminate, factor the related inventory reductions into the amount of planned ending inventory. However, a product termination is frequently coupled with the introduction of a replacement product, which may require *more* on-hand inventory to meet the higher demand levels that are common with a new product. Thus, there can be offsetting product life cycle issues that can impact inventory levels.
- *Product versions.* If the sales and marketing staff want to offer a product in a number of versions, the business may need to keep a certain amount of each type of inventory in stock. Thus, an increase in the number of product versions equates to an increase in ending inventory, and vice versa.
- *Seasonal sales.* If a company experiences very high sales volume at certain times of the year, it may be more practical to gradually build inventory levels over several months leading up to the prime sales season, rather than

attempting to do so over a short period of time. This means that a gradual increase in the amount of ending inventory should be planned, followed by a sharp decline in inventory levels immediately after the selling season.

- *Supply chain duration.* If there is a plan to switch to a supplier located far away from the company, be aware that this calls for having a larger safety stock of finished goods on hand, so that deliveries to customers will not be impacted if there is a problem in receiving goods on time from the supplier. This is a common problem, as many companies have switched to lower-cost foreign suppliers. Conversely, switching to a supplier located nearby can compress the delivery distance so much that one can safely lower the amount of ending inventory to reflect the reduced risk of not receiving deliveries on a timely basis.

- *Working capital reduction.* If management wants to increase the amount of inventory turnover, this reduces the amount of cash invested in working capital, but also has the offsetting effect of leaving less inventory in reserve to cover sudden surges in customer orders. There is a general trend toward increased inventory turnover.

All of the preceding factors can have an impact on the amount of planned ending inventory. If more than one factor is impacting a business, there may be conflicting issues that make it more difficult to plan ending inventory levels. For example, a switch to a JIT system would likely reduce inventory, but a management decision to keep more inventory on hand for faster customer order fulfillment would have an opposite effect. Consequently, it can be difficult to sort through the differing issues to arrive at an appropriate level of planned ending inventory.

If the ending finished goods inventory level is being deliberately altered because of any of the preceding issues, be sure to document the associated reasoning and include it in the notes attached to the budget, so that users of the budget understand the reasons for the change.

Impact of Changes in Ending Inventory

The amount of inventory shown in the ending inventory budget impacts a number of other elements of a company's budget. In particular, be aware of the following issues:

- *Inventory increase.* If the amount of ending inventory is increased, the production budget must include a ramp-up in production costs, which in turn will require a greater expenditure for direct materials, and possibly an investment in more fixed assets to increase the capacity of the production line. Higher purchasing volumes may allow the procurement staff to obtain some direct materials at a lower cost. The greater investment in inventory will also require more working capital, which can increase the company's need for additional financing.

- *Inventory decrease.* If the amount of ending inventory is reduced, the planned amount of production will decline. This may require the layoff of some direct labor employees, with attendant severance expenses. Lower purchasing volumes may require the procurement staff to buy goods at higher prices. The reduced investment in inventory will shrink the amount of working capital needed, which may in turn reduce the need for any additional financing. Reducing inventory levels tends to make obsolete inventory items more apparent, so there may be an increased cost of goods sold related to the recognition of obsolete inventory.

The Ending Finished Goods Inventory Budget

The ending finished goods inventory budget states the number of units of finished goods inventory at the end of each budget period. It also calculates the cost of finished goods inventory. The amount of this inventory tends to be similar from period to period, assuming that the production department manufactures to meet demand levels in each budget period. However, and as noted in the "Ending Inventory Concepts" section, there are a variety of reasons for altering the amount of ending finished goods inventory. If so, it is useful to create separate layers of ending inventory in the budget that reflect each of the decisions made, so that readers of the budget can see the numerical impact of operational decisions.

In the following example, we assume that changes made in the immediately preceding budget period will continue to have the same impact on inventory in the *next* budget period, so that the adjusted ending inventory in the last period will be the starting point for our adjustments in the next period. We can then make the following adjustments to the unadjusted ending inventory level to arrive at an adjusted ending inventory:

- *Internal systems changes*. Shows the impact of altering the manufacturing system, such as changing from an MRP II to a JIT system.
- *Financing changes*. Shows the impact of altering inventory levels in order to influence the amount of working capital used.
- *Product changes*. Shows the impact of product withdrawals and product introductions.
- *Seasonal changes*. Shows the impact of building inventory for seasonal sales, followed by a decline after the selling season has concluded.
- *Service changes*. Shows the impact of changing inventory levels in order to alter order fulfillment rates.

If management is attempting to reduce the company's investment in inventory, it may mandate such a large drop in ending inventory that the company will not realistically be able to operate without significant production and shipping interruptions. These situations can be spotted by including the budgeted inventory turnover level in each budget period, as well as the actual amount of turnover in the corresponding period in the preceding year. This is shown in the following example as the historical actual days of inventory, followed by the planned days of inventory for the budget period. Comparing the two measurements may reveal large period-to-period changes, which management should examine to see if it is really possible to reduce inventory levels to such an extent.

EXAMPLE

Quest Adventure Gear has a division that sells electronic signaling devices for lost hikers. Quest wants to incorporate the following changes into its calculation of the ending finished goods inventory:

1. Switch from the MRP II to the JIT manufacturing system in the second quarter, which will decrease inventory by 250 units.
2. Reduce inventory by 500 units in the first quarter to reduce working capital requirements.
3. Add 500 units to inventory in the third quarter as part of the rollout of a new product.
4. Build inventory in the first three quarters by 100 units per quarter in anticipation of seasonal sales in the fourth quarter.
5. Increase on-hand inventory by 400 units in the second quarter to improve the speed of customer order fulfillment for a specific product.

The ending finished goods inventory unit and cost calculation follows:

(units)	Quarter 1	Quarter 2	Quarter 3	Quarter 4
Unadjusted ending inventory level	2,000	1,600	1,850	2,450
+/- Internal system changes	0	-250	0	0
+/- Financing changes	-500	0	0	0
+/- Product changes	0	0	500	0
+/- Seasonal changes	100	100	100	-300
+/- Service changes	0	400	0	0
Adjusted ending inventory	1,600	1,850	2,450	2,150
× Standard cost per unit	$45	$45	$45	$45
Total ending inventory cost	$72,000	$83,250	$110,250	$96,750
Historical actual days of inventory	100	108	135	127
Planned days of inventory	92	106	130	114

The days of inventory calculation at the bottom of the table shows few differences from actual experience in the second and third quarters, but the differences are greater in the first and fourth quarters. Management should review its ability to achieve the indicated inventory reductions in those quarters.

The ending finished goods inventory budget shown in the preceding example is quite simplistic, for it assumes that the same inventory policies and systems are to be applied to a company's *entire* inventory. For example, this means that management wants to increase inventory levels for *all* types of inventory in order to increase customer order fulfillment speeds, when in fact there may only be a need to do this for a relatively small part of the inventory.

To adjust inventory levels at a finer level of detail, consider creating a budget that sets inventory levels by business unit or product line. It is generally too time-consuming to set inventory levels at the individual product level, especially if demand at this level is difficult to predict.

Direct Materials Budgeting Overview

Direct materials are those materials and supplies consumed during the manufacture of a product, and which are directly identified with that product. Direct materials can be a large proportion of the total costs of a company, so it is critical to be especially careful when constructing the direct materials budget. The following sections present three ways to compile a direct materials budget – either by rolling up costs based on production estimates and bills of material, or by extrapolating historical costs into the budget period, or by a combination of the two. We also address several anomalies to be aware of when creating this budget.

The Direct Materials Budget (Roll up Method)

The direct materials budget calculates the materials that must be purchased, by time period, in order to fulfill the requirements of the production budget, and is typically presented in either a monthly or quarterly format. The basic calculation for the roll up method is to multiply the estimated amount of sales (in units) in each reporting period by the standard cost of each item to arrive at the standard amount of direct materials cost expected for each product. Standard costs are derived from the bill of materials for each product. A bill of materials is the record of the materials used to construct a product. A sample calculation is:

Sample Calculation of the Cost of Direct Materials

	Quarter 1	Quarter 2	Quarter 3	Quarter 4
Product A				
Units	100	120	110	90
Standard cost/each	$14.25	$14.25	$14.25	$14.25
Total cost	$1,425	$1,710	$1,568	$1,283
Product B				
Units	300	350	375	360
Standard cost/each	$8.40	$8.40	$8.40	$8.40
Total cost	$2,520	$2,940	$3,150	$3,024
Grand total cost	$3,945	$4,650	$4,718	$4,307

Note that the preceding example only addressed the direct materials *expense* during the budget period. It did not address the amount of materials that should be purchased during the period; doing so requires that the planned amounts of beginning and ending inventory also be factored into the calculation. The calculation used for direct material purchases is:

+ Raw materials required for production
+ Planned ending inventory balance
= Total raw materials required

- Beginning raw materials inventory
= Raw materials to be purchased

The presence or absence of a beginning inventory can have a major impact on the amount of direct materials needed during a budget period – in some cases, there may be so much inventory already on hand that a company does not need to purchase any additional direct materials at all. In other cases, and especially where management wants to build the amount of ending inventory (as arises when a company is preparing for a seasonal sales surge), it may be necessary to purchase far more direct materials than are indicated by sales requirements in just a single budget period. The following example illustrates how beginning and ending inventory levels can alter direct material requirements.

EXAMPLE

Quest Adventure Gear plans to produce a variety of large-capacity water coolers for camping, and 98% of the raw materials required for this production involve plastic resin. Thus, there is only one key commodity to be concerned with. The production needs of Quest for the resin commodity are shown in the following direct materials budget:

	Quarter 1	Quarter 2	Quarter 3	Quarter 4
Product A (units to produce)	5,000	6,000	7,000	8,000
× Resin/unit (lbs)	2	2	2	2
= Total resin needed (lbs)	10,000	12,000	14,000	16,000
+ Planned ending inventory	2,000	2,400	2,800	3,200
= Total resin required	12,000	14,400	16,800	19,200
- Beginning inventory	1,600	2,000	2,400	2,800
= Resin to be purchased	10,400	12,400	14,400	16,400
Resin cost per pound	$0.50	$0.50	$0.55	$0.55
Total resin cost to purchase	$5,200	$6,200	$7,920	$9,020

The planned ending inventory at the end of each quarter is planned to be 20% of the amount of resin used during that month, so the ending inventory varies over time, gradually increasing as production requirements increase. The reason for the planned increase is that Quest has some difficulty receiving resin in a timely manner from its supplier, so it maintains a safety stock of inventory on hand.

The purchasing department expects that global demand will drive up the price of resin, so it incorporates a slight price increase into the third quarter, which carries forward into the fourth quarter.

It is impossible to calculate the direct materials budget for every component in inventory, since the calculation would be massive. Instead, it is customary to either calculate the *approximate* cost of direct materials required, or else at a somewhat more detailed level by commodity type (see the later discussion of the 80/20 method). It is possible to create a reasonably accurate direct materials budget by either means, if there is a material requirements planning software package that has a planning module. If the production budget is entered into the planning module, the software can generate the expected direct materials budget for future periods. Otherwise, the budget must be calculated manually.

If the roll up method is used, the unit volume of materials is being based on the quantities listed in the bill of materials for each item. It is a fundamental principle of materials management that the information in bills of material be as accurate as possible, since the materials management department relies on this information to purchase materials and schedule production. However, what if the bill of materials information is incorrect, even if only by a small amount? Then, under the roll up method, that incorrect amount will be multiplied by the number of units to be produced in the budget period, which can result in quite a large error in the amount of materials used in the budget. If management is intent upon using the roll up method, it is difficult to avoid this problem, other than by scheduling periodic audits of the bills of material to verify their accuracy.

The Direct Materials Budget (Historical Method)

In a typical business environment, there may be a multitude of factors that impact the amount of direct materials as a percentage of sales, including scrap, spoilage, rework, purchasing quantities, and volatility in commodity prices. Many companies are unable to accurately capture these factors in their bills of material, which makes it nearly impossible for them to create a reliable direct materials budget using the roll up method that was described in the last section.

In such cases, an alternative budget calculation is the historical method, under which it is assumed that the historical amount of direct materials, as a percentage of revenues, will continue to be the case during the budget period. This approach means that the historical percentage of direct material costs is simply copied forward, with additional line items to account for any budgeted changes in key assumptions.

Under the historical method, adjust the projected amount of sales for any increase or decrease in production that is required for planned changes in the amount of ending inventory, and express the result as adjusted revenue. Then multiply the adjusted revenue figure by the historical percentage of direct materials to arrive at the total direct materials cost required to achieve the production budget. Despite the need for these adjustments, it is still much easier to create a direct materials budget using the historical method than by using the roll up method.

EXAMPLE

Quest Adventure Gear finds that its last direct materials budget, which was created using the roll up method, did not come anywhere near actual results. This year, Quest wants to use the historical method instead, using the historical direct materials rate of 32% of revenues as the basis for the budget. To avoid having the company become complacent and not work toward lower direct material costs, the budget also includes adjustment factors that are expected from several improvement projects. There is also an adjustment factor that addresses a likely change in the mix of products to be sold during the budget period. The budget model is:

	Quarter 1	Quarter 2	Quarter 3	Quarter 4
Projected revenue	$4,200,000	$5,000,000	$5,750,000	$8,000,000
+/- planned ending inventory change	-400,000	+100,000	+250,000	-350,000
Adjusted revenue	$3,800,000	$5,100,000	$6,000,000	$7,650,000
Historical direct materials percentage	27.1%	27.1%	27.1%	27.1%
+ / - Adjustment for product mix	+3.4%	+4.0%	+1.8%	-0.9%
- Adjustment for scrap reduction	0.0%	0.0%	-0.2%	-0.2%
- Adjustment for rework reduction	0.0%	-0.1%	-0.1%	-0.1%
= Adjusted direct materials percentage	30.5%	31.0%	28.6%	25.9%
Total direct materials cost	$1,159,000	$1,581,000	$1,716,000	$1,981,350

The problem with the historical method is that it is based on a certain mix of products that were sold in the past, each possibly with a different proportion of direct materials to sales. It is unlikely that the same mix of products will continue to be sold through the budget period; thus, applying a historical percentage to a future period may yield an incorrect direct materials cost. This issue can be mitigated by including an adjustment factor in the budget (as was shown in the preceding example), which modifies the historical percentage for what is expected to be the future mix of product sales.

The Direct Materials Budget (80/20 Method)

The Pareto principle holds that about 80 percent of the effects come from 20 percent of the causes. Or, stated in terms of direct materials, it can be expected that 80 percent of all direct material costs come from 20 percent of the materials used in a company's products. The Pareto principle can be used as the basis for engaging in the detailed budgeting of 20 percent of all materials; then cluster the remaining 80 percent of materials used into a lump sum that is estimated in a more general manner, such as by a historical average. We call this the 80/20 method.

The 80/20 method is derived from the two preceding methods, because the roll up method is used to derive the amount of those direct materials comprising 80 percent of costs, and the historical method to estimate the remaining amount of materials. It is common to find that commodity purchases are heavily represented in the roll up portion of this budget, since these items typically comprise a large part of the cost of a product.

The effort required to create the direct materials budget using this method is about midway between the requirements of the other two models, since it includes elements of both. The 80/20 method is used in the following example.

EXAMPLE

Quest Adventure Gear has created a new division that produces lightweight equipment for extreme adventure racers. Quest is using the 80/20 method to derive the direct materials budget for this division. Rip stop nylon and webbing are the key commodities used in the products of this division, and so are included in the roll up portion of the budget. There are a large number of other materials whose cost is calculated in a lump sum, using the historical percentage method. The purchasing department expects to be able to centralize purchases with a smaller number of suppliers as the year progresses, thereby achieving a 0.1% reduction in non-commodity costs in each quarter after the first quarter.

	Quarter 1	Quarter 2	Quarter 3	Quarter 4
Adjusted revenue	$451,500	$471,600	$503,850	$506,250
Direct materials – roll up method				
Rip stop nylon (square yards)	10,000	10,250	10,000	9,900
Rip stop nylon unit price	$8.00	$8.00	$9.00	$9.00
Rip stop nylon total cost	$80,000	$82,000	$90,000	$89,100
Webbing (feet)	10,250	10,625	10,250	10,125
Webbing unit price	$4.00	$4.00	$4.00	$4.00
Webbing total cost	$41,000	$42,500	$41,000	$40,500
Total direct materials – roll up method	$121,000	$124,500	$131,000	$129,600
Direct materials – historical method				
Historical direct materials percentage	6.7%	6.7%	6.7%	6.7%
+/- Adjustments	0.0%	-0.1%	-0.2%	-0.3%
= Adjusted direct materials percentage	6.7%	6.6%	6.5%	6.4%
Total direct materials – historical method	$30,250	$31,125	$32,750	$32,400
Grand total direct materials	$151,250	$155,625	$163,750	$162,000

Note in the budget how the purchasing manager of Quest estimates a commodity price change for rip stop nylon as of the beginning of the third quarter, and notes this change in a separate line item. Also, note that the historical direct materials percentage in the historical method section of the budget does not include the cost of the materials already estimated above it in the roll up portion of the budget.

Anomalies in the Direct Materials Budget

In this section, we discuss how to handle two issues in the direct materials budget – how to budget for changes in commodity prices, and for the cost of materials lost by various means.

If commodity prices tend to change by large amounts and at irregular intervals, it will be difficult to reflect these changes in a full-year budget. This is a particular problem when a certain commodity comprises a large part of the raw materials of a business, as is the case with corn syrup for candy manufacturers and resin for the manufacturers of plastic products. In these situations, the following choices are available:

- *Probability basis*. If there are several possible changes in commodity prices and a probability of occurrence can be assigned to each one, multiply the

215

probability of occurrence by each pricing scenario and add the results together to arrive at a probability-adjusted commodity price.

- *Rolling forecast.* If commodity prices have a large impact on a company's financial results, consider revising the budget once a quarter to reflect the best estimates of commodity prices. Not doing so might result in a budget that is not even remotely achievable, if commodity prices head in an unexpected direction.

- *Multiple versions.* Create several versions of the budget, each using a different commodity price. Though this approach is good for providing management with models of different scenarios, it will result in an unwieldy budget.

- *Budget vs. actual adjustment.* When creating budget versus actual reports, the accounting department can segregate the commodity expense in a different line item, so that management can view the results of the company, excluding the impact of the commodity prices over which it has no control.

Any of the preceding alternatives can be selected to match an entity's specific circumstances. We prefer the rolling forecast approach, since it preserves the integrity of the budget over the short term and relies on a single budget version that is relatively easy to maintain.

There are a variety of additional costs that are sometimes included in the cost of direct materials, such as scrap, spoilage, rework, and inventory obsolescence. These costs are usually included in a lump sum in the cost of goods sold, because there are no systems in place to track them individually. This can present a problem when constructing a budget, because there are both normal (expected) and abnormal (unexpected) amounts of these costs, and some of them may not recur in the future. Thus, not tracking them separately will result in the inclusion of abnormal expenses in the budget. Consequently, if there are tracking systems in place to monitor scrap, spoilage, rework, and obsolete inventory, use them to report these items separately. With this additional information available, it should be possible to budget for normal expenses, while avoiding the inclusion of abnormal expenses.

The Role of the Direct Materials Budget

It is important to understand that the direct materials budget is not used by the procurement department for its daily purchasing tasks. The department uses a combination of the production schedule, on-hand inventory balances, and bills of material to determine its purchasing needs. If the company uses a material requirements planning (MRP) system, the computer derives exact purchasing quantities from these information sources for the procurement staff. In some cases, the MRP system may even automatically place orders with suppliers.

Since the procurement department is not relying on the direct materials budget, it is not necessary to include an inordinate amount of cost or unit detail in the budget – no one is going to use the information. Instead, it is much more efficient to aggregate information in the budget, probably at the level of a few key commodities and then a subtotal for all other direct materials. If it is necessary to engage in detailed calculations to derive the aggregated amounts, restrict these calculations to a subsidiary-level document that a typical user of the budget will not see.

Summary

All of the inputs to the inventory-related budgets described in this chapter are compiled by departments other than accounting. Nonetheless, the accounting staff is frequently asked to manage the assembly of the budget. Given this responsibility, it is necessary for the accountant to not only understand how these elements of the budget are created, but also to have some knowledge of which conceptual underpinnings of an inventory-related budget are not realistic, particularly in regard to inventory turnover levels and constraints. If a preliminary version of a budget contains unrealistic elements, the accountant should forward the issue to management, noting all concerns and requesting another iteration of the budget model.

Chapter 23
Inventory Measurements

Introduction

The inventory asset can represent a company's largest investment. As such, management should be well aware of how this investment is being used through the examination of a variety of measurements, most of which are calculated and provided by the accounting staff. In this chapter, we address the general concepts of inventory turnover and obsolete inventory, along with several ancillary measurements that are designed to focus attention on whether the amount of inventory on hand is the correct amount, and what to do with any excess inventory.

Related Podcast Episode: Episode 27 of the Accounting Best Practices Podcast discusses inventory measurements. It is available at: **accountingtools.com/podcasts** or **iTunes**

Overview of Inventory Measurements

Inventory is technically considered an asset – at least, it is categorized as such on a company's balance sheet. However, it can be considered a liability, since inventory is not easily liquidated, can become obsolete in short order, and can physically clog a facility to such an extent that it interferes with operations. Because of the liability aspects of inventory, all of the measurements in this chapter are intended to spotlight when a business has too much inventory – not when it has too little.

The traditional measurement of inventory is turnover, which is a comparison of the amount of inventory to sales, to see if the proportion is reasonable. We also subdivide this measurement into turnover for raw materials, work-in-process, and finished goods – each of which can be applicable under certain circumstances. When using inventory turnover measurements, keep in mind that the results will be largely based on the manufacturing system in place, as well as purchasing practices. For example, a practice of buying in bulk and using a "push" production system will inevitably lead to lower inventory turnover, while just-in-time purchasing and a "pull" production system will be associated with much higher turnover results.

We also discuss inventory accuracy, which is an enormously important concept. Inventory records must be as close to 100% accurate as possible, or else there will be major issues with the ability to meet scheduled production targets and fulfill customer orders in a timely manner.

Our last remaining major area addresses the concept of excess inventory. There should be measurements for detecting any inventory that is either clearly obsolete or which has aged past a certain number of days. These items will likely require disposition at a reduced price, so we also address the amount of returnable inventory and the rate at which its value is likely to decline over time. These concepts should be built into an ongoing process of identifying and selling off inventory at a rapid clip, so that no excess funds are stored in inventory that is unlikely to provide an adequate return on investment.

Average Inventory Calculation

Average inventory is used to estimate the amount of inventory that a business typically has on hand over a longer time period than just the last month. Since the inventory balance is calculated as of the end of the last business day of a month, it may vary considerably from the average amount over a longer time period, depending upon whether there was a sudden draw-down of inventory or perhaps a large supplier delivery at the end of the month.

Average inventory is also useful for comparison to revenues. Since revenues are typically presented in the income statement not only for the most recent month, but also for the year-to-date, it is useful to calculate the average inventory for the year-to-date, and then match the average inventory balance to year-to-date revenues, to see how much inventory investment was needed to support a given level of sales.

In the first case, where the intent is to avoid using a sudden spike or drop in the month-end inventory number, the average inventory calculation is to add together the beginning and ending inventory balances for a single month, and divide by two. The formula is:

$$(\text{Beginning inventory} + \text{Ending inventory}) \div 2$$

In the second case, where an average inventory figure is needed that is representative of the period covered by year-to-date sales, add together the ending inventory balances for all of the months included in the year-to-date, and divide by the number of months in the year-to-date. For example, if it is now March 31 and management wants to determine the average inventory to match against sales for the January through March period, the calculation would be:

January ending inventory	$185,000
February ending inventory	213,000
March ending inventory	142,000
Total	$540,000
Average inventory = Total ÷ 3	$180,000

A variation on the average inventory concept is to calculate the exact number of days of inventory on hand, based on the amount of time it has historically taken to sell the inventory. The calculation is:

$$365 \div (\text{Annualized cost of goods sold} \div \text{Inventory})$$

Thus, if a company has annualized cost of goods sold of $1,000,000 and an ending inventory balance of $200,000, its days of inventory on hand is calculated as:

$$365 \div (\$1,000,000 \div \$200,000) = 73 \text{ Days of inventory}$$

Though useful, the average inventory concept has some problems, which are as follows:

- *Month-end basis.* The calculation is based on the month-end inventory balance, which may not be representative of the average inventory balance on a daily basis. For example, a company may traditionally have a huge sales push at the end of each month in order to meet its sales forecasts, which may artificially drop month-end inventory levels to well below their usual daily amounts.
- *Seasonal sales.* Month-end results can be skewed if a company's sales are seasonal. This can cause abnormally low inventory balances at the end of the main selling season, as well as a major ramp-up in inventory balances just before the start of the main selling season.
- *Estimated balance.* Sometimes the month-end inventory balance is estimated, rather than being based on a physical inventory count. This means that a portion of the averaging calculation may itself be based on an estimate, which in turn makes the average inventory figure less valid.

Inventory Turnover Measurements

The turnover of inventory is the rate at which inventory is used over a measurement period. This is an important measurement, for many businesses are burdened by an excessively large investment in inventory, which can consume the bulk of available cash. When there is a low rate of inventory turnover, this implies that a business may have a flawed purchasing system that bought too many goods, or that stocks were increased in anticipation of sales that did not occur. In both cases, there is a high risk of inventory aging, in which case it becomes obsolete and has reduced resale value.

When there is a high rate of inventory turnover, this implies that the purchasing function is tightly managed. However, it may also mean that a business does not have the cash reserves to maintain normal inventory levels, and so is turning away prospective sales. The latter scenario is most likely when the amount of debt is high and there are minimal cash reserves.

In this section, we address the classic inventory measurement, which is inventory turnover, followed by the calculations for each component of inventory – raw materials, work-in-process, and finished goods.

Inventory Turnover Ratio

To calculate inventory turnover, divide the ending inventory figure into the annualized cost of sales. If the ending inventory figure is not a representative number, use an average figure instead. The formula is:

$$\frac{\text{Annual cost of goods sold}}{\text{Inventory}}$$

One can also divide the result of this calculation into 365 days to arrive at days of inventory on hand. Thus, a turnover rate of 4.0 becomes 91 days of inventory.

EXAMPLE

An analyst is reviewing the inventory situation of the Hegemony Toy Company. The business incurred $8,150,000 of cost of goods sold in the past year, and has ending inventory of $1,630,000. Total inventory turnover is calculated as:

$$\frac{\$8,150,000 \text{ Cost of goods sold}}{\$1,630,000 \text{ Inventory}}$$

$$= 5 \text{ Turns per year}$$

The five turns figure is then divided into 365 days to arrive at 73 days of inventory on hand.

Raw Materials Turnover

If a large part of a company's total inventory investment is in raw materials, it may be useful to focus attention specifically on this area with the raw materials turnover measurement. This measurement is of interest to the purchasing manager, who is responsible for maintaining the flow of goods into the production area. This measurement can also be used by the engineering manager, who can focus on designing products that use common parts already found in stock. Raw material turnover is of particular interest in just-in-time environments where the intent is to drive the investment in raw materials down to a level very close to zero.

To calculate raw materials turnover, divide the dollar value of raw materials consumed in the period by the average amount of raw materials on hand through the period, and then annualize the result. For example, if the measurement is for a one-month period, multiply the result by 12. The calculation is:

$$\frac{\text{Dollar value of raw materials consumed in period}}{\text{Average dollar value of raw materials inventory}} \times 12 = \text{Raw materials turnover}$$

There are a few situations in which raw materials turnover can be further refined. Consider the following possibilities:

- *Obsolete inventory.* A high proportion of obsolete raw materials may be keeping the turnover figure from being improved. If so, run a calculation of which items have not been used recently, and forward this list to the purchasing staff to see if the indicated items can be sold off. Then run the turnover measurement without the obsolete items.
- *Overnight delivery costs.* The turnover figure can be artificially reduced by paying extra to have raw materials delivered through an overnight delivery

service. If this is happening, track the cost of incoming freight in conjunction with the raw materials turnover measurement.

EXAMPLE

Aberdeen Arquebus sells its old gun replicas in a highly seasonal business, where most purchases are made in the spring, in anticipation of the summer battle re-enactment season. Accordingly, the owner exerts considerable pressure on the purchasing staff to minimize raw material levels, so that there are few raw materials left in stock after the selling season is complete. The following table shows the results of this effort by quarter, where production ramps up in the fourth and first quarters, followed by a rapid decline in the second quarter.

	Quarter 1	Quarter 2	Quarter 3	Quarter 4
Raw materials consumed	$380,000	$210,000	$85,000	$420,000
Raw materials inventory	$254,000	$93,000	$28,000	$335,000
Raw materials turnover	6x	9x	12x	5x

Note: The results of each calculation are multiplied by four to annualize results.

Work-in-Process Turnover

An excessive amount of work-in-process inventory is a strong indicator of an inefficient production process. When production is not well-organized, clumps of inventory will pile up throughout the production area. Conversely, a just-in-time system can operate with very small amounts of work-in-process inventory.

To measure work-in-process turnover, divide the annual cost of goods sold by the average cost of work-in-process inventory. The calculation is:

$$\frac{\text{Annualized cost of goods sold}}{\text{Average work-in-process inventory}}$$

This is the most difficult inventory turnover figure to compile, for there is usually no formal system for tracking specific units of inventory through the production process, as well as the state of completion of each unit. If so, compiling this measurement is nearly impossible. However, if there is a formal tracking system in place, the average work-in-process figure may be available through a standard report.

Another issue with work-in-process inventory is its extreme variability. The amount in process may vary to a noticeable extent on a daily or even hourly basis, so the use of an average inventory level is advisable.

EXAMPLE

Creekside Industrial is in the throes of a manufacturing system changeover, from a manufacturing resources planning (MRP II) system to a just-in-time system. The production manager wants to be sure that the company is realizing the full benefits of the transition, and so authorizes the compilation of before-and-after work-in-process turnover measurements. The results are:

(results are annualized)	MRP II Turnover	Just-in-Time Turnover
Cost of goods sold	$16,500,000	$15,900,000
Average work-in-process inventory	$1,375,000	$795,000
	12x	20x

The measurement comparison reveals that Creekside has experienced a notable drop in its work-in-process investment as a result of the switch to a just-in-time system.

Finished Goods Turnover

There are situations where a company may have quite a large investment in finished goods inventory in comparison to its sales level. This situation most commonly arises for one of the following reasons:

- *Fulfillment policy.* Senior management wants to differentiate the company from its competitors by offering a fast fulfillment rate for all customer orders, which can only be achieved with a large amount of finished goods on hand.
- *Seasonality.* Sales are highly seasonal, so the seller increases its finished goods during the months prior to the selling season, in order to meet demand.
- *Obsolescence.* Some portion of the finished goods inventory is obsolete, and so is selling at a very low rate.

To calculate finished goods turnover, divide the dollar value of finished goods consumed in the period by the average amount of finished goods on hand through the period, and then annualize the result. For example, if the measurement is for a one-month period, multiply the result by 12. The calculation is:

$$\frac{\text{Dollar value of finished goods consumed in period}}{\text{Average dollar value of finished goods inventory}} \times 12 = \text{Finished goods turnover}$$

One issue with finished goods turnover is how costing information is compiled. The cost of finished goods is comprised of the costs of direct materials, direct labor, and overhead. These amounts can vary if there are changes in the standard costing methodology that a company employs. Also, these costs can be fraudulently altered in order to increase the amount of ending inventory, thereby reducing the cost of goods sold and increasing profits. Thus, the costing methodology can have an impact on finished goods turnover.

EXAMPLE

The senior managers of Billabong Machining want to ensure the highest level of customer satisfaction by promising order fulfillment on 99% of all orders placed within one day of order receipt. Given the large array of widgets that Billabong offers for sale, this pledge requires the company to maintain an inordinately large investment in finished goods. The following table reveals the finished goods turnover rate before and after the fulfillment policy was begun.

(results are annualized)	Before Fulfillment Policy	After Fulfillment Policy
Finished goods consumed	$4,800,000	$5,100,000
Finished goods inventory	$400,000	$1,275,000
	12x	4x

Given the massive decline in turnover, the management team might want to rethink its decision to fulfill customer orders so quickly, especially since sales have not increased much as a result of the decision.

Inventory Accuracy Percentage

A business relies upon the accuracy of its inventory records to maintain its production and customer fulfillment systems. For these records to be truly accurate, they must contain accurate information in the following areas:
- Quantity on hand
- Location of inventory
- Unit of measure
- Part number

If any one of these items within an inventory record is wrong, the entire set of information can be considered sufficiently incorrect to render the entire record useless. For example, the inventory quantity may be completely accurate, but if the location code is wrong, the materials handling staff cannot find the item. Or, if the part number is wrong, a component cannot be used. Consequently, the inventory accuracy formula encompasses all four elements.

To calculate inventory accuracy, divide the number of *completely* accurate inventory test items sampled by the total number of all inventory items sampled. An accurate inventory test item is considered to be one for which the actual quantity, location, unit of measure, and part number matches the information stated in the inventory record. If even one of these items is found to be incorrect, the entire item tested should be flagged as incorrect.

The formula for inventory accuracy is:

$$\frac{\text{Number of completely accurate inventory test items}}{\text{Total number of inventory items sampled}}$$

EXAMPLE

An internal auditor for Radiosonde Corporation conducts an inventory accuracy review in the company's storage area. He compiles the following incorrect information for a sample test of eight items:

	Audited Description	Audited Location	Audited Quantity	Audited Unit of Measure
Alpha unit	No	No		
Beta unit	No			
Charlie unit		No		
Delta unit	No	No		
Echo unit		No		
Foxtrot unit	No			No
Golf unit				No
Hotel unit				No

The result of the test is inventory accuracy of 0%. The test score astounds the inventory manager, who has been focusing solely on quantity accuracy. Even though the quantity counts did indeed prove to be accurate, the inventory records were well below expectations for the other data items.

Excess Inventory Measurements

If a company maintains any inventory at all, it is quite likely that some portion of this investment is obsolete. A business needs to have an ongoing inventory evaluation system that highlights obsolete items, as well as a well-defined system for disposing of these items as quickly as possible, and at the highest price. In this section, we address several variations on obsolete inventory measurement, as well as how to focus attention on the opportunity cost of not disposing of inventory in a timely manner.

Obsolete Inventory Percentage

When a company has a significant investment in inventory, one of the more essential accompanying metrics is the obsolete inventory percentage. This measurement is needed to derive that portion of the inventory that is no longer usable. The percentage should be tracked on a trend line and compared to the results of similar businesses, to see if a company is experiencing an unusually large proportion of inventory problems. Actions taken that relate to this percentage can include:

- Changes in the reserve for obsolete inventory, if the percentage is varying from the long-term trend.
- Changes in the amount of activity to disposition obsolete inventory in a manner as advantageous to the company as possible.
- Actions taken to reduce the underlying causes of obsolescence, such as buying in smaller quantities, switching to a production system that is based on customer orders, and better management of engineering change orders.

To derive the obsolete inventory percentage, summarize the book value of all inventory items which have been designated as not being needed, and divide it by the book value of the entire inventory. The formula is:

$$\frac{\text{Book value of inventory items with no recent usage}}{\text{Total inventory book value}}$$

The main problem with this percentage is figuring out which inventory to include in the numerator. Whatever method is chosen should be used in a consistent manner, so that trends in the percentage can be more reliably tracked over time.

EXAMPLE

The warehouse manager of Mole Industries wants to investigate the extent of obsolete inventory in his warehouse, so that he can remove items and consolidate the remaining inventory. He prints a parts usage report from the company's manufacturing resources planning system that only shows the cost of those items that are in stock and which have not been used for at least two years. The total cost listed on this report is $182,000, which is 19% of the total book value of the entire inventory. The warehouse manager brings this high percentage to the attention of the purchasing manager, who immediately contacts suppliers to see if they will take back the obsolete items in exchange for a restocking fee.

Percent of Inventory Greater than XX Days

A variation on the obsolete inventory percentage is to track the amount of any inventory that is older than a certain number of days. If an inventory item exceeds the threshold, it could be targeted for return to the supplier in exchange for a restocking fee. This approach is particularly useful when a company has instituted just-in-time deliveries, but still has excess inventory on hand from before implementation of the new system.

The precise number of days used for the threshold in this measurement can vary, based on several factors. Consider the following:

- *Warehouse-specific.* If tighter inventory controls are being implemented at just one location, set a minimal threshold for that facility in order to target the largest possible amount of inventory for disposition.

- *SKU-specific.* If a particular stock-keeping unit (SKU) is being targeted for reduction, set a minimal threshold just for that item. This is particularly common for any SKUs for which a company has a large amount of funds tied up in inventory.
- *Class specific.* The measurement can be restricted to just raw materials, in order to focus on tighter purchasing practices. Alternatively, it can be restricted to just finished goods, in order to focus on production scheduling and sales forecasting issues.
- *Early warning.* Analysis of obsolete inventory may have shown that any inventory over a certain number of days old is more likely to eventually be designated as obsolete. Thus, the threshold can be set for a certain number of days prior to when inventory is usually declared obsolete, which gives the company early warning to draw down these stocks.

The steps required to calculate the percent of inventory over a certain number of days are:
1. Set the threshold number of days and the inventory type to be measured.
2. For the block of inventory to be measured, determine the dollar amount of all inventory items exceeding the threshold number of days.
3. Divide the aggregate total from the second step by the total dollar amount of inventory. Note that this should be the ending inventory balance (not an average balance), since the inventory figure derived in the second step is as of the ending inventory date.

The calculation of the percent of inventory greater than XX days is:

$$\frac{\text{Inventory dollars greater than XX days old}}{\text{Total inventory valuation}}$$

This measurement can be misleading in two situations, which are:
- *Seasonal production build.* A company may build inventory levels throughout the year, in anticipation of a short selling season. If so, the amount of all types of inventory may appear inordinately old with this measurement. In this situation, consider only using the measurement immediately after the selling season, to identify the extent to which inventory items did not sell.
- *Production schedule.* Certain raw materials may only be used in specific products, for which production runs are only scheduled at relatively long intervals. If the measurement is generated just prior to such a production run, it could reveal what may appear to be an inordinate amount of raw materials on hand. This issue can be spotted by comparing the production schedule to any items appearing in an initial version of the measurement.

EXAMPLE

Rapunzel Hair Products sells a hair spray that has been proven to lose much of its hold characteristics after six months in storage; at that time, any remaining stocks cannot be sold, and so are thrown in the dumpster. Accordingly, Rapunzel's sales manager requests that an inventory report be generated that aggregates the percentage of this inventory that is more than 90 days old, so that coupons can be issued in a timely manner that will spur additional sales of the hair spray. For example, as of the end of the last month, the ten products that use the hair spray formulation, and which were more than 90 days old, had an aggregate book value of $80,000. Since the total hair spray inventory value was $1,000,000, the percent of inventory greater than 90 days old was 8%.

Returnable Inventory Valuation

Only a portion of all excess inventory can be returned to suppliers. Other items are too old or damaged to be returned, or suppliers refuse to take them back, even for a restocking fee. Management should be aware of the total dollar amount of returnable inventory, since the amount of cash that can be realized could be of considerable use to the company. This measurement usually takes the form of a report, which itemizes in declining dollar value the amount of inventory that can be returned, based on the expected disposal price, net of any restocking charges.

A key concern with the returnable inventory valuation is not to include in the report any items for which there is a reasonable short-term prospect of usage. Otherwise, the company will incur a restocking charge to return items to a supplier, followed shortly thereafter by the repurchase of the same items at their full retail price.

One concern is whether to include in the valuation report any items for which suppliers only offer a credit, rather than a cash repayment. If the company does not expect to make any further purchases from a supplier that only offers a credit, the credit is essentially useless. In this case, it is better to exclude such items from the report.

Opportunity Cost of Excess Inventory

Most companies have pockets of excess inventory on hand. This inventory may be obsolete, or there may simply be more on hand than the company can reasonably expect to use or sell in the short term. In these situations, the purchasing department should be working on ways to disposition the goods in exchange for the largest possible amount of cash. The disposition value of inventory almost always declines over time, so there is an opportunity cost associated with not actively pursuing inventory dispositions. To measure the opportunity cost of excess inventory, follow these steps:

1. Compile the units of inventory that must be disposed of.
2. Estimate the disposal price that the company can obtain for these units if it were to do so today.
3. Estimate the rate at which the disposal price will drop on a monthly basis.

4. Estimate the direct cost of holding the inventory on a monthly basis.
5. Multiply the disposal units by their estimated disposal prices, and multiply the result by the monthly rate of price decline. Add the incremental cost of holding the inventory.

The calculation of the opportunity cost of excess inventory is:

$$((\text{Disposal units} \times \text{Disposal price}) \times \text{Price decline \%}) + \text{Inventory holding cost}$$
$$= \text{Opportunity cost}$$

When deriving this opportunity cost, be careful not to include fixed costs in the inventory holding cost, such as the cost of warehouse utilities. The only relevant inventory holding costs are those that will be eliminated if inventory is sold off – thus, only completely variable holding costs should be considered.

An issue that will likely arise when this measurement is presented to management is the amount of loss the company will record on its books as a result of an inventory disposition. The correct response is that the company should be recording an updated obsolete inventory reserve each month, irrespective of whether the inventory is disposed of. Thus, the only decision remaining for management is whether to hold onto old inventory or sell it now and convert it to cash at whatever prices the company can obtain.

While there are a number of estimates involved in this measurement, it is still one of the best ways to get the attention of management regarding the cost of holding onto inventory for longer than is necessary.

EXAMPLE

Green Lawn Care sells battery-powered lawn mowers, for which the selling season is quite short. In the current season, the sales department estimates that the company will have 5,000 excess lawn mowers. The company can expect to sell these units for $200 right now (August), and can expect this price to decline by 5% in each successive month. There is also a holding cost of $2 per unit, per month, since the company is renting storage space for the units from an independent warehouse. Based on this information, the opportunity cost of excess inventory is:

$$((5,000 \text{ Disposal units} \times \$200 \text{ Disposal price}) \times 5\% \text{ Price decline}) + \$10,000 \text{ Holding cost}$$
$$= \$60,000 \text{ Opportunity cost}$$

In short, the company stands to lose $60,000 for each month in which it does not dispose of the excess lawn mower inventory.

Summary

It may appear that all inventory measurements are designed to draw attention to an excessive investment in inventory. This is largely true, but can also represent a problem, for *some* investment in inventory is usually needed. If inventory levels are drawn down to near zero, the logistics and production functions of a business must be precisely tuned to operate correctly at such a minimal level. If not, the business will likely experience continually-stalled processes that interfere with its ability to produce and sell goods to the satisfaction of its customers. Consequently, the accountant should not present these measurements to management with an implied emphasis on a continual reduction in inventory – the existing inventory level may be just fine.

The intent of this chapter was to establish a tight focus on just those measurements pertaining specifically to the inventory asset. In reality, inventory crosses over with several functional areas – product design, purchasing, and production. Consequently, the accountant may need to review these other areas to find additional measurements that have a tangential impact on the inventory asset.

Glossary

A

Administrative overhead. Those costs not involved in the development or production of goods or services.

Advance pricing agreement. An agreement between a company and a taxing authority, in which the company outlines the procedure it will take to establish transfer prices.

B

Backflushing. The concept of recording raw material withdrawals based on the number of units produced.

Bill and hold. A situation where the seller recognizes revenue from a sale, despite not shipping the related goods to the buyer.

Bill of materials. A list of the parts required to build a product.

Blanket purchase agreement. A purchase order that allows for repetitive purchases within a specific period of time.

Book value. An asset's original cost, less any depreciation or impairment that has been subsequently incurred.

By-product. A product that is an ancillary part of the primary production process, having a minor resale value in comparison to the value of the primary product being manufactured.

C

Carrying amount. The recorded amount of an inventory asset, net of any write-downs.

Channel stuffing. Using special deals to sell more goods to customers than they need.

Consigned inventory. Inventory owned by a business, but stored at the location of a reseller.

Contra account. An account that offsets another, related account with which it is paired. If the related account is an asset account, the contra account is used to offset (reduce) it with a credit balance.

Contribution margin. The margin that results when all variable costs are subtracted from revenue.

Cost layering. The concept that different tranches of costs have been incurred to construct or acquire different clusters of inventory.

Cost pool. A grouping of individual costs, typically by department or service center. Cost allocations are then made from the cost pool.

Cross docking. Moving goods from the receiving area to the shipping area, with no storage in-between.

Cycle counting. The practice of continually reviewing inventory records for accuracy, and correcting any underlying problems found.

D

Direct materials. Those materials and supplies consumed during the manufacture of a product, and which are directly identified with that product.

Drop shipping. When goods are shipped from a supplier to the ultimate customer, with no handling by an intermediary seller.

E

Economic order quantity. A formula used to derive that number of units of inventory to purchase that represents the lowest possible total cost to the buyer.

Engineering change order. A document specifying a change to the composition of an existing product.

F

Finished goods. Those goods ready for sale to customers.

First in, first out. A cost layering concept that assumes the first units acquired are the first units used.

G

Gross margin. Revenues less the cost of goods sold. The gross margin reveals the amount that an entity earns from the sale of its products and services, before the deduction of any sales and administrative expenses.

Gross profit method. The use of the historical gross margin to estimate the amount of ending inventory.

H

Historical cost. Costing based on measures of historical prices, without subsequent restatement.

Hybrid system. A costing system that combines elements of the job costing and process costing systems.

I

Inventory. Tangible items held for routine sale, or which are being produced for sale, or which are consumed in the production of goods for sale.

Item master. A record that lists the name, description, unit of measure, weight, dimensions, ordering quantity, and other key information for a component part.

J

Job costing. A system for compiling those costs associated with a specific job or project.

Joint cost. A cost which benefits more than one product, and for which it may not be possible to separate its contribution to each product.

Just-in-time. A set of concepts that focus on minimizing waste within the production process by only manufacturing products as needed.

K

Kitting. The assemblage of parts for inclusion in a production job.

L

Last in, first out. A cost layering concept that assumes the last units acquired are the first units used.

LIFO layer. A cost per unit ascribed to certain units of stock under the last in, first out method of inventory costing.

Lower of cost or market. The concept that inventory items should be recorded at the lower of their cost or the current market price.

M

Manufacturing overhead. All of the costs that a factory incurs, other than direct costs.

Material requirements planning. A push-based planning system that orders parts and schedules production based on an estimate of customer demand for goods.

N

Net realizable value. The estimated selling price of an item in the ordinary course of business, not including any costs of completion and disposal.

Normal capacity. The production volume a business expects to achieve over a number of periods under normal circumstances.

O

Obsolete inventory. Inventory items for which there is no longer an internal use or external demand.

Overhead absorbed. Manufacturing overhead that has been applied to products or other cost objects.

Overhead rate. The overhead for a specific reporting period, divided by an allocation measure.

P

Period cost. A cost that is charged to expense in the period in which it is incurred, because the cost was consumed during that period.

Periodic inventory system. The updating of inventory records only at set intervals, using a physical count.

Perpetual inventory system. The updating of inventory records on a continual basis, based on every inventory-related transaction.

Physical inventory. A manual count of the on-hand and off-site inventory, including raw materials, work-in-process, and finished goods.

Process costing. A costing system used in situations where large quantities of the same item are manufactured.

Purchase order. A legal authorization for a supplier to ship goods or deliver services to a buyer, under the terms stated in the purchase order.

R

Raw materials. Base-level materials intended for conversion into finished goods.

Reorder point. The inventory unit quantity on hand that triggers the purchase of a predetermined amount of replenishment inventory.

Retail inventory method. A method used by retailers to derive their aggregate ending inventory, based on the relationship between the cost of merchandise and its retail price.

Return merchandise authorization. An authorization extended to a customer, allowing the customer to return specific goods to the seller.

Rework. Any product that is initially found to be faulty, and which is then repaired and sold.

S

Safety stock. Extra inventory maintained to mitigate the risk of a stockout.

Sales order. An internal document used to describe the contents of a customer order.

Scrap. The amount of unused material that remains after a product has been manufactured.

Shrinkage. An uncontrolled loss of inventory.

Split-off point. The point in a production process after which a final product can be determined.

Spoilage. Produced goods that are defective.

Standard costing. The practice of substituting an expected cost for an actual cost in the accounting records, and then periodically recording a variance between the expected and actual cost amounts.

Sunk cost. An expenditure made in a prior period, which will not be affected by any current or future decisions.

V

Variance. The difference between an actual measured amount and a basis, such as a budgeted or standard amount.

W

Work-in-process. Unfinished inventory that is either currently in the production process or waiting in queue for additional finishing work to be performed.

Index

100% count analysis 39

Administrative overhead 97
Affiliated group definition 147
Auditing, inventory 26
Average inventory 219

Backflushing 23, 41
Bar code scanning 20
Bill of materials 210
Budget
    Direct materials 210
    Production 202
By-products
    Costing concerns 126
    Definition of 124
    Pricing of 125

Control group analysis 38
Controllable variance 72
Controls
    Intercompany 177
    Inventory valuation 178
    Production 181
    Purchasing 161
    Receiving 168
    Record accuracy 24
    Shipping 174
    Warehouse 180
Corrective action system 27
Cost layering 49
Currency translation adjustment 113
Cycle counting 34

Data collection methods 19
Data entry backlog 22
Direct materials budget
    80/20 method 214
    Anomalies 215
    Historical method 212
    Role of 216
    Roll up method 210
Disclosures 128
Dollar-value LIFO 53

Employee accuracy factors 17
Ending inventory budget
    Changes in 207
Environmental accuracy factors 16
Expected dispositions method 103
Expensing method 107

Finished goods turnover 223
First in, first out method 50
Fixed overhead spending variance 70
Fraud
    Labor costs 183
    Materials costs 184
    Overhead costs 188
    Prevention 193
    Revenue 189
    Risk factors 192

Goods in transit 134
Gross profit method 44

Hybrid costing system 92

Intercompany controls 177
Internal revenue code 139
Inventory
    Accounting for 3
    Auditing 26
    Cycle counting 34
    Definition of 1
    Disclosures 128
    Naming conventions 18
    Policies 196
    Reconciliation 40
    Record errors 14
    Reports 25
    Theft 190
    Transactions 6
    Valuation controls 178
Inventory accuracy percentage 224
Inventory greater than XX days 226
Inventory record accuracy 206
Inventory turnover ratio 220

Job costing

Accounting for 79
Actual overhead costs 81
Job closing 84
Labor accounting............................. 80
Overview of 77
Standard overhead costs................... 82
Subsidiary ledger usage................... 85
When not to use.............................. 78
Joint costs, allocation of 124
Journal entries
Acquired inventory 131
Backflushing 131
Bill and hold................................. 132
Consignment 132
Cost recognition 130
Count adjustments......................... 136
Cross docking............................... 133
Drop shipping............................... 133
Kitting 134
LCM.. 135
Obsolete inventory 135
Overhead allocation 136
Receiving 137
Sales 137
Scrap & spoilage 138
Just-in-time production.......................... 8

Labeling accuracy issues 17
Labor efficiency variance 68
Labor rate variance 67
Last in, first out method....................... 51
Link-chain method............................... 55
Lower of cost or market rule 110

Manufacturing overhead....................... 97
Manufacturing resources planning 206
Material requirements planning.............. 7
Material yield variance 66

Negative inventory balance 26

Obsolete inventory.............................. 103
Obsolete inventory percentage 225
Opportunity cost of excess inventory . 228
Overhead rate 99
Overhead rate averaging..................... 101

Periodic inventory system 10
Perpetual inventory system.................. 12
Physical count improvements.............. 33

Physical inventory count...................... 30
Pick to light.................................... 21
Policies, inventory............................ 196
Pricing of joint cost products 125
Process costing
FIFO method.............................. 90
Overview 86
Problems with............................. 95
Standard cost method.................... 89
Weighted average method 87
Product life cycles............................ 206
Product versions, number of 206
Production budget
Issues 203
Layout...................................... 202
With multiple products 205
Production controls 181
Pull system 8
Purchase price variance...................... 65
Purchasing controls........................... 161
Purchasing process........................... 159
Push system.................................... 7

Qualified liquidations........................ 142

Radio frequency terminals 20
Rate variance................................... 65
Raw materials turnover 221
Receiving controls............................. 168
Receiving process 166
Reconciliation of inventory.................. 40
Record keeping, inventory 29
Reports, inventory............................. 25
Reserve method................................ 105
Retail inventory method...................... 45
Returnable inventory valuation 228
Rework
Accounting for............................ 120
Definition of 118
Reporting of............................... 119
RFID 21

Scrap
Accounting for............................ 120
Definition of 120
Seasonal sales.................................. 206
Shipping controls 174
Shipping process 171
Simplified dollar-value LIFO............. 144
Specific identification method 59

237

Split-off point 123
Spoilage
    Abnormal 117
    Definition of.................................. 115
    Normal 116
    Sale of 117
Standard cost, creation of 61
Standard costing
    Accounting for 63
    Attainable basis 62
    Historical basis 62
    Overview of 61
    Theoretical basis............................ 63
    Variances....................................... 65

Transactions... 6
Transfer pricing
    Adjusted market price 152
    Contribution margin pricing........... 153

Cost plus basis 153
Market price....................................151
Negotiated prices 152
Overview of....................................149
Problems with 155
Tax impact 156

Variable overhead efficiency variance ..70
Variable overhead spending variance ...69
Variance analysis, problems with 71
Variance reporting.................................75
Variance types.......................................65
Volume variance 65

Warehouse controls.............................180
Weighted average method.....................58
Working capital reduction...................207
Work-in-process turnover 222

CPSIA information can be obtained
at www.ICGtesting.com
Printed in the USA
LVHW101404110319
610216LV00011B/157/P